**Samson Blinded:
A Machiavellian Perspective
on the Middle East Conflict**

by Obadiah Shoher

Table of Contents

Foreword to the Second Edition

In the first edition of this book, I wrote about Palestinian claims, "Some chances lost cannot be regained." That equally applies to the Jews.

Present Israel is doomed. A nation defined in religious terms cannot survive in a secular state. Religious Jews despise Western culture and alien religious practices in the Promised Land; secular Jews dislike outdated religious rites. Reformism gained strength in America and is poised to invade Israel, subverting the religion. The socialist state suffocates enterprising Jews, and welfare programs dilute their work ethics. Democratic centralism suppresses the strongly opinionated population. Military expenditures have reached an economic dead-end.

Why are the Jews, who waged such asymmetrical warfare against the British seventy years ago, now sheepishly obedient to the Israeli government? One reason is a much stronger security apparatus in Israel than in the Mandate Palestine. More importantly, people shrink from the uncomfortable realization that their government is their worst enemy, an apathy that dooms their country.

Egyptian society is boiling. Support for the Muslim Brotherhood visibly grows, and that radical group already controls the largest body of the parliament. Many adherents are moderates, but so it was before every revolution. Moderates clear the way to power for radicals who often begin their rule by butchering the moderates. Ageing Mubarak is losing his grip on his country and the people sense that. Democratizers further destabilize the situation by demanding the transparent election framework that will bring to power the Islamists, the only group untainted by corruption and perceived as able to combat it. Egypt barely controls its South, and a despised and corrupt police is both powerless and unreliable. Decades of propaganda etched, in the minds of two generations, Israel as the archenemy. Restitution of Sinai was not enough; they want revenge. Israel did not demilitarize Egypt when she could have, and now the enemy is coming back with a vengeance, armed with nuclear bombs.

Iran strives for Middle East dominance, a hard take for a non-Arab Shiite country. Nuclear technology is a must for the Iranian military, and Persian pride will not let them accept inferiority to Arab Egypt in this important aspect.

Pakistan exports nuclear technology and scientists, and no one outside that country knows the whereabouts of all its bombs. The secular Pakistani elite is unstable, and Islamic politicians ascend the election ladder.

Islamic Algeria has firmly embarked on the nuclear path. The terrorist state of Libya conducts its nuclear program in the utmost secrecy, and Israel's age-old enemy, Syria, takes fundamental steps in the same direction. North Korea will sell its A-bomb to cash bidders, even if they're terrorists. Muslim countries have obtained nuclear weapons, which will inevitably detonate in Israel.

Ancient Judea lingered in existence after Israel fell. Creating a small, ethnically and religiously homogeneous state of Judea can prolong Jewish presence in the Promised Land. A small state, however, will not survive among the surrounding sea of hostility.

Modern Israel is not unique. Jews tried to reestablish their country several times in the past two millennia. A third of the Jews died in the Holocaust; wiping out another third in Israel would be apocalyptic. Glorious nuclear suicide or evacuation to relative safety of the Diaspora?

Modern Jews were given a chance to return, but flouted the wise biblical instructions on the scope of their state. Jews did not drive away the hostile aliens and the Arabs fought back. Jews had no heart to destroy the enemies and the enemies developed nuclear weapons. Most of all, Jews created a society bereft of Judaism — a Western democracy with no claim to the Promised Land, and no place in the land.

Foreword to the First Edition. On hate.

Several reviewers classified this book as hate literature. This cannot be true, as hate is irrational and I argue for pure rationality; hate veils itself in morality while my policies are stripped from any notion of moralizing; hate is wasteful while my aim is efficiency. Hate is like any ideology: silly, costly, and going nowhere. *Hate* is a political label: it is politically correct to hate communists, but not, say, Muslims.

I am indifferent to Muslims as to any Gentiles who observe Noahide laws, find Arabs mildly amusing as any indigenous culture, and deeply respect the terrorists as determined soldiers.

I suggest many policies which aim at these groups. But any political book advocates against someone; discrimination is central for politics. Even alliances are formed generally against someone. Republicans want more votes at the expense of Democrats, and attack them to that purpose. My recommendations involve threats of violence, but international politics is always built around such threats; balance of power is the only proven strategy for maintaining peace. My editors and I carefully re-worded possibly ambiguous propositions, and made sure the book never advocates violence per se, but only threatens reprisal for others' violence. The aim is to mitigate violence, not launch it.

Nazis hated Jews; Hutu and Tutsi hated each other; Catholics at some point hated Protestants. The hatred, no doubt, run along the lines of economic competition, but the final concept was distorted beyond any semblance of rationality. To follow the first example, a reasonable idea to prosecute swindler Jews evolved into expulsion of all Jews, only remotely useful for Germans, and into entirely unreasonable mass murder. Vengeance, however, tends to cross the line and become hatred. It is an interesting subject, but beyond the scope of book about rational ends and means. We cannot afford to hate enemies; we must act efficiently.

I do not hate Neo-Nazis. They are just enemies, and must be dealt with rationally. I dislike anti-Semites, but cannot object to their opinions as long as they remain passive. Xenophobia is all too human. How many Jews tacitly dislike Gypsies? I do not blame Gentiles for not helping the Jews; how many Jews helped Rwandese? I do, however, believe in the biblical "chosen-ness" of the Jews, and, accordingly, their inherent difference from other peoples. That does not make me a racist, but makes me to hate many Jewish violations of Or Hara'ayon. Jews who offend non-hostile Gentiles are guilty. I would rather see hysterical reviews of my book by anti-Semites than glowing reviews of some Jews who see only imperial ambitions in the book. I equally despise condemnations from Jews who reject even questioning the historical right to the land. Unwarranted self-righteousness, lack of compassion to the underdog, the despising of Gentiles while at the same time requiring them to support Jews—these traits of many Jews I really hate.

I am liberal—in the traditional sense of the word before leftists usurped it. I dislike irresponsible idealists who in the worst totalitarian manner shut out voices of realism, and keep their heads in the sand of theoretical ideology. These totalitarian moralists are bad for us, but catastrophic for the next generation which will suffer the crisis the idealists created—the crisis we still can defuse.

Theory

Most of us want to believe that peace is the natural state of humanity. At the very least, we prefer to see it as a lasting solution, interrupted sometimes by readjustments in the balance of power by means of armed conflicts. But in the real world, we have to make choices. It is not uncommon to prefer ideological or religious values to one's own life. Preference is a matter of value judgment; there is no objectively best option. Indeed, in the Ten Commandments, fundamental to modern Jewish, Christian, and Muslim cultures, the religious prescriptions precede the prohibition of murder. Killing enemies in war is not prohibited.

Once people are ready to die for their values, their religion may condone killing for them, since the commandment of negative reciprocity— Do not do unto another what is hateful to you—is satisfied. It is not hateful to die, and therefore not prohibited to kill.[1] That approach attached moral legitimacy to scores of wars, notably the Crusades, but also recent ideologically inspired wars, down to the Falklands. Rational—or honest— minds might argue that the causes for wars are usually silly or superficial, that enmity is forced on people on both sides otherwise content with each other. But that is a different issue, namely, do soldiers really need to die for the goals they fight for? Why does the traditional interpretation of *You shall not murder* exclude from the prohibition executing criminals and killing in war? Because people are normally ready to die to save their neighbors or their country. Reciprocity allows them to kill.

The prohibition of murder's place *following* the religious rules in the Ten Commandments suggests the subordination of life to ideology. Both the case law of the Hebrew scriptures and the prescribed punishments for religious transgressions support that conjecture.

The parties to the Arab-Israeli conflict have shown in numerous wars that they are ready to die for the cause, an attitude not limited to the military. Israeli civilians stand ready to suffer daily losses from suicide attacks, and Muslim civilians likewise have no trouble sacrificing themselves. The maiming of thousands of locals in Osama's attacks on the American embassies in Africa raised no domestic outcry. Israeli rhetorical condemnations of the terrorists and Arab denouncements of Baruch Goldstein[2] aside, only the facts matter: Israelis and Muslims are ready to die for religious or nationalist causes. War is lamentably acceptable to both.

Consider the application of *You shall do nothing to your neighbor you do not want him doing to you.* No one wants to give way in any

---

[1] Moses ordered the execution of 3,000 people, 0.5% of those who joined Exodus, for worshipping the golden calf. He suppressed the Apis bull' cult to consolidate a nation. Many other nations fought on ideological grounds.

[2] A radical Jew who shot Arabs in a mosque.

conflict, whether bargaining in the marketplace or fighting on the battlefield. Should the buyer pay the asking price without question? Would the seller like someone imposing a price on him? Should he not refrain from imposing prices on others? The two parties would have to bargain since neither should impose a price. The dilemma is superficial. The commandment is fulfilled so long as both parties agree on how to resolve the conflict. A gambler's winnings at cards or on the stock market fits the definition of stealing, because someone loses without being fairly compensated, but such wins are not criminal, since both parties played the game willingly. Arabs condone war as a means of resolving conflicts, so the Israelis are justified in fighting them, since both accept the use of force to resolve conflicts. Mahatma Gandhi and Nelson Mandela turned the tables by renouncing violence and turning world opinion against violence done to them. Muslims see their best hope in asymmetric warfare, which justifies Israel's military ventures.

Why doesn't normal market bargaining lead to violence? Because neither party is a monopolist. It is easier to buy elsewhere or wait for another buyer than to risk a fight. The situation is different when monopolists bargain. They have to reach an agreement, at almost any cost. Such disputes can be violent. The dispute over jurisdiction is a monopolistic bargain: the Palestinians have assets the Israelis want, namely territory.

If the Israelis and the Palestinians set out to settle their differences from two irreconcilable sets of axioms, they would never reach an understanding, but conflicting interests are not conflicting axioms. People deal daily with others whose interests conflict with theirs and resolve the conflicts without resorting to violence.

There are many acceptable axiomatic systems of conflict resolution. Israel solves other conflicts through trade, diplomacy, or public relations. People choose the costlier—riskier, more intrusive—means only after they exhaust the less costly ones. Can Israel be sure she has exhausted diplomacy in her conflict with the Palestinians and their allies? The answer involves a highly subjective judgment, based largely on the cost-benefit ratio of either means—which is different for both parties. Powerful Israel can go to war easily, so accepting resolution by violence is no great leap, and historically, Arabs have also forgone goodwill negotiations for the more immediate means of combat.

If both parties agree on the means of resolution and choose one based on feasibility and expediency, they proceed from similar axioms, and each treats the other the way both expect and accept.

The notion of means should be treated broadly. In the marketplace, one side cannot insist the other not borrow to pay or buy elsewhere. When the parties are of disparate size, such as mega-corporations and their customers, the smaller cannot demand that the bigger act small and desperate to sell. The "means" might be defined in terms of the rules the parties accept. When both sides circumvent *Thou shalt not murder* by using the reciprocity rule to make murder *acceptable killing*, they cannot argue about how to do the killing. Israel cannot complain about terrorism, nor can the Palestinians about helicopter raids on terrorist enclaves in crowded cities.

To put it differently, if the Arabs are ready to fight for jurisdiction instead of appealing to the British Mandate Administration or the United Nations, they should expect the Jews to fight too. Whether military means can be avoided remains to be seen—but peace is unlikely for now.

There are other means of conflict resolution, like competition in humility, for example, but philosophical dispute in such a case is futile, since life does not operate by elegant mathematical formulae, whether in humility or anything else. As Mao Zedong remarked, a statement may be both true and false at the same time, when people value their own interests and their enemies' differently. Fear, the product of force, is the only common denominator for all people.

Righteous people can be just and treat others as they want to be treated—the positive formulation of the commandment. Compromise based on consideration of others' interests and aspirations, not the cost-benefit ratio of war, is theoretically possible. Politics has never achieved such a thing, however. Establishing a precedent of just conflict resolution would be a greater contribution to humanity than re-establishing the biblical state. Should the Israelis miraculously opt for that solution, opportunist Arabs would exploit their weakness. There is no chance either party will strive to be objective, just, compassionate, and considerate.

Popular opinion pardons some killing as long as the ideology behind it suits them, as contemporary approval of the Crusades shows. Only egregious murder is disgusting—the Holocaust, the French slaughter of the Algerians, the Rwandan atrocities. The West condemns the terrorist attack on the World Trade Center, where people see the damage as disproportionate, but the Islamic world does not. They see the loss inflicted as partial payment for the death and, humiliation of countless Muslims. On the other hand, many in the West see Palestinian guerrilla terrorism as an acceptable response to Israeli aggression.

People are ready to kill and persecute for things much less than national conscience. Police shoot escaping pickpockets, and courts imprison people as non-violent as tax evaders. Both in international relations and in law enforcement, killing is mostly a threat kept credible by occasional realization. Killing of petty criminals or Palestinian protesters would be extremely unjust if *all* of them were killed. But only few people die in each group. Threatening them with minuscule chances of being killed is a proportional response to their violence, which also involves only a minor chance of killing. In effect, criminals' sentences consist of assured but moderate (jail sentence) and of improbable but harsh (a small possibility of being killed) components. The product of the highest severity of killing, multiplied by the minor chance of being killed, is reasonable.

"Justified" killing may still not be just, even though rationalized, e.g., when it's a matter of impassioned differences between people of opposing ideological bent. A Quaker pacifist would consider any killing in any war immoral and unjust, but throughout history people have been ready to kill *en masse* to convert others, religiously or politically. The readiness of militant Jews to conquer a tiny plot of land in which to practice their religion is not uncommon. On the contrary, what *is* without precedent in history is the restraint the rest of the world urges upon them. The countries that recently fought to control the places so insignificant for their national conscience as Grenada, Falklands, Algeria, and Chechnya, criticize Israel for holding on to Jerusalem, Judea, and Samaria. Other countries had dissipated their affection on their huge territories, and cannot understand the intensity of affection the Jews feel to the Temple Mount.

Any comparison can be subjected to *reductio ad absurdum*. Many compare Eretz Israel[3] to the *Lebensraum* the Nazis demanded. In that quest, the Nazis purposefully exterminated Jews and Gypsies and reduced Slavs to serfdom. Israeli Jews occupy a tract of land smaller than a county in many states, land around which their national identity and hopes have revolved for millennia, the land every Jew prays to return to: "Next year, in Jerusalem!"[4] The proper comparison is the Russian defense of Moscow, Leningrad, and Stalingrad or the British defense of London in WWII.

Indeed, a century ago most of the population of Palestine (but not, significantly, of Jerusalem) was Arab. But democracy, the best system of majoritarian decision-making (itself a questionable concept, as many philosophers including Plato recognize), is not perfect. Consider California, where the white non-Hispanic population is no longer the majority. Suppose other ethnic groups, projected to reach a super-majority by 2050, amend the state constitution, relegating Caucasians to inferior status by declaring Spanish the official language. Would anyone challenge the right

---

[3] The land Jews claim for Israel as based on religious considerations.

[4] Jewish population never ceased in Jerusalem, constituting a majority in the 19th century. In 438, the Roman Empress Eudocia issued an edict lifting the ban on praying at the Temple site; in 464, Emperor Julian announced his intent to rebuild the Temple; in 614, Jews and Persians recovered the city and held it for several years; many Jews lived there in 1099 when massacred by crusaders. Jews were not negligible in Palestine, totaling about 56,000 in 1918.

Ancient Jews, living throughout Roman and Persian Empires, annually sent their half-shekel contributions to the Temple without compulsion. Jews do not move to Israel because of economic devastation, military indecisiveness, political vacillation, and religious Talmudic orthodoxy. Israel is culturally alien to them. Still, Israel occupies a prominent place in Jewish consciousness. Russian Jews, assimilated, oppressed, ignorant of Hebrew and Judaism, flocked to Golda Meir on her visit to Moscow. Assimilated American Jews underwrite Israeli government bonds, and the U.S. politicians see them concerned enough with Israel to vote depending on these politicians' views of the Middle East conflict.

of Caucasians to fight for their own jurisdiction within California? Many would not. Ethnically, religiously, and even ideologically diverse states that fail as melting pots dissolve. Who was there first and who came later does not matter; much of Israel was not settled fifty years ago. A coherent and importantly distinct group living compactly is entitled to sovereignty, or at least it makes sense to give them sovereignty to keep them from living in perpetual conflict with their neighbors. What, except anti-Semitism, denies the same logic to the Jews in the Middle East?

Cruel measures are sometimes the kindest

The cruelty of the stronger increases suffering in the short run but decreases it over the long term by stopping wars sooner and crushing the will to fight. Low intensity perpetuates conflicts. Tolerating enemies is provocative. That notion is unpopular with shortsighted democratic politicians, but it is the only practical approach for the oldest living nation on earth. [5]

Americans used that approach with Japan, killing many with two nuclear bombs to save even more and tens of thousands of American soldiers in an invasion of the Japanese home islands, even though the United States could have demonstrated the nuclear threat without actually bombing.[6] Israel, however, cannot effectively threaten her opponents—either by nuclear deterrent, which long ago lost its credibility because of the international outcry against its use, or by conventional war, which American pressure would stop as soon as Israel began to win. The call for morality in international relations precludes the use of the balance of power to resolve conflicts. Formerly, stronger states restored the balance of power in their favor by warfare. Now they succumb to weaker but supposedly equal neighbor states, as does Israel when it withdraws from Arab lands or America when it gives in to trade demands and defaulted loans. Morality is a restriction, and impedes the efficiency of military efforts.

Machiavelli: goodness and cruelty

Niccolò Machiavelli affirmed that two ways lead most directly to peace: destroy a people's will to fight by either utter goodness or by utter cruelty, usually expressed as extermination. The second option is impractical in the ostensibly humane modern world, which abhors suffering. That luxury corrupted the Romans is obvious, but to say the same of modern Western civilization is taboo. The recent examples of Russia,

---

[5] Neither Chinese, nor Indians were originally homogenous like the Jews since at least the Exodus, but lived in perpetually warring states, spoke different languages, and were religiously distinct.

[6] When Truman shrunk from employing nuclear weapons in Korea, he opened the door to murderous regimes in China and North Korea which annihilated hundreds of times more people than would have died in nuclear attacks.

India, Vietnam, Afghanistan, and Algeria show that impoverished people are willing to fight for principles, to bear and to inflict suffering. Only weakness, the fear of material loss, or the hope of preserving the status quo by accommodating adversaries weakens that will.

The desire for peaceful coexistence runs aground on two problems. First, it accommodates evil alongside merely diverse views. Only Nazi atrocities and threats brought the major powers to declare war. Later, the civilized world hesitated a long time before it stopped the massacres in Rwanda and Yugoslavia. The distinction between justice and mercy blurs into nonexistence. Second, the desire for accommodation is hypocritical: compromise gives way to confrontation when either party hopes to avoid loss; the embargoes on Iraq and Cuba inflict considerable suffering without endangering Americans. The Americans were not brutal in Iraq[7], but heavy fighting or orders relieving them of responsibility would have evaporated the civil gloss.

The Torah says that one can feel compassion only for a neighbor, a well-known member of a closed group with shared values. The mass media bring distant people together, creating the illusion of a global neighborhood. Mistaking timid civility for humane concern and compassion is either a mistake or hypocrisy. Few people are really compassionate toward all, and their example is important but futile. Compassion to aliens is superficial, and people rarely act upon it.

Conquest by virtue is ambiguous, since in the view of her neighbors, Israel would show virtue by getting out of the Middle East altogether. Israel has designed various agricultural programs to help poor Arabs in other countries, and the status of indigenous Arabs in Israel is comparatively high; but Arab popular opinion calls that a sign of Jewish weakness, not of goodwill. People need to denigrate their benefactors to preserve self-esteem, attributing hidden motives and hating them.[8] The help is taken for granted, and its cessation or decrease causes bitterness. The "good" option is unrealizable, hardly ever attempted by practical statesmen, and never successful. No regime that comes to power by force can sustain itself by grace without first exterminating its enemies. Goodness as a device

---

[7] The isolated trials of American soldiers underscore the legalistic notion of brutality which does not tolerate killing fatally wounded enemies to end sufferings or cruelty to interrogated military prisoners.

[8] Western Europeans show no gratitude to America for saving them from the red plague during the Cold War, and revisionists charge the United States with drawing Western Europe into confrontation with the Soviets. Palestinians are not grateful to the United States for pressing for their independence or Egyptiansfor rejecting the Franco-British bid to restore control over the Suez Canal. Arab politicians hardly ever acknowledge the agricultural assistance Israel provides to Palestinians.

to mollify subjugated people[9] is a theoretical construct. Machiavelli hardly discusses the statesmanship of kindness.[10]

Absolute cruelty is superficially as much an extreme as absolute goodness and should be as unrealizable if the object of application of either were immutable. Cruelty, however, eliminates the object itself by destroying opposition and dispersing potential supporters to other countries where they are eventually assimilated and lose nationalist aspirations. Sufficient cruelty can often reduce the dissident population to conformity. Goodness, on the contrary, emboldens dissent—exactly the case with Palestinian nationalism.

Israel, therefore, is left with the most ineffective yet apparently most common third option, low-intensity violence dragging on and on in the futile attempt to avoid acting inhumanely while forcing people to forsake their interests. The aim is to wear the enemy down on various fronts: economy, human resources, the popular will to sustain losses in life and excessive taxation, and the goodwill of foreign sponsors. That path may eventually lead to peace as people grow used to Israel's existence and the enemy's aggression dissipates. Hostilities would not cease even after centuries of coexistence if fresh grievances occurred continuously, as in the case of Catholics and Protestants in Ireland. Mutual acceptance depends on assimilation, or at least the blurring of important differences. Since Jews strive to remain distinct from others—a major source of the hatred of them throughout history—Israelis should not expect time to heal Arab wounds and discontent. In any case, prolonged suffering is more painful than any reasonable speedy solution.

Unlike Arab dictatorships, Israel faces the problems of any other democratic country, including popular resistance to heavy taxation for military purposes in peacetime. Low tolerance to human loss is another factor, though military superiority has so far allowed Israel to come off—in statistical terms—almost unscathed. Another important factor, the goodwill of the United States, is available now but could end quickly if Arabs finance an effective public-relations campaign. Money, a malleable press and public relations agencies, and grassroots anti-Semitism are there. The Vietnam War demonstrates the possibility of stopping American military intervention by appealing to popular opinion.

---

[9] Using goodness for subjugation is not necessarily hypocrisy, though there would be nothing wrong if it was. Living side-by-side with the Jewish state tremendously benefits Palestinians in economic terms. The British developed India, and other Europeans developed their ex-colonies as well.

[10] How authoritative is Machiavelli? But how could he be authoritative in the culture dominated by moral idealists who hijacked the name of liberalism? Not his authority is the issue, but whether his prescriptions were ever refuted. They were not. Machiavelli failed as the head of militia because of the objective limitations, and this book does not address his military ideas, anyway. Besides, teaching is different from practicing; good teachers of arts are often mediocre painters.

The seemingly irresolvable situation has, however, a solution, a combination of the first two options. Israel should drive the Palestinians into Jordan and Lebanon and treat the other Arabs with kind indifference but react with cruelty to any violation of her interests. Negotiators know an opponent is much more likely to give way if pressured from the beginning and then offered a way out. Human nature often leads one to seek the friendship of a strong and haughty neighbor. In both personal and international relations, a strong, accommodating neighbor can provoke hatred. People find satisfaction in attacking a weak giant or at least showing him disregard. When the giant is likely to punish the attack, the best bet is to associate with him. As the saying goes, "If you can't beat 'em, join 'em."

Prudence suggests starting peaceably and disguising plans. As Benjamin Franklin remarked, "A spoonful of honey will catch more flies than a gallon of vinegar." That, however, hinges on the possibility of enforcing the situation deceit obtains: the flies get *stuck* in honey. In the real world, the flies would revolt against the forces of adhesion and the person who lured them in, crying injustice and asking others to help them get away. Jews already tried honey when they agreed to the 1947 partition and peaceful coexistence with the Arabs, though the original plan earmarked all of Palestine for the Jews. That did not work, because the Arabs wanted it all. Once the flies corral one spoonful of honey, they look for more. Once terrorists demands are met, they increase. The Jews act the same way. Settlement could be achieved only as equilibrium of power: more demands less resolutely supported and stiff opposition to further concessions.

Realism, not superficial morality

Passionate (one might say, neurotic[11]) Jews are neither cold politicians like the British[12] nor disciplined soldiers like the Germans nor fearless like the Spanish.[13] The typical Jew is no statesman. So why should Israel make things worse by revealing her weaknesses and exacerbating them with soul-searching and reluctance to admit the most evident things about the way states are created?

Often misunderstood, Machiavelli, one of the greatest humanists of the Renaissance, left a message to future generations. He disdained government force and war; he admired just, wise rulers. He considered murder and deceit distasteful but natural, but like a good surgeon, he saw

---

[11] Cowardly would be another word, amply describing the panic of the Israeli General Staff in the first days of the Yom Kippur War.

[12] Or strong and cynical like the Arabs. I cannot forget the photo of the first President Bush standing before Saudi King Fahd, who remained seated supposedly because he was ill. The posture of many Arab politicians is stunning compared with the groveling of their Israeli counterparts.

[13] Or so hold the traditions about their national characteristics.

the need to do repulsive and painful things quickly and effectively. It is better to live and let live, but if you decide on territorial expansion and war, at least do it knowledgeably. Strategists as far removed in time as Sun Tzu and Clauzewitz shared that attitude. Politics is a cold-blooded game with no place for moralizing and hesitation for the victors. Be coherent and single-minded; smother the weakness of humanism, and weaken the enemy by inducing him to act according to moral rules while you disregard them as fiction, inapplicable in crises. Israel has yet to accept and adopt the truth of warfare. Right now she rolls down the dangerous road recently traveled by Nazi Germany, hysterically imposing unrealizable political objectives on a strong army.

There is no way to peace except to gain the enemy's respect. Bernard Lewis relates a legend about an Arab ruler who said, "Among my people, I aroused respect untainted with fear and love untainted with disrespect." Perhaps possible in an enlightened monarchy, democracy's policy swings preclude such politics. Israelis, hated European aliens among Middle Eastern peoples, cannot arouse such feelings and might hope at best for respect engendered by force and fear. And Arabs,[14] who equate strength with arrogance and hauteur, understand that and would take any other policy for weakness. While few Arabs hated Jews a century ago, they despise them now, because the Israelis combine weakness with anti-Arab ambitions, the worst mix possible.

Fear is the standard—in fact, the only—instrument that lets states exist. Even people who believe in "state by consent" agree that government's most important functions, such as taxation, law enforcement, and defense, ride on the fear of reprisal for non-compliance. Force and the fear of force undergird the balance of power, to which the United States subscribed after Wilson's homilies failed. The most we can hope for in international relations is the judicious and adequate use of power or the threat of it. The Americans stole a piece of Mexico but not of Canada because of their cultural affinity with the latter. They spared Haiti because there was no profit in controlling and upgrading the alien population, not to mention damaging their international image. Arabs will agree to Israeli annexation if they admire her the way Mexicans admired the United States. Lacking this sense of inferiority, Arabs will resist encroachment, as the Canadians did.

No easy way out

Hard lines often repel people who have lived all their lives in democratic countries and prefer indecision and tolerance, expecting the legal system to work, the citizenry to behave reasonably, the courts to be just, and the police to protect and serve. That does not happen in most

---

[14] Sephardic Jews, who both think like Arabs and understand how Arabs think, vote for the right-wing Likud, traditionally associated with strong anti-Arab policy.

countries. The hard-liners in many countries who argue against compromise with perceived evil and for harsh action against it, are not extremists but rather realists who realize that civility will not solve the problem.

I lived in the former Soviet Union and also in Arab countries, all ugly dictatorships. I have spent much time among Palestinians and have several Palestinian friends. Many Palestinians I know still have the Bedouin respect for the strong and disdain for the weak. When Jordan killed eight thousand Palestinians in a couple of days, it aroused little concern; indeed, Palestine has good relations with Jordan. But Palestine continually carps at Israel, specifically because it has unconsciously found a weak spot, namely Israel's rhetoric of morality and her attempt to wage a moral war. Quick, cruel action would stop the war and save lives, as actually happened in Dir Yassin, the Arab village destroyed during the War for Independence by a joint Irgun-Lehi-Palmach operation. Though civilian casualties among the villagers who refused to evacuate were unavoidable and women and children anywhere near Arab fighters were killed, Israeli soldiers shot down between sixty and two hundred people in heavy urban combat, saving scores of thousands of lives by stopping the war and causing the Arab civilians—misinformed by their mass media which reported the fight as a massacre—to flee. That was not good, but it was necessary.[15] Statehood, war, and conquest are ugly, but if there is a national resolve to embark on that path, it should be done efficiently[16] without inflicting prolonged sufferings on one's own or the subdued. Crush the will to fight, drive them away, and live peacefully.

Sovereignty over non-assimilated people is not invulnerable but prevails until the aggrieved are able to rebel, as in Ireland or Chechnya. Citizens let police protect their property from anyone who refuses to recognize their legal rights. The police are fairly efficient against minor law-breakers, but countries are big and their relations to each another less clear than that of owner to thief, so they cannot rely on some international police force for automatic intervention or arbitration. States have to stand ready to protect their holdings, especially if the citizens back the military effort. Sovereignty is sustained by the ability and will to fight for it.

---

[15] Joshua ben Nun could not resettle Canaanites far away, and was told to kill them, a prescription Machiavelli would agree with. Dispersing the Palestinians might preclude future claims: likely, they will assimilate.

[16] Popular opinion is not always right. It is our duty to argue and otherwise work against wrong and immoral policy at every stage of its implementation. As long, however, as such policy, not outright criminal, is carried into action, it makes complete sense to hone it to the utmost effectiveness (lack of moral restraints) in order to reach the goal faster and with less suffering.

Create a credible threat, act brutally

Paper agreements are broken as often as they are signed—unless they are enforced. Lebanon revoked the peace agreement it signed in 1983 a year later. Arabs are notoriously flexible about promises and generally have little respect for agreements. Peace is established on the battlefield and sustained by threat. Defense is a tactical device, ineffective long-term. The threat required may be small when people are tired of war, as in the case of Alsace-Lorraine after World War II, but the threat must be strong and credible with poor and aggressive people like the Arabs who are highly tolerant of suffering.

Defense hardly ever wins peace; the threat of *offense* does. Arabs will not make peace with Israel unless they fear attack. They are comfortable in thinking Israel will not attack them and have no reason to negotiate, especially when certain concessions are involved. Arab disinterest in peace means changes in Israeli military doctrine.

Among the reasons countries make peace are economic benefits (there are none in the present case) or fear. Present Israeli policies give Arabs nothing to fear. Even when they attack first, Israel wages war humanely without inflicting unbearable loss of life or destruction of property. Even in 1967, the Arabs' nightmare, Israel took only non-essential land.

Every offensive war—and Israel's wars are technically offensive, since they aim to settle Jews on land the Arabs held before 1948—succeeds only when important enemy territory is conquered or threatened. Modern warfare enables territorial control by air force and tank divisions, two Israeli specialties. Thus, Israel need not overextend herself conquering vast tracts of land.

The negotiations with Syria over the Golan Heights showed how little bargaining power Israel has. She offered to return most of the Golan Heights, keeping only the ridges needed to maintain first-warning stations and to prevent Syria from firing directly on the Jewish valley below. Predictably, Syria demanded all the Heights. Why would it do otherwise? Syria does not need peace or economic relations with Israel. On the contrary, Syria blackmails the United States by threatening Israel. What does it take to make a country cede conquered territory? the threat of continued economic loss or military operations. A disadvantageous status quo can be accepted *de jure* only if things threaten to get worse, that is, only if peace prevents further aggression. If Israel wants to retain the Golan Heights, she should take or threaten to occupy a much larger territory and then offer a trade.

The Arabs may be forced to seek peace by other measures as well. They should be advised that Israel would annex any territory occupied in retaliation for terrorist attacks permanently—including the Palestinian autonomous regions. And Israel may have not much time to advance on that path, since only Egypt maintains current Middle Eastern stability, and that will change as soon as Islamic radicals succeed the current leadership—and 94% of Egyptians polled supported the 9/11 attacks. In fact, 40% of Arab Britons cheered the attacks. The percentage was probably higher if the truth were known, since many British Arabs were uncomfortable expressing admiration for the nation's enemy.

Arab mentality and discontent

People tend to respect and even enjoy those who defeat but do not oppress them. Israel should consider that as she insults the Arab world by oppressing Palestinians instead of defeating Arabs. To say that Arabs are totally different from Westerners is incorrect. Westerners have historically shown similar cruelty and treachery, but Arabs are cruel and treacherous in the present day, and that makes the difference between the West's current world-view and theirs.

The ever-growing disparity between Arab and Western capabilities also angers Arabs. While a free and enterprising people would have sought to bridge the gap by raising themselves, Muslims—rather like socialists—try to lower others. That is the source of their aggression and terrorism. Unable to achieve economic dominance, they contend in the military sphere. Losing in conventional military operations against tiny Israel, they resort to terrorism.

The struggle adds apocalyptic dimensions to the Muslim self-image: they did not blame God for past economic failures, and the current abundance of petro-dollars is no proof of his favor now. Early military successes established the truth of Mohammed's teaching in his followers' eyes. Arab failure on the battlefield today comes dangerously close to demonstrating that Islam is exhausted. In the hope that more devotion and self-sacrifice will incur divine favor, Muslims preach all-out war against the whole world. Such hysteria cannot last long, especially in the world of MTV values. The next generation of Arabs, like the communists before them, will likely succumb to Western mores, thus obviating the struggle against Israel. If Israel holds on a few decades more, she can win without war.

Peaceful relations with Arabs are possible

In the end, both Jews and Arabs need peace and normal relations with each other. That is not impossible. Many states become friends after protracted hostilities—the United States and England or France and Germany for example—but first the shooting war must stop and time pass. If Jews and Arabs had a common enemy, the waiting period would shorten drastically, as post-World War II politics demonstrated, when Germany and France became allies and the Soviets and Western Europe became enemies. Since, however, the only likely candidate would be Christian, *ergo* Western, taking on such an enemy for the sake of accommodating the Arabs makes no sense for Israel.

24

The other Arabs do not care about the Palestinians

To explain their position to the outside world, Arabs invented a reason for a non-peace solution: the Palestinian problem. That is ludicrous, since the other Arabs hate Palestinians[17] and ostracize Palestinian emigrants settled in their countries. The P.L.O. fomented nationalist unrest and otherwise meddled in Jordan, Lebanon, and Tunisia, though even that is forgotten with the demand for a Palestinian state, not even in question in the early 1970s when Anwar Sadat offered Israel peace. Minor Arab contributions to the Palestinian cause show solidarity on the surface but perpetuate the Israeli-Palestinian conflict in substance.

Arab countries have no reason to make peace

In a notable but commonly ignored example, Egypt concluded a peace treaty with Israel in return for repatriated territory. Other Arabs have no reason to seek peace with Israel. They do not need peace for economic reasons. They lose nothing by preserving the armistice. Israel does not threaten them, hence, there's no cause for them to desire peace.

From the Arab point of view, Israel looks weak in repeatedly asking for peace. She ignores the Arab mentality. Arabs must be forced to the peace table. Israel should turn the tables and change the rules. She does not need an armistice now. She should abandon it and tell the Arabs they have three months to negotiate and resettle the Palestinians or hostilities will resume.

Israeli interests and policy in the Arab world

What are Israel's interests? Defining them too vaguely eventually leads Israel to one of two extremes. If she overextends herself, Israel will go abroad "in search of distant monsters" and eventually bankrupt herself in foreign operations. If she does not guard her interests adequately, Israel's threat of deterrence will deteriorate and provoke more enemy attacks. Although it is tempting to insist on full normalization of relations with her neighbors, the approach would lead nowhere, since the notion is vague. Considering intra-Arab tariff agreements and preference policies, Israel will be drawn into endless disputes about opening Arab markets, which will always be more open to other Arabs, and trade relations with Israel will remain less than normal. A customs union with Israel is unacceptable to Arabs, whose weak economies would be swamped by Israeli exports, and Israel would not welcome an influx of Arab *Gastarbeiter*. Opening foreign markets is neither unprofitable nor uncommon—witness Great Britain's relentless pursuit of commercial interests by military means. Indeed, Britain

---

[17] This relation is two-way. Even given the background of Arab insouciance over the Russian incursion into Muslim Afghanistan, the P.L.O. was the only Islamic organization to support the Soviets.

would not have allowed a boycott such as the Arabs' on Israel. The proper policy, however, seems to be *laissez-faire*. Israel cannot dictate Arab economic policies and preferences. That leaves two practical definitions of national interest: military—no Arab military or terrorist territorial violations—and economic—no discrimination against Israeli companies compared to other non-Muslims. Economic benefits likely do not justify the expenses of a large-scale war, especially since the Arab markets are relatively minor and oil is available elsewhere. This reasoning, to be sure, refers only to protracted war. Only an overwhelming initial strike and the establishment of local police enforcement, supported by the threat of aerial attack with weapons of mass destruction, makes sense while the Arabs possess oil. That, however, means crushing all resistance. The model is Roman punitive expeditions, not the current American involvement in Iraq.

Should Jews decide that economic interests in small Arab markets justify maintaining a standing army, that decision may become a proper objective. Military threats to protect economic interests were common until the 19th century in those nations that needed standing armies anyway to control their empires. Maintaining an army solely to promote economic interests in the Middle East is economically unjustifiable. The really large markets, however, usually belong to NATO members or affiliates, against whom Israel can hardly use force. The profit from such small markets would not pay the bill but would rather cost the Israeli economy its technological edge through addiction to low-end, low-profit, low-tech markets guaranteed by military power.

Territory is not worth lives, but sometimes there is no choice

No piece of land, much less sovereignty over it, is worth lives. Taking that approach to its logical conclusion, however, means Jewish withdrawal from the Middle East. The objective, therefore, is to maximize Jewish landholdings without significantly raising the death toll. Wars cause deaths, not only traditional pitched battles but terrorist acts. Because I'm inherently partial, I prefer measures to reduce the loss of Jewish lives, even at the expense of Arabs, but if the Arab death toll can be minimized without harming Israel, I would support it. I would never, however, put leftist dogma masquerading as liberal morality before Jewish lives.

Arabs coexisted peacefully with small Jewish communities for centuries, but now Jews are so sufficiently strong and culturally diverse a group that Arabs would not tolerate them even in an autonomous region in a federal state. Few governments in history have accepted large alien minorities as citizens without trying to assimilate, disperse, or subdue them. Nations often antagonize a weak but defiant neighbor, especially if it was once strong and aggressive.[18] If the Israelis dismantled their state, Arabs

---

[18] The key is defiance, persistence in being arrogantly different. Jews spark anti-Semitism, while native Americans cause no similar feelings.

would likely prey on them. The humiliation of losing its statehood would break the Jewish nation's spirit and ignite anti-Semitism.[19] The option of stateless coexistence with Arabs is now closed, and the Israelis must have a viable state, and viability expands as much as possible without increasing Arab resistance, worldwide opposition, and major loss of life.

Should the Israelis fight for the present state, surrounded by recalcitrant Arab states, or should they use the Israeli Defense Force to buy land in Africa, Latin America, or Eastern Europe? Should they negotiate administrative autonomy in, say, Australia? The Jews do not need land *per se*. Agriculture is almost worthless in a modern economy, so no small area is worth fighting for. The only territory the Jews as a nation need is Eretz Israel—not for its economic significance but to achieve intangibles like religious fulfillment, national consciousness, and honor. Even in the rational world, those values seem odd only when related to Jews. People honor those who risk their lives to defend the principles they hold dear: Christianity, socialism, freedom, or sovereignty, even if that requires some killing.

Confronted with the offer of settlement in Uganda, Weizmann remarked that the British would not move their capital to Paris. The analogy startled his interlocutor: "But London is ours."

"Jerusalem was ours when London was marshes," Weizmann replied. Neither British help nor a United Nations resolution achieved the goal—only force.

Israel should restrict democracy

The possibility of democracy in Israel at present is a hopeless myth. Israel is not at peace; therefore she is at war, an ambiguous and expansive war. Trotsky's *neither peace, nor war* policy proved a disaster, and Israel rolls the same road. Democracy tolerates differences of opinion about national policy instead of requiring a unified national effort. Democracy, inherently weak and unfit for wartime, is for peacetime. The democracies of Ancient Greece waged only short, expansive wars unless they were forced to alliances in some utterly undemocratic way. They were also free from political ambiguity: everyone wanted booty. Totalitarian regimes demonstrated tremendous capacity for warfare in WWII: the United States struggled to overcome small, recently industrialized Japan and a Germany already ruined by the time the U.S. army intervened in Europe.

Many countries have realized the need to restrict freedoms and introduced wartime censorship, restricted freedom of association, and postponed elections, essentially suspending democratic processes.[20] Secret arrangements with foreign governments, disinformation, and suspension of

---

[19] The Israelis became "normal" with a state and an army of their own.

[20] The United States did not have to abrogate freedoms during the WWII because no significant group favored peace with the Germans and the Japanese.

due process complete the undeclared temporary conversion to autocratic rule within a generally agreed policy framework.

No inherent right to a state, no inviolable state

No government takes the idealist claim of the right to statehood seriously. Otherwise, Russia would let Chechnya secede, and Britain would have agreed to an independent Ireland long before it did. Taken to its logical extreme, the right to statehood would dissolve modern states into village-size communities and eventually abrogate the host states. The anarchist's dream is another man's nightmare. The anarchist ideal sees ownership of land as jurisdiction over it. Where dissenters can secede and establish independent colonies, wars will be fewer, but while the concept of nation-states remains, territorial wars will continue, though progressively deterred by increasing expensive military devastation.

Jews and Arabs have different interests and will likely never define fairness the same way; however, such agreement is a prerequisite for the peaceful resolution advocated by humanists like Noam Chomsky.[21] The common interest that arises from sharing enemies is unlikely today when an enemy of the Jews is almost automatically a friend of the Arabs, as were the Nazis.

It is difficult to imagine a shared goal sufficiently important to unify the adversaries. Economically, Israel is less attractive to Arabs than old partners like Britain and France or influential ones like the United States and, increasingly, China and Japan. For political guarantees and military aid, Arabs can apply directly to the United States without reference to Israel. Neither side is interested in formal peace, preferring armistice and minor unrest, which bring both Israel and the Arabs from the strategic periphery into the focus of world affairs and pays dividends in economic and military aid, unnecessary for peaceful coexistence but advantageous for strong governments. A foreign enemy distracts people from local problems, letting Arab dictatorships and Israeli socialism survive.

Jews have claimed Jerusalem as their eternal capital for two millennia; their national consciousness centers around it. They want the city, but ideologically motivated Arabs also want it now. Where's the solution acceptable to both? Neither trusts the traditional broker and both suspect the United States of pursuing its own interest. The balance of power, the equilibrium point of many military and moral forces, settles such disputes, not someone's idea of justice, as opinions differ. Any peaceful solution would be arbitrary and therefore unacceptable to many. In minuscule Jerusalem, a hundred yards is a league. Why should the Palestinians have only the West Bank instead of all their pre-1948 territory,

---

[21] Regardless of how misguided and idealistic are Chomsky's views, I deeply respect him as a voice of conscience, reminding us of morality where we prefer efficiency and of compassion where we pursue self-interest.

28

including today's Israel? Why should the Jews agree to partition instead of claiming the Promised Land in its entirety, including all of Palestine? The answer hinges on the equilibrium of force, the route David took to conquer the Temple Mount.

If religious justification seems flimsy, consider the arguments other states offer for their existence. The desire of enlargement is an obsession and a driving force of many states. If that objective is universally acceptable, which one is not? Why was splitting along religious lines acceptable in Yugoslavia and Indonesia but not in Israel? If African tribes hardly out of the Stone Age are entitled to sovereignty on their ancestral lands, how much more are the Jews? If world opinion accepts the suppression of the long-standing nationalist aspirations of weak minorities, the Spanish Basques or the Russian Tatars, why not suppress the hardly three-decades-old nationalism of a non-nation with no distinctive culture, i.e., the Palestinians? Why do the people who set up the Christian Kingdom of Jerusalem during the Crusades condemn Israeli control of the city? If white settlers displaced the aboriginal Americans and Australians to create viable states, why should Jews not do the same? If no state objected to the creation of Saudi Arabia by conquest, why refuse a similar justification for Israel? If ethnic populations were relocated from Poland and Czechoslovakia to pacify Germany, why reject a similar approach in Palestine?

Questioning the Jewish right to the land ignores the crucial issue: what right do Arabs have to it? Jews bought land from individual Palestinians. No one was evicted, nor was private ownership violated. Much of the territory was unused desert and marsh before the Jews made the land productive and valuable, acquiring the right of homestead. As for state control of unused, untitled land, the Palestinians never had a state—the Turks, then the British, controlled the land—nor were the Palestinians recognized as a nation, a recognition which would have let them claim tribal sovereignty over the land. By the time the colonial powers turned the territory over to the locals, they *de facto* included not only Palestinians but Jews as well. The only reason Britain decided to split the land earmarked for Israel into two countries was to settle the nomadic Arabs even Jordan did not want. The Jews did not seize the land from Palestinians; neither had a formal claim on it.

Many mistakenly believe Palestinians today lay claim to land they once owned. Rather, the Palestinians claim they lost jurisdiction over a country they never had. Before the rise of Palestinian nationalism in the 1970s, the rioters and guerrillas were anti-Jewish, not pro-Palestine. If private ownership of some land means jurisdiction over the whole country, the Jews who bought land had a better claim to Palestine in 1947 than the indigenous Arabs who largely lacked title. But private ownership of land is unrelated to jurisdiction even over that parcel, let alone over any wider entity. The Arabs claimed more land than they actually needed and already

29

had in Palestinian dominated Jordan. The Jews had to force an accommodation.

Respect even for private property is limited: in times of famine, the survival instinct prevails and food storages are routinely sacked with no public outcry. Since many people value religion and ideology above life, property rights are *a fortiori* subjected to religious values. Even if Jerusalem actually belonged to the Arabs, the Jews were justified in taking it over, because of all religions, Old Jerusalem is central only to them. Golgotha is more important to Christians than the Temple site, and Muslims have no scriptural connection with the place at all after Mohammed reoriented Muslim worship to Mecca. Private property is not an issue in the conflict; Israel generally respects Arab ownership of particular buildings and land. Assertions to the contrary usually refer to the nationalization of unowned land and a hostile environment for Muslim owners. Driving other people away is better than living in hatred. Significantly, the war has little to do with Israeli political freedoms, since it is not a sure thing that the Arabs would have refused them those rights. Nor does the war pursue religious aims, since several kinds of worship flourish in Israel. The war is oddly about government and municipal control over territory.

Borders are graphic representations of the current power equilibrium. They are in constant flux and always have been. The attempts of nation-states to sanctify borders to preserve a status quo beneficial to them are futile. If the Palestinians are ever strong enough, they will squeeze Israel out. Israel should do likewise.

While Arabs naturally prefer to see the land they settle inviolate, Jews want that land as the center of their national ambitions. A ridiculously small part of Arab holdings in Dar Al Islam is the ultimate secular goal of Jews.

For centuries, countries have fought to reach a situation where further border adjustments are not worth wars. The rights to life and property should be preserved for Palestinians as long as that does not involve attacking Jews. But there is no *right* to have a country, let alone a country within specific borders; that is done by force. The violence, moreover, is not endless. A few crushing defeats can change a nation's mind, especially when a good economy switches the focus of ambitions, as was the case with France under Napoleon and later with Germany. A balance of power struggle is usually bloodless.

Indeed, that would have happened if Jews had been honest with the Arabs in 1948 when Israel was founded. The Arabs accepted the medieval Christian Kingdom of Jerusalem,[22] created by brute power for the familiar

---

[22] That they usually called the city Aelia Capitolina rather than her Arabic religious name Al Quds (the Sacred), demonstrates that they attached little religious value to the place. Saladin's recapture of the city a century later was only a by-product of his war of expansion. Soon after, Saladin turned the city over to the Christian

goal of profit. If 20th century Jews had used force, the Arabs would have had no problem, but the Jews made a crucial mistake: they attempted to justify their claims not by force but by religion. It is one thing to say to someone, "Give me this thing, because I'm stronger and will kill you if you do not." It is quite another to argue that you want to take this thing for ideological reasons which are irrelevant to him. He will not only find counter-arguments but will also develop the will to fight, because as he sees it, your position is wrong and his, right. People are more sensitive to infringement of religious values than of their compatriots' property interests. Ideological reasoning provoked the Arabs, yet was probably irrelevant to most Jews, as their support for settlement in Uganda instead of the Middle East at the dawn of the Zionist movement showed. Many, probably most, of Israel's founders were socialists and thus secular. Religious justification of an invasion of the Middle East meant nothing to them and deceived the rest. The fact is, the Jews took the land because they wanted it and could take it. That is reasoning, not justification. They need no one else's help, as they did not in campaigns so widely separated in time and yet so similar as Joshua ben Nun's conquest of Canaan and the 1948 War of Independence.

No viable state has ever been created, let alone sustained, peacefully.[23] All desirable land was settled in antiquity. If the Jews wanted a state, driving indigenous peoples away or subjugating them was the only option, the only viable way the countries are created. More recently, Germany was consolidated from homogeneous kingdoms—with a common language and culture—only by blood and iron. Less than fifty years ago, the French killed millions in the futile effort to preserve their colonies. Other nations established their states in blood long ago and now have the luxury of moralistic piety. Israel cannot afford morality at this stage of the state's formation. It is impossible right now to deal with the Arabs humanely and democratically. There is no need to cast the creation of a state, an amoral entity, in moral terms. The creation of Israel was not fair to the Palestinians nor could it be, since it robbed them of land they considered theirs. But since the Israelis decided to do it, they should do it wholeheartedly, without making excuses, offering reparations, or saying the Palestinians abandoned their villages of their own free will. They should not seize significant territories from the Arabs, then offer to return them for a flimsy paper agreement.

---

emperor Frederick II, and it languished in obscurity into the 19th century when Zionist immigration brought it to the fore of Arab politics.

[23] Some, as Singapore, were peacefully established in peculiar circumstances not paralleled in the Middle East. Many ex-colonies were set up as states by their former masters. Most are still too young to permit conclusions, but no fundamental change of the principle that force creates states is likely.

The question is not some idyllic justice unknown in international relations based on power, but the normal, generally accepted way of doing the business of statehood. No one is singled out for prosecution for a crime everyone commits; why single out Israel for admonition and reproach? How can the *modus operandi* of every state known to history be called a crime? A crime is an exceptional wrong. Statehood itself might be viewed as bad, but Israel's birth pains are milder than most others'.

A world used to popular contract, mutual accommodation, and peaceful resolution of disputes would be wonderful. No such thing exists, however, as America's first European settlers learned from the natives. All nations were created in bloodshed and are sustained by power; anything on paper is inevitably irrelevant. Israel cannot be built on agreements with the Arabs. International agreements are the legal by-products of inhumane military victories.

No historical right

Justification of an Israeli state by historical right is sheer nonsense. If Jews have a right to return after two millennia, Arabs have even more right to return after fifty years. The Jews, moreover, were not forced out of Judea any more than the Arabs from Israel. Facing a hostile regime, both chose to emigrate.

The Israelis need not appeal to a twenty-century-old historical right. Indeed, there is no such thing as a historical right. Ancient Egypt, Mesopotamia, Rome, and Turkey learned that painful lesson about the same land. American Indians don't rule their country now. Thirty years of occupation since the Six-Day war of 1967, coupled with the indigenous population's abandonment of the land and *de facto* Israeli sovereignty, is a much more valid argument.

Might does not make right, but why care about the right? Arabs won't consider Jewish national longings, and Jews are deaf to the prohibition of ceding Islamic land. Rights exist only in a given system of axioms, and are not valid for outsiders. Between groups, power is the only argument, moderated by the prohibition of atrocities.

Israel appeals to some Christians by recalling her biblical right to the land, forgetting that most Christians believe they themselves replace the Jews as the New Israel. In any case, the land is destined for some Israel, whether old or new, and not for Muslims, who make a religious point of oppressing Christians.

Serbs and Bosnians are still enemies after six hundred years. It takes only a few hotheads to stir people up. Palestinian will always remember what they perceive as Israeli injustice. The most expedient solution is to expel the Palestinians, disperse them, and pressure them into assimilation with other Arabs. Jews preserved their national aspirations in the Diaspora because of Jewish distinctiveness. Palestinians lack a persistent sense of a unique identity. Life in a small remnant of their

32

country contiguous to Israel would remain a continuous humiliation to them. The notion of continuing the guerrilla warfare would be too present, too tempting. If the Palestinians stay where they are now, the conflict will go on, not because the people on either side are inherently bad, but because a conflict that involves nationalist ambitions cannot be arbitrated; and even if it could, enough people on both sides would not be satisfied, leaving the fire smoldering, ready to flare up on the slightest pretext.

This book often presents contradictory advice, such as either transferring Haram esh-Sharif to Arab diplomatic jurisdiction or destroying the mosques there. Either option is workable. Whichever one prefers is a subjective choice. Israel must at last choose *a* policy, adhere to it, and work to bring it to life, instead of floundering about, losing lives and money and effort and goodwill.

If there is a decision to expand, it should be carried out intelligently and efficiently. *If* Jews want their own state, it cannot be a multi-ethnic democracy. *If* war threatens, Israel should strike first. Evil ends should not be exacerbated by prolonged means. Israel has shied from the problem for decades, only because she is uncomfortable with the solution—unwilling to pose clear questions and see clear answers, losing thousands of lives and spending hundreds of billions of dollars.[24] The solution this book suggests is inhumane, but current policies are cumulatively worse.

The feasibility of conquering the Arab states

In a war to repel aggression, Israel should require unconditional surrender, a bit of age-old wisdom lost on Israeli politicians who repeat the WWI error of leaving humiliated enemy to re-arm. The habit of settling for an armistice is supremely damaging and costly. Armies love victory; indecision is demoralizing.

Israel must occupy the capitals of enemy states. To avoid loss of Israeli personnel, that goal should be carried out in two stages. The first is the aerial destruction of economically significant objects and the devastation of the capital itself. Enemy civilian losses should be ignored, since the people willingly participated in the war by accepting and supporting their governments. Second, a local collaborative government should be installed, supported by a few Israeli mechanized ground troops and the threat of further air assault. Its aim should be to exact reparations in oil. There would be no need to guard the whole country, as the Americans do in Iraq, just the oil wells and pipelines. After some years of humiliation, Israel might agree to local elections based on a constitution prohibiting major military development, much as the United States did in post-World

---

[24] In 1994 dollars, including U.S. aid. Estimates for cumulative losses from 1948 exceed a trillion dollars when accounting for GDP losses from conscription and displacement of economic resources, embargo, and other indirect costs.

War II Japan. Given how poor the Arabs would be without oil, Israel would have enough power to enforce her demands.

Should conquered lands and revenues be restored at all, or should they be annexed? Victorious nations do not usually return occupied territory, even if it is not economically or militarily valuable. Different considerations have dictated rare exceptions. The United States granted Philippines sovereignty to maintain its image of an anti-imperialist popular democracy that keeps its promises. Preserving the distant, heavily populated land as a colony against the wishes of its people was unfeasible, especially since the Philippines agreed to let the American military bases stay.

If a state occupies foreign land to trade later for normalization of relations, it must maintain credibility. Once the Arabs see they could regain lost territory without a peace treaty, they will have little reason to sign one. No country restores conquered land to a hostile neighbor unwilling to establish peaceful relations. It was very odd for Israel to give in to Lebanese and Syrian pressure. What could the political weight of a failed or terrorist state be, anyway?

Abandon the pretense of humane war

Israel must abandon morality while at war. Saving Israeli lives must be the priority, no matter the casualties among Arab soldiers, government officials, or civilians. Most Israeli politicians would subscribe to that, though Israeli strategy in Lebanon led to great Israeli casualties, because the conflict was kept to low intensity to save Arab lives—at the cost of Jewish lives, a sop to the media and perceived Israeli moral values.[25] If Israel is not Jew-centric, then all the fuss about historical rights and religious justification is hypocritical. People who fight selflessly for high ideals are often ready to sacrifice their lives. That, however, is not the case with the Jews who view themselves as the ultimate end of the Israeli state, not as a means to some political purpose. Soldiers die for fellow soldiers but not to save the enemy, military or civilian. The Israeli government should not force romanticism on its combat personnel. To sacrifice one's life to save the enemy's children and women is noble, but it cannot be forced on anyone. The Soviet Union fought to spread imperialist socialism; America, to defend democracy. Religious Jews could say that Israel has the transcendent biblical objective of establishing herself in the Promised Land, but the same scriptures tell Jews to slaughter the Canaanites. Secular Jews

---

[25] The motivation was complex, including fear of escalation. Israel's repeated overestimation of her enemies (except in 1967–73) recalls the American mistake in dealing with the Soviet Union and China: from Truman's refusal to employ nuclear weapons at Yalu out of fear, irrelevantly to humane concerns, to the low intensity of anti-Cuban efforts, to shrinking from removing nuclear arsenals from degrading Russia after the U.S.S.R. dissolution.

see no purpose for Israel except bettering their lives and are not about to die to save Arabs. Any enemy casualties are acceptable; using weapons of mass destruction is preferable to risking Israeli soldiers in close combat. Taking Nablus off the map to nail a few terrorists is clearly excessive, but destroying the house they are in from the air is better than a pitched battle.

Countries, not armies, prosecute wars. Soldiers hate the enemy, not just opposing soldiers. A requirement of not harming civilians divides the perception of the enemy schizophrenically and undermines the resolve to fight. No Western army worried about civilians until the 18th century when attitudes changed. In heavy urban battles, most inhabitants died; plunder and torture were commonplace. Romantic ideas of either knightly or Christian warfare (oxymoronic as that is) prevailed for a short time when armies were small, fighting near their kingdoms, easily re-supplied, and opponents were ready to engage in the open. Napoleon's army lived off the land, and the powers in WWII did not care about civilians in either Leningrad or Dresden, but targeted them to break the enemy. Korea, Algeria, Vietnam, Afghanistan, Yugoslavia, and Iraq all saw large civilian losses. Wars are about indiscriminate killing, especially in conflicts with guerrillas purposely mixing with the population. Civilians are spared when armies fight other armies, not whole populations. The objective then is to destroy the enemy's military capacity, and inflicting undue casualties on civilians only distracts armies, burdens them with spoil,[26] and makes conquered peoples rebellious. Exactly the opposite happens in Israel's wars, especially in anti-guerrilla operations. The Arabs are generally loyal to their leaders, especially if they oppose Israel. They support Arab armies and Arab guerrillas. Poor, uneducated societies are more coherent in their views than the Western liberals imagine. Muslims laughed at the American attempts to prove that the United States fights Islamic terrorists, not the general population; they knew there is no difference. No army is separate from the people, as was the case in the West before universal conscription. And Arabs support their armies economically. Monarchs paid for their wars; modern governments rely on taxes and military material factories. Therefore, civilians are part of the war effort—and fair game.

Advocates of a humane war strategy are often ignorant of military reality and history. Not only is half-measure warfare more prolonged and bloodier than a quick confrontation in the same situation, but any army in its rage treats civilians criminally. Military professionals recognized that grim reality when carpet-bombing Dresden, A-bombing Nagasaki, or slaughtering the fleeing Iraqi army and many civilians in 1991. Israel

---

[26] Booty became less critical for better-paid or wealthier conscripted soldiers. The commanders found plunder disgusting. Keeping a train with loot is a problem in mobile warfare. The taste for booty is ineradicable and still surfaces. Consider the Russian plunder of Germany in 1945 and Israeli and Arab claims of looting in 1948.

should not practice the utter stupidity of shielding enemy civilians at the expense of her soldiers' lives.

As the immediate Arab threat fades, it is difficult to convince Israelis to risk their lives for policies they do not support, especially when the Israeli vote splits almost evenly between two major blocks, and the opposition carps at everything the government does. The resolve to protect Israeli soldiers, never mind enemy casualties, will do a lot to stiffen the will to fight.

People fighting for cherished values can be cruel, since values are more important than the lives of a hated enemy who opposes them. Soldiers hesitate to inflict suffering when they are not sure they support the war. They give the enemy the benefit of the doubt. They are less willing to risk their own lives. Undecided soldiers fight indecisively. Therefore Israel should avoid half-wars and focus on ideologically charged conflicts and wage them without mercy.

Making Arabs Agree to Peace

Behavior that is rational in small groups does not work in complex adaptive social systems. The laws governing finite interactions do not apply to the infinite. Too many parties are involved in the Arab-Israeli conflict, too many interests clash, the actions are too unpredictable. The parties have no fixed positions. Attitudes adapt to changing circumstances, precluding systemic response.

The notion of reaching peace through good-faith negotiations is a rationalist fantasy not unlike a centrally planned economy. Neither decrees nor any number of people voting set the prices and demand, but rather myriad market interactions are in play, many of them imperceptible or seemingly irrelevant. Price setting involves a lot of mini-confrontations, sellers refusing to take less, buyers refusing to pay more. Not goodwill but the relative market power of suppliers and consumers set prices. The invisible hand—innumerable conflicts, power exchanges, exhaustion— makes peace, political or economic. Kindness might work in small groups but does not on the large scale where it cannot be tailored to each person's perception and builds rancor, not goodwill.

Preparing for a drawn-out war when nearly everyone is talking about peace is odd in the extreme. We figure that two reasonable people can always reach a mutually acceptable solution. To suggest otherwise is counter-intuitive.

The Israeli situation differs from the model of two reasonable people arguing. At issue is a monopoly both parties want—or think they want. Partition is humiliating, as if the Mongols demanded joint jurisdiction over the Kremlin with the Russians because the Mongols controlled their homeland for centuries. The possession of Jerusalem was a sensitive issue for Christendom for centuries until the religious cynicism of the 19th century arose. For Jews and Arabs, the city is also a political concern. The parties to the conflict are not two. Not all the world's Muslims will sign the peace treaty, and asymmetric warfare will let them ignore it to pursue their goals. There are no courts and police to enforce the agreement; U.N. guarantees did not prevent the war in 1967, and NATO's protection is dubious. Israel lacks the depth of defense necessary to wait for support to materialize. Another difference is that crowds do not think rationally. The soldiers on either side might not see each other as enemies, but mobs do. Soldiers facing death might forget indoctrination; people who support terrorists from safety of their homes are prone to hatred. Countries reach agreements, but Israel is not fighting a country. Guerrillas have no reason to honor treaties, and they do not fear reprisal.

The nations of Europe, which share religion, ethnicity, and culture, have fought each other for centuries for every imaginable reason, regardless of treaties and alliances. The latest sixty years of peace make some think it will last forever, though it took, first, a dangerous common enemy, the U.S.S.R., and now common trade adversaries, the United States and East Asia, to make it gel. Europeans are educated, hard-working, law abiding, and prosperous; none of that generally holds for the Arabs. Domestic wars became economically unfeasible for Europeans only decades ago, and their ideological and ethnic differences are now blurred. Jews, on the contrary, want to preserve their difference from the Arabs, which is ample ground for hatred. Israeli kings who achieved tactical victories over their neighbors, undoubtedly thought they established lasting peace—until the reversal came in a few decades. The Middle East will continue as perpetual battleground.

The United States took California from Mexico, yet Mexican Americans do not blow up buses. Mexico accepted the loss of California because the Americans never offered to return it, claimed historical justification for the annexation, or asked humane Mexicans to pity European refugees to the New World. Americans were powerful and proud of it, therefore admired. Palestine, even if a state, can relate to Israel as Mexico relates to the United States: admiring and hoping for more job opportunities. Israel, however, does not want such attachment, as it would come at the cost of flooding the Jewish state with Palestinian immigrants.

Israel needs to make war to win peace. At their height, the Romans learned not to wait for the enemy to strike first but launched preemptive campaigns, usually with the limited objective of de-militarizing the enemy and installing a friendly ruler. In his dictum, *Qui desiderat pacem, praeparet bellum,* Vegetius Renatus criticized the policy of waiting passively for barbarian incursions. Pacifism is the end, not a means.

The subsidies to Muslims should stop, as neither payments for good behavior nor sanctions that punish violence work. Once people realize someone will pay them to keep quiet, the asking price goes up. Force backed the *pax romana,* but money cannot buy peace. The United States has often tried to buy allegiance, only to watch its money end up in hostile hands, and breeding hostile minds. Money is not everything—and nothing compared to ideology.

If both Israel and the Arabs risked losing aid and either side declared a cease-fire, the other side would blackmail by threatening hostilities. Even if they gave in to economic sanctions, they would resume hostilities once the money stopped. America's Arab clients will turn on their benefactors in the hatred that dependence generates.

Germany did not repent after WWI, even though the Allies did not invade the homeland and practically abrogated reparations; but the Marshall Plan changed its tune *after* the devastation of WWII.

Force is the only convincing argument in no-holds-barred, no-guarantees international relations. Good behavior cannot be bought or even defined. If it means cessation of hostilities, Israel would be happy to preserve the status quo with an armistice, but the Palestinians cannot accept that—except to buy time and find the money to finance the next round.

Few soldiers go to war for ideology, and those who do forget all about it on the battlefield. Israeli soldiers generally do not hate Muslims, though many despise them. Tellingly, second-generation Israeli Jews of Arab origin hate their ethnic brethren far oftener, nearly as much as Arabs hate Israelis. Overcoming hatred is a major problem on both sides, but it won't happen any time soon. Both need an external enemy to blame their problems on. Only prosperous societies can live without enemies, and the Palestinians are desperately poor.

Voluntary settlement is not possible. Some Arab militants will not accept even the most reasonable solution, a Palestinian state on the West Bank and in Gaza, autonomy for Muslim sites in Jerusalem, and compensation for seized property. Islamic radicals demand the right of return for the refugees' descendants, autonomy for Israeli Arabs, and a boycott and perhaps evacuation of the Jewish state. They will be few, and most Arabs will accept the offer; but suicide operations require no army. No peace treaty can improve Israel's military status quo, though it might foster goodwill between Jews and Palestinians that could be nurtured into cooperation.

Israel has the option of settling with the Arab countries and then dealing with the terrorists and, purportedly, reducing her military requirements. Whether the Arab countries could be made to sign a peace treaty is not clear—so far they make more demands than compromises. Muslims would remain hostile to Israel, not letting her demobilize. Time dulls hatred, but it rekindles when new generations forget the past. Israel is the Arabs' perfect enemy, non-threatening yet a good excuse for internal failures, and social upheavals will resurrect enmity. Israel is a foreign object in the Middle East, and the Muslims will try to cast her out.

Objectives of Peace

Israel does not need peace

An Arab-made peace with Israel would exist only on paper; in Islam, *jihad* is a perpetual obligation. The military jihad is interrupted only temporarily by truces, and a truce is what Israel has now. Arabs see themselves as morally bound only by lawful agreements—and a peace agreement with an infidel state in Dar al-Islam is by definition illegal and allowed only to deceive infidels. That Jews are not infidels in Islam, but enjoy special status, will pose no difficulty for radical imams; Israel is not a theocracy, but a secular state, and thus in their minds infidel, promoting the Great Satan's values. Few Muslims concede that jihad is an outdated, unrealizable obligation like those common in mature religions or reinterpret it as peaceful competition. Fundamentalist guerrillas who oppose settlement with Israel see jihad as a military obligation and would honor no indemnity of the West. Arabs have always violated cease-fires with Israel; why imagine they would observe peace treaties? Normalization would not help: Russia, Germany, and the Great Britain had perfectly normal relations days before the World War I.

If Israel would define why it needs peace, rather than demanding it, she could calculate feasible concessions. Peace is not required for salvation. On one hand, no large-scale war with the Arab coalition looms, and on the other, some authoritarian ruler bent on war can start a war regardless of any paper treaty. The people in the rich Arab countries that can afford an expensive war are accustomed to prosperity and do not seek a fight.

Israel can agree to an armistice. America and the Soviet Union ended several wars—Japan, Afghanistan; Korea, Vietnam—without formal peace agreements. Peace is irrelevant even for economic purposes: should Israel become an attractive financial center, Arabs will find ways to invest there. They have already solved the ideologically much bigger problem of investing for interest at all, prohibited by Islamic usury laws.

Peace is important only if Israel wants to become a regional superpower and needs an unburdened economy, stability, and good relations with her neighbors. Even then, peace does not lead inevitably to fully normalized relations, witness the situation with Egypt. Indeed, it is unrealistic to expect Arabs to start treating Jews as equals or superiors after centuries of *dhimmi*-ship[27] and known weakness. Israel must first become economically and culturally attractive to Arabs. Then a diplomatic solution will follow.

---

[27] *Dzimma,* resident Jewish and Christian aliens in the Muslim world, generally protected but with considerably restricted rights.

Israel can sustain neither modern war nor a credible threat

The politics of warfare must stop, since Israel cannot depend on military means forever. Even assuming a ratio of Jewish casualties to Arab casualties of 1:100, the Israeli population would be wiped out in any confrontation involving large-scale use of chemical, biological and nuclear weapons. Israel's population is much more concentrated than its enemies' and much more vulnerable. Moreover, military expenditures have brought the country to an economic dead end. Weapons are more technologically advanced than average goods, and the cost of weapons rises faster than the GDP. Poor economic development and increased military costs will at some point mean Israel can no longer finance her defense. Even the Soviet Union, which ignored its people's welfare, could not sustain the arms race. Protracted warfare devastates Israel, causing emigration and undermining the aim for which Israel was established. Whatever the objective, Israel must strike quickly and decisively to force the Arabs to accept Israeli terms—or acquiesce to theirs.

An end of belligerence is imperative

There is an important political reason for ending hostilities. The political fragmentation brought about by the departure of the authoritative figures of modern Israel's early history creates a situation where quick decisions, especially difficult ones, are impossible. Indecision impedes military action, particularly preemptive action, so important for a small country without much depth of defense in a protracted low-intensity war. Whatever Arab intentions, peaceful or not, tiny Israel is little more than thirty years past a major war, twenty years after a confrontation with Lebanon, and surrounded by large, aggressive neighbors professing a belligerent strain of Islam and uninterested in peace negotiations. Some of them maintain large standing armies, and all are obtaining modern weaponry. The Israeli government would be crazy not to maintain military readiness—though nothing will be of any effect without depth of defense.

No developed country can sustain the cost of defense in a war of attrition. The minor destruction Israel causes hardly bothers Palestinians. Israel uses significant resources to answer low-cost guerilla actions. Egypt mobilized repeatedly to exhaust Israel with reciprocal mobilizations.[28] The mass media make every incident significant, raising anxiety levels. Israel should use attrition wherever possible (against the Saudis, for example) and resist it through preemptive destruction of enemy forces.

Low-level breaches of an armistice are rarely intended to annoy the opponent but more often are either military operations *per se* (the war of attrition) or preparation for a larger conflict. Israel has not profited from armistices and need not limit her response to provocations. Attacking an

---

[28] Why waste a good mobilization? If the army is almost assembled anyway, destroy the enemy's military assets to discourage new provocations.

unprepared enemy upon the first reasonable provocation is better than waiting for escalation and imminent war. Zero tolerance to truce violations would have prevented the Yom Kippur War. An enemy's regrouping or rearming signals the end of any truce. Israel should have attacked Gaza when the first Hamas troops assembled there.

The creation of a Palestinian state would not bring peace

That Israeli recognition of a Palestinian state will lead to peace with other Arab countries is wishful thinking. Arabs list recognition of Palestine among other prerequisites for peace with Israel. Many Arab groups declare openly that recognition is not enough: Jerusalem must also be partitioned. There will be no end to Arab demands. Since Arabs do not want Palestinians living among them, they will demand the right of return to Israel for the descendants of refugees and, taking a cue from Jewish Holocaust organizations, will demand reparations for refugees. The only peace Israel should consider is a comprehensive agreement settling all disputes with all Arab states. Unfortunately, no recent Israeli government has insisted on that self-evident requirement.[29]

A settlement would eliminate neither hatred nor the danger to Israel from guerrilla warfare but only make large-scale war less plausible—though still possible if Israel punished Arab terrorist sponsor states. The conflict would not likely subside, as long as Israel offers an attractive vent for Arab grievances. Perhaps the guerrillas would turn against America instead. Indeed, they lost interest in Russia after evicting its troops from Afghanistan and returned only when Chechnya offered irresistible provocation. These considerations are, however, irrelevant. Israel should not pursue non-essential policies. She should not acquire land she does not need. If there is a good reason to hold territory, it must be held, and the guerrillas should be dealt with. If Israelis do not want to defend the territory, it is not essential and must be shed.

The argument that Muslim insurgents hate the West, not for its values but for what it does to them, is tautology. Even if America withdrew from global politics, it would remain a large part of the global economy and culture and always act internationally on its values. While Al Qaeda now concentrates its propaganda on U.S. military presence in the Muslim world, a total American withdrawal would only mean Arabs would find another focal point of hatred: satellite broadcasting, movie content, fast food chains (attacked even in Europe), stock and money markets, and agricultural exports. Military withdrawal from Muslim hot spots would not solve the

---

[29] Even such an agreement would be worthless unless the Muslims become assimilated into the Western world view and stop seeing Israel as a foreigner in an Islamic land. The Christian Kingdom of Jerusalem believed that all its problems were settled for a century, until the unexpected rise of Islamic consciousness swept it away with Saladin's army.

problem for America. Arabs launched an oil boycott against the West with the resultant price hike ostensibly because of the Israeli conflict with Egypt. Decades after the settlement, Arabs—even those dependent on the United States for protection—continue to increase the prices.

The story of Tunbs, one of three tiny islands involved in an inter-Arab dispute,[30] shows that Arabs cannot formally accept even minor border adjustments unless they are imposed by some major power. The islands are rather like Israel: economically insignificant land far from the core territory of Arab rivals not under any threat. Iran and Israel offered significant political concessions and aid. In response, the Arabs stiffened their position as the best strategy of improving their bargaining position and esteem. The conflicts kept them prominent in foreign affairs, and major powers courted them. The emirs involved agreed to Iran's *de facto* annexation of the islands, yet objected to save face. They also asked that the British, not the Iranians, expel them. Likewise, Arabs would have no problem if the United States prohibited a Palestinian state, but they protest if Israel, their neighbor and supposed equal, delays Palestinian statehood. The British cared not a whit about the annexation, if only it were done without much fuss, as the Americans likely feel about the Palestinian issue. If the Tunbs dispute among Muslim powers lasted for decades, how much dimmer are the prospects of a settlement with Israel?

No Palestinian state without a pan-Islamic peace agreement

Agreeing to a Palestinian state without Israeli membership in NATO and peace treaties with all Arab countries is impractical. Otherwise, Jerusalem would be the new stumbling stone and the new reason for Arab support of the guerrillas. Having seen the effectiveness of guerrilla warfare, Arabs will hardly stop at Jerusalem. Nothing precludes them from demanding the abolition of the Jewish state.

Israel should not let up on the Palestinians until a comprehensive agreement is achieved. A cease-fire is psychologically dangerous, because it is hard to convince people to go back to war after a hiatus. A cease-fire with the Palestinians will not only drive many Israelis, no longer willing to tread the dangerous path of expansion, to the political left, but will also impair the national resolve to fight, should hostilities reemerge.

The inadmissibility of vacillation

The Israeli Defense Force wins wars; the Israeli government is generally good at negotiations. Only the absence of a grand strategy lets belligerency drag on for almost six decades. Israel may choose to shrink her borders, or she may choose to expand. In the latter case, she has the relatively easy military choice of Palestine and South Lebanon, the

---

[30] Iran contested three minuscule islands, Tunbs and Abu Musa, from Ras al Khaimah and Sharjah (now UAE), respectively.

42

politically incorrect choice of Jordan, and the hard military choice of the Sinai. She could give in to all demands and either abandon the idea of a large standing army or sacrifice the economy to political and military ambitions. Settlers may leave the occupied territories, confine themselves to a network of defended settlements, or maintain control over the whole place. The means are available to sustain any policy. Moderately foolish policy is better than no policy. Nothing is so costly in lives, material, reputation, and public resolve as constant wavering. A policy must be devised, agreed upon and unambiguously fixed as the Basic Law.

Israeli vacillation is provocative

Israeli vacillation provokes Arabs. First, the wavering curve's nadirs offer the Arabs clear clues of what Israel might accept. Subsequent greater demands are not credible and induce the Arabs to demand ever further concessions. Second, indecision makes everyone afraid. Having a powerful but unpredictable neighbor leads Arabs to beef up their arsenals and launches a spiral of violence.

Israel's errors recall Germany's before World War I: concentration of military might, regional dominance, absence of clear objectives, and aggressive, unpredictable policy that threatened potential enemies. Israel's mistakes have provoked an arms race, cemented the Arab coalition, obviated internal Arab disputes, and united Arabs to oppose the common enemy. Many Jews claim they do not intend to threaten the Arabs, but the issue at hand is Arab perception of events.

Jews must state their objectives clearly in terms of self-interest, follow a predictable policy, and stop panicking her neighbors who never know what Israeli is up to at any given moment. If, however, Israel decides upon the aggressive course, she should not threaten. Attack the designated targets immediately. Do not let the Arabs prepare and the U.S. intercede. Governments rarely give way to threats, certainly not autocratic governments and not in religious matters. To delay aggression would greatly increase the cost of victory.

Vacillation damages the Israeli psyche, too. Israeli government officials in office must stop stating their private views on the peace process publicly. If they do not agree with state policy, let them leave office and promote their viewpoints. Government policy should be coherent. People who adopt radical ideological goals may want to adhere to them, though not practice them immediately. People remember the most far-fetched suggestions. In the present case, it is peace at almost any cost versus keeping the territories at almost any cost. That polarizes and radicalizes society, both sides ignoring the middle options, but middle options are often the reasonable ones. Though most Arabs did not demand a Palestinian state thirty years ago, now even most Jews agree to it. Israeli society must agree on a path to normalization—offense, defense, or peace for concessions— and stop wavering.

Vacillation is costly and politically detrimental

Oscillations between the desire for peace at any cost and the desire for expansion create ineffective policy. Israelis today are discussing the equivalent of Sadat's 1972 offer. Begin was looking to give up the Sinai in return for recognition of *de facto* Israeli jurisdiction over the West Bank territories. In the end, Sinai bought a dubious peace with Egypt, but Egypt was ready to accept Israel anyway, a matter of Arab acceptance of political reality. Therefore a moderate Egypt asked only for the return of the Sinai, while fundamentalists disregarded the agreement, anyway. Consequently, Israel would have risked little by keeping Sinai, valuable not only for unprecedented depth of defense, but also as the approximate extreme of Eretz Israel, theoretically the ultimate goal of Israeli policy. Egypt would eventually have agreed to divide the Sinai with Israel, if not immediately then after some years. As almost every country has at one or another point of its history, Egypt acquiesced to force. It lacked sovereignty for millennia, its statehood relegated to a semi-mythical time of the pharaohs. Only decades ago, the British re-shaped Egypt as they wished, as its straight, arbitrarily drawn borders show. Egypt also abrogated its claim to Gaza and the Negev. Partition of Sinai would have left Israel with oil wells in the isthmus, the reserves the Jews were exploiting when the Camp David accords transferred the Sinai to Egypt. Israeli leaders submitted to international pressures and lost sight of their primary objective. Concessions have not led either to normal Israeli-Arab relations or Israeli dominance.

Israeli wavering damages her image before the world opinion. Foreigners know very little about the history or subtleties of the Jewish-Arab conflict. Israeli indecisiveness proves to them that she is wrong, that even she doubts her policies.

Piecemeal compromises blur objectives

Concessions obscured the objective of peace when only short-term goals were in sight. Exchanging territory for peace makes sense if it means liquidating Israel's immense standing army and freeing the economy from military pressures. But peace with Egypt did not reduce the Israeli army, since other enemies remained. The same army could have kept the Egyptians at bay without conceding most of the territory Israel held at the time. Any other country would consider such a loss of territory a defeat, not a political gain—most certainly so if the territory was historically significant for the national conscience. Joshua did not trade the Promised Land for peace treaties.

Israeli acceptance of compromises on Sinai, Golan, and Gaza only prompts the victorious enemy to ask for more concessions. Peace is best achieved in a single agreement, when one side has a lot to trade in and the other is desperate to recover territorial losses. The more territory Israel gives to Arabs under interim agreements, the less her bargaining power and the less Arab interest in settling the conflict.

The fallacy of minor concessions

Although all the Arab demands could be settled somehow or other, giving in to them all would reduce Israel to insignificance. Concession is futile and leads only to more demands, until the Jews would eventually find themselves in the sea. The fallacy of an endless chain of minor compromises, none with a clear offsetting gain, shows in the fact that though Israel refused Sadat's 1971 offer of normalization with the Arab world in return for Sinai and the Golan Heights,[31] in the thirty-odd years since, Israel agreed to return most of the territories but has not achieved peace with her Middle East neighbors. She continues that policy now, transferring Gaza and the West Bank to the Palestinians without a peace treaty with other Arabs, most of whom stated previously that the Jewish settlements in Palestinian regions were the only impediment to peace after 1976. Although not exactly appeasement, acquiescing to demands certainly provokes more than would a one-time settlement undergirded by the goodwill of the *stronger* power.

Arabs have long since spotted its willingness to make concessions as Israel's national weak spot, and they pound it with their *intifada*. Although Israel has the right to agree to whatever concessions she wishes, she should do so as the strongest power dispensing favors, not giving way before the demands of others.

Abandon half-measures

A clear understanding of policy makes the futility of half-measures transparent. What is the point of settlements in the occupied areas? They were introduced on the assumption that no Israeli government would abandon so much investment; the restoration of Sinai—an object of major Israeli investments—to Egypt showed that is not the case. Israel, however, continued to build new settlements on the West Bank. They will not anchor the occupied territories for Israel but rather make the territorial question worse, as previously useless land becomes investment property. They are of little military value: after the Arabs built mobile armies, area defense is not viable. Settlements, in need of defense, will become liabilities in a major conflict.

The acquisitions would be defensible if they could be maintained under the current democratic political structure. Settlements are no way to acquire territory: they are at odds with Israel's professed desire for peace,

---

[31] Though the offer was formulated as the return to pre-1967 borders, Sadat did not care about the Palestinians or their land and probably not about a partitioned Jerusalem, either. Sadat could not force other Arabs to cease hostilities with Israel, but they would not have risked war at that stage without Egypt.

and ultimately a cowardly means and exactly the opposite of Machiavelli's prescription. The settlers themselves are not cowards. They live surrounded by enemies, but the government uses their villages as a pretense for claiming the land instead of taking it by military means. Other than the biblical justification, the settlements are indefensible. Israel uprooted a dense network of Arab villages in her territory in 1948 and 1967 and helped the inhabitants leave. If Israel abrogates her biblical claim, refuses to use force, and acquiesces in the establishment of a Palestinian state, what's to keep the Palestinians from driving Jewish settlers out? In other words, most people object to the settlements because they undermine the 1948 U.N. territorial mandate. I object to them because they are ineffective and provocative and strengthen support for the U.N. two-state plan.

Jews need not exterminate the locals as Joshua supposedly did, behavior not readily reconcilable with the tolerance the Torah teaches.[32] Israel has clear guidelines in dealing with Palestinians: the Ten Commandments, which prohibit murder and robbery but not killing in a war for the Promised Land, nor do they prohibit running people off, provided the land and other property is justly compensated. Those who compare Israeli policy with the Nazis should imagine the Germans moving the Jews to Switzerland forcibly but compensating them for their real estate.

If the Jews intend to keep the occupied territories, they should do it the only effective way, by occupying the land, annexing it, driving the Arabs out, fencing it off, and facing the international consequences. In all probability, friends and foes alike would let it pass after a brief period of ostentatious antagonism to satisfy their liberals and fundamentalists. Nobody cares about the Palestinians. Everyone wants the issue to go away. If Israel acted illegally and ruthlessly—but quickly and effectively—in a few years, most nations would accept the *de facto* situation, just as they agreed to Israel's acquisition of Jerusalem contrary to the U.N. resolution. All modern borders were established by violence, except in artificial ex-colonies like Iraq, where violence still reshapes demarcation lines.

The shock of two world wars was not enough to end warfare. World War I left deep demographic and economic scars on European nations, but only twenty years later they were ready for another war of unprecedented scale. The United States suffered vast human and material losses in World War II, yet jumped into the Korean War in only five years and the Vietnam War little more than a decade later. World War II had relatively little bearing on Africa, though it exhausted the empires into releasing their colonies, and almost none on Arabs and Latin America.

---

[32]The Torah prescribes restraint toward slaves and help for enemies who are one's co-religionists. Hatred of idolaters is a divine prerogative, not to be enforced by Jews in some kind of *jihad*. Killing the Canaanites was a separate commandment precisely because it was hard to justify based on the other commandments. Many archeologists doubt the extermination ever took place.

World War II did not change the pattern of state relations. The chemical, biological, and nuclear deterrents are responsible for the current sixty years of relative peace. They do not, however, deter poor, uneducated Muslims ruled by autocrats who kill more of their own than a nuclear attack would.

Many people believe the Americans tend to side with the weak and thus would turn against an Israel that bullies Palestinians. Few other nations behave so, and Israeli actions would likely get the tacit approval of Great Britain at least. American idealism is largely a self-serving myth.[33] Many Americans, feeling safe in trans-Atlantic isolation, resent violence and are prone to compassion, but their support has often been misplaced. They defended Vietnamese against a freely supported government, and Iraqis against a dictator voted for in a recent referendum. Acquiescence in Pinochet's butchery meant to relieve Chileans from Allende's inflation. The Americans lauded Oliver North for defiantly covering the support of Nicaraguan contras fighting against local socialists who bullied the population with free health care and education. The Americans remained isolationist until Franklin Roosevelt dragged the country into the war by hook and by crook. The United States officials returned at least one ship of Jewish refugees to Europe because of the problems with their immigration documents. So much for compassion for the weak guy. In Yugoslavia, Americans defended one set of scoundrels against the other. Both Muslims and Christians committed atrocities, and the United States entered the conflict against ex-communists. Idealistic—or so wanting to be—U.S. public opinion restrains the government's antisocialist policy when it leads to supporting odious dictators, and the government even condescends to that opinion when the communist threat in a particular country is eliminated. But economics drive United States foreign policy: an economy open to foreign trade and investment, paying its debts even if to a dictatorship. When neither ideology nor the economy is in question, the United States enters conflicts reluctantly, as in Rwanda, only when public pressure forces it to play international gendarme, a role model for realpolitik cases. Political liberalization is a by-product of the American drive for free markets—but not always, as American support of Diem, Trujillo, Pinochet, and other ugly characters shows. Since annexation would solve the Palestinian problem and advance economic liberalism, the United States would approve Israeli action in that direction. Even without United States support, Israel proved her ability to wage wars successfully on her own. Good strategic planning, preemption, and her current technological edge assure Israel's victory in the unlikely event of an ensuing conflict— and the guerrillas will hardly balk at detonating an A-bomb in Tel Aviv as soon as they get one, anyway. Israel does not need American support to

---

[33] Unlike Jewish self-awareness as the chosen people, which is passive , the similar American notion is increasingly active. Pushing others toward paradise does not work.

demilitarize the Arabs. A dominant Israel would enjoy United States support like never before. The successful 1967 war led the U.S. government to reevaluate its relation with Israel; the devolution of Sinai prompted it to closer ties with the emerging strong Egypt.

If you decide on annexation, carry it out. Do not weep, offer condolences to Arabs, or blame the army or the government, and do not allow refugee camps in any country to start up as a journalists' Mecca. Be prepared to kill protesters, drive refugees far away (Dir Yassin may prove a small exercise in dealing with quasi-armed civilians), and force neighbor countries to absorb them. Major Muslim states may attempt to show solidarity, and Israel must be ready for war. That, however, is unlikely, since wealthier Arabs will be relieved of the Palestinian problem, if Israel forces weaker states like Jordan and Lebanon to assimilate them. The violence is insignificant by Arab standards which disregarded thirty to a hundred thousand Kurds killed[34] by Saddam Hussein in quashing an insurgency and hundreds of thousands Iraqis by Iranians; twenty thousand Muslims, terrorists along with civilians by Hafiz Al Assad; an estimated 1.5 million dead in Afghanistan civil war and the same number in Sudan; forty thousand in the Algerian Islamist revolt and also in Tajikistan; two hundred Muslim civilians killed by Al Qaeda in bombing two United States embassies; hundreds shot by Shah Mohammad Reza Pahlavi's troops in a single demonstration; and eight thousand Palestinians butchered in Jordan and another thousand of them dead in Lebanon; the Islamic government of Iran marched teenage soldiers through minefields, an alternative to sapping.[35] Annexation would bring Israelis the credentials of a strong nation in their neighbors' eyes.

Israel should establish *de jure* recognition of the status quo by annexing the land legally without discussions about the future of the territories.[36] Treating the matter as settled is the best way to settle it. If, however, Israel intends to give the territories away, then she should leave and forget about it. If guerrillas come from there, stop issuing visas to Arabs. Replacing them with Asian and Eastern European Christian *Gastarbeiters* would reduce the costs of Israeli entrepreneurs: Palestinians in Israel earn higher wages than many Eastern Europeans and Asians.

---

[34] About twenty people are wounded per each dead in modern armies with good medical care. Absent of it, wounded-to-casualties ratio in Muslim wars is closer to the ancient 3-4:1 norm, perhaps 8-10 wounded per each casualty.

[35] Muslims do not care for their coreligionists. Hardly any Muslim group thanked the U.S. for stopping the murder of Muslims in Yugoslavia at the expense of détente with Russia and much of Eastern Europe. However, many Islamic groups vociferously condemned some imagined American complacency in the atrocities committed against Yugoslavian Muslims.

[36] The land Israel took in the 1967 war, and Palestinians claim for their state. Calling these territories "occupied" tendentiously presupposes that Palestinians have more right to Judea and Samaria than do the Jews.

Temporary immigrants, furthermore, do not require pension plans, and the Israeli government would save on security precautions.

The current policy is stupid. It is not even a policy but rather an absence of policy. Israel spends for three ends without achieving even one. She controls the occupied territories as if she intended to hold them. She gives them away as if she agrees to Palestinian sovereignty. And she sponsors further settlements, so Jews can somehow cling to the land even if Israel abandons it. The last notion is truly ridiculous. If the Arabs controlled the land, they would drive even the stoutest settlers away by cutting the roads and harassing them. The United States managed an airlift only with great difficulty when the Soviets cut the land routes to West Berlin. Hundreds of Israeli settlements cannot be supported by airlift, and attempts to secure the roads would restore Israeli possession of Palestine.

Economically impotent, forgotten by all, Palestine would drift into insignificance, another failed state whose best people emigrated. Major guerrilla groups would join the government and moderate, serious anti-Western terrorists could not hide there under Israel's nose, and sporadic violence would be reduced to boring routine. Jews might start buying land in the West Bank and settling there under nominal Palestinian jurisdiction. If Palestine refused to let religious Jews settle there, Israel would be justified in expelling Muslims. The Palestinians would likely agree to have Jews as resident aliens, if only to solve the problem of autonomous settlements. Clashes would ensue, Israel routinely interfering to protect her citizens in Palestine when the local authorities failed. Palestinians would find that the best way to stop clashes and Israeli reprisals is to wall the Jewish villages off and give them administrative autonomy. Such settlements, only formally under Palestinian jurisdiction, would expand in size and number: the Palestinians might object to foreign settlements but not to law-abiding, legally immigrated resident aliens who happen to be Jews. The settlements would be stable and attract more Jews to Palestine. The Palestinians could not pursue a similar policy in Israel, because land there is much more expensive, and Jewish owners usually refuse to sell or lease to Arabs. Israel should spread the blame for the settlements by inviting Christians to settle in the religiously significant areas connected to the Israeli highway system. The Vatican would likely not agree to such provocation, but less scrupulous groups would.

Delaying the solution makes the problem chronic and harder to cure

Protracted confrontation with Arabs causes systemic deviations in Israeli society—in economy, morale, and politics. Short efficient war would have left no lasting distortions. Long neglected problems, like chronic illnesses, require harsher solutions than were available initially. Although some kind of coexistence with indigenous Arabs was once possible, now that Israel has given them hope for their own state, there is no painless way back. Israel must either give them the territory or destroy the Palestinian settlements and exile them far away—not to refugee camps in neighboring countries. Jordan and Lebanon, unhappy with refugee camps as a source of anti-government and guerrilla unrest, would readily accept an Israeli ultimatum to disallow them. Forced cultural assimilation should accompany deportation: Palestinians are not sufficiently different from Arab Muslims to constitute a distinct culture.

Does Israel want economic and social progress in Arab countries?

Israel has to decide how to affect Arab countries. Israelis may help the Arabs build prosperous democratic states where people grow averse to war. The instantaneous artificial democratization of feudal Arab societies, however, is futile, as we are seeing in Iraq; in the best-case scenario, it would take decades. Germany, though nominally a monarchy, rigorously adhered to the rule of law and had parliamentary experience, crucial factors in transforming into democracy. In Japan, hierarchy, respect for authorities, and little difference in the political parties' platforms (because critical issues are few) keep the country essentially autocratic under an umbrella of electoral democracy. Arabs are best compared with Russia: no rule of law, religious (Arabs) and ideological (Russians) hypocrisy, contempt for authorities, widespread corruption, technological backwardness, aggressiveness, high tolerance to suffering, and zeal. So far every Russian attempt at becoming a democracy has failed, despite almost ninety years of elections after the downfall of the monarchy. People need certain qualities to keep governments at bay and prevent the slide into autocracy—basic political education, love of freedom, respect for the law—qualities that take time to acquire. That is especially relevant to Palestine: mild autocracy may keep violence at bay, while democracy would bring the Islamists to power, both because they are the only morally untainted group and because they can promise an influx of subsidies from Saudi Arabia and Muslim charities worldwide.

Jews have already tried to develop Palestinians economically and showed some progress in agriculture, though none in other sectors. The failure is understandable from a historical perspective. Arabs have lagged behind Westerners for centuries, with no technological progress in Muslim lands. Even medieval Arab science consisted largely in translating and digesting works by Greek authors. Despite all the perks Arab governments provide to students and businessmen, both scientific research and non-oil business in those countries are close to nil, and whatever small trading activity there is involves Indian immigrants. In the United Arab Emirates, Kuwait, Saudi Arabia, and Libya, locals are employed almost exclusively in government sinecures; on the West Bank, they have lived on welfare for three or four generations. A bit more progress, though minor, came in Westernized Turkey and Egypt, but overpopulation, the emigration of educated people, the wave of fundamentalism, and an influx of rural population to urban areas overcame it. It takes time for people to acquire the skills of Western civilization and culture. Most Arabs are only thirty years from camels and primitive farming and generations behind Europeans in that regard.

Another approach would be for Israel to fuel the internal religious and class strife in the Arab world. An easy political option would be to flood the Arabs with American proposals on political, economic, and cultural matters, forcing a lively debate on them. There are many ways to support—money, printing presses, international media coverage, recognition, weapons—or discredit political parties during elections. United States observers could raise an outcry about the inevitably rigged elections.

The first candidates for Israeli support are the Shia, increasingly oppressed by spreading Wahhabism, and immigrant workers. The time is ripe, further, to destabilize Saudi Arabia: the welfare the royal family passes out has decreased as population has increased,[37] and the people could be made resentful of the House of Saud. The easiest would be to supply the Arabs with obsolete weaponry and ammunition and let them kill one another, then introduce puppet regimes, or to install an Israeli peacekeeping administration. Finally, Israel could simply annex its territory, from which a large part of the population would have fled already. Annexing and exiling the remaining indigenous population is more practical, since administration by international mandate or by local traitors would only foment nationalism. But it is wrong to do either intermittently, to promote stability first, and then provoke internal conflict.

That is, the Israelis may say one thing and do another,[38] for example, support democratic grassroots movements in the Arab world in

---

[37] It is only in knowledge-based economies that population increase develops the stock of knowledge leading to a rising GDP, even the per-head GDP.

[38] Deceit, though denounced in modernity when people became too lazy to discern it and too weak to risk suffering from it, was noble among ancients. Deceit, the old charge leveled against the Jews, would not provoke anti-Semitism, unless one believes this was the actual reason for the hatred, not a mere rationalization. The Torah prohibits deceit in court only to the detriment of one's neighbors. Talmudic rabbis taught that a Jew should not deceive even gentiles, but their views refer to civil relations, certainly not to warfare. No one doubts the applicability of deceit to military affairs—and Israel is at war. There is a long history of lying even to one's allies, especially when the alliance is one of convenience: the British issued memorandum to Stalin of April 19, 1941, warning him of an impending British pact with Germany which would allow the Nazis to turn their forces against the U.S.S.R.; the idea was to push Stalin into an alliance with the British and a preemptive strike against the Nazis. Governments at war routinely lie to their own people; democracy does not work in wartime. Even soldiers are not told the truth about upcoming operations. Israel surely has less obligation to world opinion. Bureaucratically executed deceit is even worse than its absence. Recall the memorandum of the U.S. Joint Chiefs of Staff of 1962 on justification for U.S.

order to destabilize the situation and offer an alternative to Islamic fundamentalism. If that worked, the democratic Arab states would redistribute the wealth, greatly diminish the state's power, and at the same time make the people more wary of Israeli retribution and thus less belligerent. Wealthy people are peaceful; wealthy governments, militaristic. To feed the Arabs democratic ideology is easy, but it should be packaged as a return to true Islamic roots of equality and communal decision-making. When lying, it is important not to believe the lie and to keep track of the real objective. The policy should be to weaken the Arab states, not destroy them, because destruction would clear the way for guerrilla domination on the ruins of failed states. To that end, Israel might support NGOs advocating human rights in Arab countries. The West should not make human rights in the Arab world a policy cornerstone, since acquiring the appropriate political culture would take Arabs a long time; but freedoms should not be sacrificed, since many Arab opinion-making intellectuals and students long for them, and the general population would also like more liberties. Small but widely publicized liberalization efforts would create good will for the West.

No people becomes liberal overnight. Japan, the textbook example of democratization, is an oligarchy with touches of technocratic autocracy. Turkey and Bahrain, the most Westernized Muslim countries, are far from responsible popular democracies. Since Muslims are not ready for democracy, enlightened autocracy under rulers like Hosni Mubarak of Egypt or King Hussein of Jordan is an option. The Egyptian and Jordanian rulers respect law and cannot be likened to demagogues like Ayatollah Khomeini. Yet the game is dangerous even with authoritarian leaders, because they may shift to fundamentalism if their support base weakens. The religious establishment is the biggest coherent group in the Muslim world and influences democratic elections; Pervez Musharraf of Pakistan relies on the clergy. When regimes are overthrown, power goes to the *ulema* by default. The support game damages Israel in the case of dictatorships. Enemies trained against other enemies tend to be aggressive in general and in time turn against their sponsors, as the Afghan Taliban did to the Americans who armed them. Alliance with the devil is short-term. No country can achieve long-range success by promoting totalitarianism for short-range tactical reasons but will incur the subject population's hatred and see a drift to fascism of some kind. Better to seek and foster potentially

---

military intervention in Cuba, concerned with setting up a pretext for invasion. There is nothing inherently wrong in lying to the public in order to justify overrunning an enemy (Soviet, in this case) outpost, something that requires no extraneous justification in the first place. But being ready to violate international law and to fake a *casus belli*, the JCS staff could not bring itself to violate the rules of paperwork processing, archiving the implicating memorandum. Secret operations are by definition illegal. They should be recognized and handled as such.

powerful and ideologically amenable small groups among the enemy that would oppose and undermine the radical *ulema's* claim to be the only alternative to corrupt local regimes. A common mistake of supporting one party only must be avoided: any party in the corrupt environment invariably becomes corrupt, and *ulema* emerges again as the only honest opposition. Rather, many parties should be supported simultaneously to dissipate the protest votes. Support should not be half-hearted, such as only produces resentment, but substantial and unambiguous.

That reasoning has an important exception of limited application. Sometimes acting against a stable, democratic country like Egypt under Mubarak is problematic, although the necessity of destroying its chemical, biological, nuclear arsenal is clear. In those cases, an internal coup offers justification for an Israeli attack, since weapons of mass destruction might fall into the hands of rogues—though even then the cost-benefit ratio of supporting a coup is questionable.

That doubt is not, however, an absolute prohibition. Collaboration, especially tacit collaboration, with dictators is a valuable tactical tool. Sensible dictators generally shy from foreign involvement. Dictators can hardly risk arming their people and stirring up the will to fight, for fear it might turn on them. The expansionists Caesar, Augustus, Attila, Genghis Khan, Napoleon, and Hitler enjoyed popular support. When Iraqi support for Saddam became acquiescence, he could no longer risk large military exploits. The Arab monarchs and dictators are concerned with their own survival, pressing Israel to create an external enemy. They started wars in 1967 and 1973 to reestablish credibility of rhetoric. Semi-democratic Iran and the P.L.O. crowd[39] threaten Israel more than the authoritarian Arab states. Israel should not get involved in supporting and setting up oppressive regimes, since the collaboration would not last long, and drawbacks would soon outweigh benefits. Israel should support only regimes with a good grip on their local affairs—in their conflicts with other Arabs.

America should give up promoting democracy in Syria if Assad reins in the Islamic Jihad at home and Hezbollah in Lebanon, especially if Hezbollah grew nationalist and anti-Syrian. Intervention should come only if a regime causes trouble internationally, like harboring terrorists, not for its domestic policies. The best idea is not to meddle with Muslim societies but to exploit changes by offering minimal support to people with acceptable objectives. Politicians rarely possess such skills.

As the imperially established borders enclosing different Arab tribes and faiths collapse, Israel can reduce military expenditures since she would not need to maintain cutting-edge weaponry against emerging small

---

[39] The Iranian government, for all its authoritarian policies, is still more or less freely elected. The Abbas regime, although autocratic, is democratically chosen from the host of other factions, such as Hamas and PIJ.

states. Small and failed states do not develop nuclear weapons. There is no reason to support dictators for fear of a failed state *per se*; they would fail anyway. Rather, strategists should consider whether a failed state could be reorganized, as was Yugoslavia. Dividing Iraq into Shia, Sunni, and Kurdish mini-states could work, especially if the United States agreed to relocating the Turkish Kurds in Iraqi Kurdistan. Turkey would love to be rid of troublesome people, and Kurds could not oppose relocation.

But do Muslims not deserve freedom and democratic government? Israel does not care. Her interests, not the concerns of others, dictate her policy. Many, like socialists, accept limited freedom as long as governments guarantee welfare and pensions. Many people value ideology or loyalty above freedom, especially poor people who have little use of freedoms, and strive for esteem through communal attachment and hatred. People value only freedoms they win. The Arabs do not want democracy imported from Israel or the United States.

Fostering dissidents and insurgents, Israeli and American bureaucrats must overcome affinity to foreign bureaucrats that makes them distasteful to dissidents. This treacherous affiliation is well known in the relations of royal houses: Russian, German, and British monarchs corresponded civilly during the WWI slaughter. Supporting democrats and Westernizers without local followings is futile. American diplomats prop up mannerly, nicely dressed, religion-hating leaders, even if they are self-proclaimed. Promoting their values is one thing, advancing them politically is another—and wrong.

One should not expect to seed controversy among terrorist groups by dividing them along ethnic or religious lines. Guerrillas of various creeds often work together. Their leaders, used to sending their people to their death, are necessarily cynical. Bribing one group to fight another does not work. The money would go to fighting old enemies, and once a new common goal or enemy appeared, the groups would overcome their internecine hate. Many secular Jews support the ultra-orthodox settlements in the territories financially and politically. Discontent and dissent in Arab countries, however, weakens the guerrillas' financial and social base.

Promoting political and religious division in hostile countries is a correct and justified policy. Most Muslims profess fundamentalist, militant Wahhabite Islam.[40] The Saudis accept the faction as their state religion and finance everything Wahhabite, from schools to guerrillas abroad. Wahhabism, however, is a theologically questionable 18th century innovation posing as the teaching of the medieval Islamic radical, Ahmed ibn Taymiyya, a controversial figure repeatedly jailed for his unorthodox views. By declaring other Muslim rulers apostates, Wahhabism suits the

---

[40] While the clerical bureaucracy tends to interpret this doctrine conservatively (less aggressively), the likes of bin Laden who infuse Wahhabism with a new spirit of struggle are likely to prevail.

Saudi dynasty. It is not the only school of thought in Islam and has produced little scholarship. Israel might support Islamic factions through foreign foundations to dissipate Wahhabi authority and remove an important motive of Arab aggression. Israel should keep a watchful eye on theological developments in Islam, since Wahhabism might eventually become a conservative state religion and marginalize the radicals.

While Saudi financing accounts for the proliferation of Wahhabism among clerics, they objectively need fundamentalism in order to oppose secularism. Helping them find an acceptable non-Wahhabite way to counter secularism might work. The Catholic Church transformed theology into Christian culture. The process does not have to be slow. Islam might succumb to Westernization quickly, thanks to the pervasiveness and persuasiveness of the mass media.

The suggestion to support both anti-state Islamic fundamentalism and Westernizing forces may seem contradictory, but if Israel does both, she addresses different groups simultaneously to split Arab society along many lines. Fundamentalism is not sustainable in the modern world where ideas compete freely and will soon become absurd and lose many adherents. Encouraging it speeds up disillusionment. In a rare demonstration of goodwill toward America, tens of thousands of Iranians rallied in her support after 9/11. Fundamentalism's promise of an egalitarian society undermines governments when Westernization beckons. Fomenting fundamentalism, however, requires caution. If the clerics retain power for long, they will harm Israel a lot more than today's cynical Arab autocrats.

Israeli support of Islamic fundamentalism will not be a problem, since even democratically chosen fundamentalism will not last long. As in Iran, the clerics will not deliver, and the population will soon grow dissatisfied with them. Iran provides another example. France, which for years subverted the Shah and did a lot to install Khomeini, received no favor in return. Iran was even more hostile to France than to the U.S. Similarly, Israel cannot expect gratitude from the Muslim fundamentalists she would support but rather must rely on their predictable actions as part of her strategy. The support for radical Islamists, furthermore, is weak: they took only 11% of the vote recently in Pakistan. Any secular party that champions equality and the overthrow of corruption would get more votes than the religious fanatics. Since nationalist rhetoric very closely resembles fundamentalist rhetoric, people are unlikely to choose copycat nationalist parties instead of the clerics they scorn. The emergence of authentically local Westernizers like Ataturk is much more probable. The clerical states are not as bad as a superficial look at Iran and Afghanistan might suggest. In both cases, the *ulema* bureaucratized themselves shortly after coming to power, and bureaucracy led to conservatism. Iran all but stopped terrorist bombings in the West, reduced its support of guerrillas to little more than rhetoric, and leaned toward *rapprochement* with the United States.[41] Similarly, the Taliban clerics confronted the opium industry, a positive development checked by international sanctions which left illicit drugs the Afghan government's major budget source. Another benefit of clericalization is subsequent imminent secularization, since people will hardly live under fundamentalist rule in the 21st century. The trend is clear both in Saudi Arabia and Iran and seems to be the case in Afghanistan as well.

Islamic democracies present a problem, since the United States would likely support them. The nominal democracy of such countries provides an excuse for political cowardice. The United States tolerates them acquiring nuclear weapons and other weapons of mass destruction, delaying a showdown while CBN (Chemical, Biological, Nuclear) arsenals burgeon. A regime change could direct those weapons against Israel. On the other hand, promoting fundamentalism makes Israel America's only politically correct ally in the oil-rich region, while other countries cooperate implicitly. Liberal democracy will not stop Muslim support for guerrillas and war in general. Europeans kept right on warring long after the French Revolution articulated concepts of freedom and human rights. On the other hand, totalitarian regimes like the United Arab Emirates, Qatar, and Kuwait are reasonably peaceful. No political order makes people pacifist; wealth and the fear of losing it in a war does. Arabs would need decades of liberal policies to acquire distributed wealth, and therefore liberalizing them is not an immediate solution.

However Israel relates to Arab governments, all the positive programs, especially those initiated by the United States, should be addressed to the general population rather than to officials. Under the present system, financial aid buys government-to-government collaboration, not popular goodwill, since most people do not benefit. American-sponsored colleges in Arab countries, Arab students in America[42], food delivered directly to the hungry ("Grown in the USA" clearly marked in Arabic), free U.S.-sponsored newspapers, public criticism by American diplomats of local governments' unpopular actions—that should buy the West friends in the world of Islam.

In most Arab countries, where freedom of speech means criticizing the United States for shutting down terrorist Web sites, citizens cannot vent their spleen over government policies. Their grievances, most related to class conflicts, sublimate into the only permissible controversy, hatred of

---

[41] It is doubtful that the U.S. would accept such *rapprochement*. Wherever possible, suffocating the country into a change of regime *á la* the U.S.S.R. seems preferable. The problem in applying such a policy to Iran is that, unlike the U.S.S.R., Iran has few fixed expenses and could scale the debit side of its budget to decreasing income. Finishing Iran's war with Iraq was in that regard a mistake.

[42] Many short-term students, not few long-term who often move to the West.

Israel. American pressure on the Arabs to permit freedom of speech would dissipate the accumulated discontent and reduce anti-Israeli sentiment. It makes sense likewise to take a hard stand on human-rights issues (not including police abuse, indispensable for dealing with terrorists), like the status of women, restrictions of Shia and other religious minorities, bureaucratic corruption, fair distribution of oil profits, and transparent government spending. Such a policy would also build considerable goodwill for Americans among Arabs who correctly believe the West supports their oppressors with little regard for common people.

Israel should work to divide Muslims along ethnic and religious lines. Though most Islamic nations have little identity and would gladly dissolve into a pan-Muslim empire, Iranians and Azeris, Iraqis, Egyptians, Pakistanis, Kazakhs, and Tajiks have strong national identity. African Muslims, seen as inferiors in Islamic tradition, have what might be termed negative identity. Nigeria is the largest country affected by Islamic racism. The United States might nurture those countries' nationalist claims for a bigger role in pan-Islamic institutions.

Although Muslims proclaim themselves one *umma*, they share the wealth differently. Minuscule elites in Saudi Arabia, the United Arab Emirates, Qatar, and Kuwait enjoy much more income than the billion-plus other Muslims. Muslims everywhere should be incited to claim their share of oil proceeds from the immoral oil fiefdoms.

Adding insult to injury, the Saudis restrict access to the holy places they hold in trust on behalf of the whole *umma* by introducing small *hajj* quotas for various countries, preventing Muslims from entering paradise. Saudi Arabia keeps much more populous Pakistan and Bangladesh, and increasingly Indonesia, quiet by financing the local *ulema*. Using Islamic proxy organizations, Israel should expose those shrewd, inexpensive, and efficient tactics as corruption that damages those countries' national interests. Major players—the United States, France, Russia—may consider copying the Saudis and bribing influence peddlers among non-Arab Muslims through some supranational foundation. Would the local imams boycott those funds? Perhaps. Then the approach would be to educate new imams in alternative *madrassas*. Look for dissenting, venal imams and bribe them with money, invite them on lecture tours in the United States, publish their books, build mosques for them, anything to make them collaborators. The expenses are huge, but this is a war, not a cultural exchange. The West could outspend Saudi Arabia in financing moderate Islam, as it outspent the Soviet Union in the arms race.

Replacing Islam with Islamic nationalism is not the goal. Traditional terrorists like the P.L.O. or Abu Nidal were not religious. The guerrillas' current religiosity is a propaganda exercise for external consumption. Nationalism is no less murderous than religious zealotry. The West should promote only enough nationalism to break up the professed unity of the Muslim world and no more.

Yet another front is exploiting intra-Arab disputes. Although Israel does not want a head-on collision with Egypt, she can wear Egypt down by rearming Sudan's and Oman's large armies with obsolete weapons. Oman maintains trade relations with Israel, and its ruler, Qaboos bin Said, is reasonably friendly. Reacting to a military buildup, even without explicit hostile intent, would drain Egypt's economy to mobilize a mass army like Sudan's and Oman's, not a smaller and advanced, Israeli type force. An Egyptian buildup would pose no threat to Israel. Both Israel and the United States could focus on Oman, where the population is somewhat more tractable, and foster its advancement in the Arab world.

The United States invasion of Iraq eliminated the opportunity for perpetuating the Iraq-Iran conflict, which devastated two of Israel's enemies for years. The opportunity may return when the United States withdraws from Iraq and should be exploited.

The civil war in Lebanon should be abetted, if Israel has designs on that country, with arms sales to all sides. Israel may divide Lebanon with Syria, and transfer Lebanese Muslims to the Syrian North Lebanon. Lebanese Christians will form their own state between Israel and Syria. A Christian country in the Middle East will dissipate Muslim hatred now centered on Israel, and ensure Western support for anti-Islamic policies.

Israel indirectly supports India on Kashmir, but unless the Pakistani nuclear capability is eliminated, she should keep close ties with the Pakistani military. America's estrangement from Pakistan created the demand for Israeli military services and supplies.

Numerous other disputes could be exploited to sunder Muslim anti-Israeli unity.

There are sound arguments for democracy and for dictatorships in the Arab world: for controlling population, either up or down, to make states poorer and weaker; for helping or hindering economic development. The best policy is to let things run their course. In the long term, Israel only wastes her resources in working against the tide or speeding things up which are fast in a global society anyway. Instead, Israel should concentrate on destroying the immediate threats: WMDs and guerrillas.

Simplistic collectivism, aggressive religion, bad education, hatred and xenophobia are economically inefficient traits. Religiously or ideologically strict cultures are uncompetitive. Islam transfers human goals into the other world.

The pursuit of worldly objectives and individualism might not be morally superior to Islamic ethics, but the Western outlook is far more efficient than Islam in spurring technological progress and the accumulation of wealth. The gap between the West and Dar al-Islam will grow until the latter either dies out or sheds its religious baggage. Even so, without the work ethic behind several Far Eastern economies, Muslims will acquire no significant industrial wealth in the near future.

Comatose Islamic societies may live off oil. Israel needs to survive the death pangs of the moribund Islamic culture. Israeli blend of mild religiosity and moderately active working habits is remarkably sustainable.

Determine military strategy and adhere to it

Military strategy cannot countenance vacillation. Hesitation nearly caused a defeat in 1967, and led to the high casualties of 1973 when Israel did not preempt because the government was uncertain of Egyptian intentions. Even if Israelis believed the Egyptian army was only conducting its usual provocative maneuvers and not preparing for war, *any* maneuvers should not have been allowed but rather considered a *casus belli*, as in 1967. In the like situation of the Cuban missile crisis, Kennedy properly regarded the military build-up near his borders as a *casus belli*—regardless of immediate intentions—and issued a credible ultimatum. Border maneuvers are a standard device of disguising preparations for war, as the Soviets learned in 1941 when even after the German bombardment began they believed they were staging an exercise. Preemption could not be effective with SAM-5 anti-air batteries deployed along Israeli borders, but Israelis did not know it. Israel had every reason for a pre-emptive strike even earlier, when the Soviets brought the batteries to Egypt, just like the great powers opposed anti-ballistic missiles and the Strategic Defense Initiative. The biggest error—or crime—was allowing thousands Israeli soldiers to die instead of employing or emphatically testing nuclear weapons immediately. Using tactical weapons in Sinai was relatively safe for Israeli civilian centers and would not have set a precedent of attacking cities with CBN. Indecisiveness means casualties. Two causes prevent automatic reaction to aggression. Politicians want hands-on control but do not know what to do when they get it. Military professionals get hung up on the kind of rigid agreements and diplomatic triggers that drug Europe into World War I.[43] Syrian reliance on a mutual defense agreement involved Egypt in the 1967. The Arabs, however, have learned that lesson well, and no reasonable enemy follows that path. The Syrian example may be an argument to the contrary. Had Israel not only shot down a few Syrian planes but also destroyed their army, Egypt would not have stepped in.

Israel must define the limits of her tolerance to the world. Arab mobilization, border exercises and repeated skirmishes, militarizing 30-to-100-mile-wide buffer zones, and acquiring weapons of mass destruction on a par with Israel's, including long-range ballistic missiles, must be regarded as acts of war. Sinai's and Golan's depth of defense saved Israel in the

---

[43] Namely, protection treaties of Russia and Germany with Serbia and Austria, respectively. Certain of backing by major powers, these minor countries readily escalated the conflict, triggering the mutual defense treaties, a result which neither the Russian nor the German government, though hostile, wanted. The Russian and German military establishments were only too happy to act upon them.

1973, giving her time to mobilize. Military build-up allows Arabs to stage concentrated attacks at any border point, and penetrate Israel deep before the I.D.F. bring reserves for counter-attack. Preemption is Israel's only choice.

Why may Israel accumulate weapons of mass destruction when her neighbors may not? The answer is unrelated to morality or even to Israel's ostensibly peaceful intentions: the Arabs suspect that a new Israeli government may choose expansion. Israel must be able to impose her will on her neighbors to her advantage and prevent them from acquiring the means of harming her. Similarly, a small number of countries prevents others from joining the nuclear club, a policy more strictly enforced against countries with proven malicious intent and a history of aggression. A nuclear Iraq could have prevented the American attack; North Korea's claim of nuclear weapons gives her great leverage. The United States forced Iraq to destroy its missiles only weeks before the invasion. In some places, citizens may not acquire weaponry sufficient to resist the government forces if it violates people's liberties. As *dhimmi* in the Muslim world, Jews could not own arms even when violence erupted.[44] Keeping efficient military equipment away from Arabs is a practical stratagem unrelated to morality. This policy is incidentally fair: democracies constrained by liberal public opinion use weapons of mass destruction more judiciously than authoritarian states. Even if she expands, Israel will not likely use chemical, biological, or nuclear weapons against Arab population centers. The Israeli Defense Force suffered heavy casualties in Beirut street fighting instead of burning the guerrillas, the city, and the remaining citizenry down from the air. Arabs have committed many atrocities against their own people, and although the fear of reprisal would deter most Arab governments from

---

[44] While Christians treated Jews incomparably worse than Muslims, Arabs also have murdered many Jews: 5,000 in Granada in 1066, thousands in Morocco in 1465 and three hundred in late 1800s, not to say about the wholesale destruction of Jewish communities there in the 8th century, and hundreds in Libya in 1785. Arabs committed atrocities against Jews in almost every country of Middle East, and in those Muslim-controlled African countries where they could find Jews to massacre, as in Algiers. On numerous occasions, synagogues were razed, Jewish property confiscated, and they were forced to convert to Islam. In the 19th century, Jews in Algeria, Morocco, Tunisia, Egypt and Libya were only permitted to live in ghettos. Muslims treated the Jews better than did Christians not out of kindness, but because less developed Muslim societies were often organized in large empires, had less internal struggle than Christiankingdoms, and rarely depended on religion to promote political ends. Religious differences with Jews, accordingly, were not exaggerated. Poor Islamic societies were more egalitarian than the Christian, and Jews were relatively not that much wealthier than the average population. Non-Muslims were prohibited from government offices, and the Jews got fewer concessions, such as alcohol and tax farms, as led to the popular hatred in Christendom. Mohammed's instruction to treat *dhimmis* fairly also helped the Jews.

using weapons of mass destruction against Israeli civilians, some care little enough for their people to disregard retaliation. The transfer of CBN to guerrillas by Arab agencies is also a possibility and another justification for enforced demobilization of hostile regimes bent on acquiring CBN.

Arabs should not be kept from killing one another, but they should be restricted to conventional weapons and low-intensity conflicts by not being allowed to acquire technology, skills, or military supplies dangerous to Israel. Such a policy and the will to deploy overwhelming military power in case of violation would let Israel, as arbiter of the balance of power, create a precarious regional stability.

Israel is not too small for that role. Rome managed an empire of from nine to fifty million people, two orders of magnitude above the city's population. The ratio is still more favorable for Israel whose advantage against the Arabs depends not only on skill but also on superior weaponry. Alexander conquered lands entirely disproportionate to the size and population of Macedon, but overextended relative to communication and transportation capabilities, a factor which is no longer a problem. Minuscule Sweden conquered lands as far away as Eastern Europe. But France and later Germany lost wars when they overextended themselves trying to administer newly acquired lands directly. The problem of managing the occupied countries is especially relevant now, when the occupying administration is expected to act not only humanely but also actually *beneficently* to the locals. Thus in Yugoslavia and Iraq locals staged demonstrations against the coalition army which was slow to provide municipal services. Something similar regularly takes place in Palestine. Imagine Jews protesting in 70 C.E. that the Romans delayed rebuilding Jerusalem and supplying the inhabitants with clean water! An army must be good at killing people, not policing or servicing them. Armies are not nation-builders; people are. Armies are not peacekeepers, either.

The Soviet Union, relying on local regimes for expansion, was closer to the mark, but reliance on weak governments meant the burden of military and economic aid. The United States, occasionally financing its vassals, has not yet overextended its economic capacity. Americans combine the promise of protection with a credible threat of punishment for disobedience, a policy that does not require the presence of large military units everywhere. The American strategy of maintaining mobile forces in geopolitical centers, ready to reach hot spots if they appear, closely resembles the Roman strategy of settling colonies of soldiers or veterans in newly acquired lands, backed up by mobile legions in important provinces. Rome also relied on client governments that paid for protection. America often extorts economic concessions by demanding their clients open their markets to American business interests.

Great Britain's policy of supporting the weaker party in power struggles is the most feasible for Israel, requiring the least resources to create a dynamic equality where small efforts tip the scales to either side.

For centuries that policy gave Britain considerable control of Europe and to some extent worked in the colonies, which played the rulers against one another.

The biggest trap in modern colonial policy is world public opinion. Instead of conquering, Israel might create a situation in which some governments ask her for protection from their own people or their neighbors—and pay for it. She would let client governments deal directly with their own people, obviating the need for Israeli involvement in anti-civilian police actions, but keep them too weak to dominate their neighbors. Muslim public opinion attributed something like that to the United States after Desert Storm: lure Iraq into Kuwait by seeming to acquiesce, then push Iraq out without destroying it and swap protection for influence in Kuwait and Saudi Arabia. The bureaucratic government could not devise such a devilish plan, but the Muslims who subscribe to such strategies know that they work.

How long would such belligerency continue? That depends on the effort involved. Reagan brought the Soviet Union to its knees in less than a decade by applying tremendous pressure on all fronts: military (peripheral conflicts), economic (arms race), internal affairs (dissidents), diplomatic (Poland), ideological (radio broadcasts), and human rights (emigration). The key is persistence: any country, totalitarian even more than democratic, can sustain occasional extraordinary pressure. Continuous—even moderate—pressure is unbearable. Popular will breaks when people see no light at the end of the tunnel. The Soviet Union was in a death agony from birth, with rare hopeful respites. Reagan succeeded along several major lines: American propaganda made the United States attractive to the Soviet people who lost the urge to fight it; demonstrated Soviet military inferiority in Afghanistan and in space; counteracted communist expansion abroad; bankrupt the U.S.S.R. by reducing economic cooperation; and lured the Soviets to overextend themselves in arms procurement and costly help to communist clients abroad.

Israel could finish off the Muslim states in no more time, provided she exhibits the same kind of unrelenting determination, exploiting every possibility, giving no respite. No need for competition in GDP, or who can spend more. Rather make expenses asymmetric: incite demagogues in Muslim countries to demand redistribution of oil wealth, including aid to poor Muslim countries; sell Muslims expensive and useless weapons; reduce the demand for oil by using nuclear energy; and sabotage infrastructure, seizing oil wells and staging revolts in oil producing regions. An Israeli hard line will impair the credibility of Arab governments in their subjects' eyes. Ridiculing the clergy and promoting secular values would disillusion Muslims ideologically.

Determine the Territorial Objectives

What area do the Israelis want?

The definition of Israel's optimum boundaries fluctuates wildly within Israel. The millennia-old goal was the land within its biblical borders, a view not easily justified. For one thing, Israel was never that size. Samaria embodied a different strain of Judaism, possible only because Samaria was politically independent of Jerusalem. Nor did Sinai ever belong to the Israel in antiquity. In the messianic age the prophets described, Jewish control included not only all the promised borders but also the rest of the world, a notion commonly disregarded. The issue of Israel's size is moot; the question is not where Jews live (Arabs never opposed Jews settling in Muslim lands) but rather sovereignty and government control, who rules where Jews live (an increasingly obsolete notion today as multinational governments like the United Nations and the European Union evolve). Globalization is directly related to the efficiency of communication and transportation, and the process, akin to nation-states assuming control of feudal towns, will doubtless continue to blur national boundaries.

United Nations-defined boundaries reflect the fleeting balance of power in 1947 and are irrelevant today. The resolution—which hinged on the votes of Haiti, Philippines, Costa Rica, and Liberia, and was adapted to long-gone interests of major powers—is no guide to the Promised Land. Jews accepted the partition as a springboard, and Arabs did not accept it; neither side agreed with the agreement.

According to the initial British promise, Jews expected to receive all of Palestine. Then a part of it was carved out for the locals who would not move to Jordan. Then Jews decided to take control of all of Palestine and settle for whatever part of it. When the cause of Israeli independence seemed all but lost in 1947, sensible leaders persuaded others to agree to whatever territory the major powers were willing to concede to Israel through the United Nations. With their unexpected[45] victory in 1967, Israel's popular mood swung to optimism and a determination to hold the ancient land, though determination faded with the shock of 1973, when the Egyptian attack caught Israel off guard. But many Jews still believed they could take land from the weak Syrians (Golan Heights) and Palestinians (West Bank). That also proved incorrect, and now, under international pressure and unwilling to suffer guerrilla warfare, many Israelis are ready to return to pre-1967 borders. With the West Bank overcrowded, Palestinians might seek a part of the Negev desert the Israelis developed. Some sort of partition of Jerusalem is probable, if not political then perhaps

---

[45] By pure luck, Arab armies were not prepared for a preemptive strike and were surprisingly weak in aerial and tank warfare.

administrative, with separate mayoral jurisdiction for Jewish villages and Arab villages in Greater Jerusalem and visa-free travel between Arab and Jewish communities. Whether the Arabs would seek to reduce Jews to *dhimmi* status under administrative autonomy is an open question, but the scenario is plausible if the Israelis continue making minor concessions and diluting the national resolution to fight.

Israelis never decided on the acceptable fight. In case of a major invasion or WMD terrorism, should they exhaust all human and material resources or avoid apocalyptical confrontation by resettling, if not in Uganda then in Australia or Arizona? Jews or the land, what is more important and in what proportion? Ad hoc decisions might come too late.

Why does Israel need the territories?

To determine the immediate goal, one must first define the overall purpose. Why does Israel need the territories? One motivation is esteem: a powerful nation is respected. Since Israel could easily take land from Syria, Lebanon, and/or Palestine, run the inhabitants off, and hold the land at little expense, expansion is a valid option. Before the notion of "humane war" appeared fifty years ago in Korea,[46] no nation acting rationally has returned lands taken from a weaker neighbor, especially in response to aggression. Seeming irrationalities sometimes have good reasons, like a previously weak colony acquiring arms and resolving to use them or the devaluation of raw materials which cease to justify the military expense of holding onto colonies. No country has returned territory significant to its national consciousness, especially with no significant military threat involved. Israel had good reason to hold onto a buffer zone with Egypt.

The State of Israel is ridiculously small, minuscule compared to most Arab states artificially carved from larger entities. Even after the demise of the Ottoman Empire, Britain and France originally divided the region into only three countries: Iraq, Palestine, and Syria, and later subdivisions served to appease local puppet dynasties. Israel's size is unnatural and poses a clear danger in the age of weapons of mass destruction, especially if the Arab states merge into fewer, larger entities.

Seemingly rational but mistaken pretenses often mask the goal of increasing national prestige. Consider a few of them. Military purposes? Another few dozen kilometers are insignificant in the age of air warfare. When Israel held the West Bank territories, guerrillas operated mostly in those territories and in border settlements inside Israel. When Israel gave the land back to the Palestinians, the terrorists moved into Israel proper. Infiltrating disputed territory is easier than infiltrating Israel. With

---

[46] European Christian governments sometimes tried to spare civilians even a few centuries ago, but the definition of "sparing" was limited to refraining from mass murder and large-scale robbery. Napoleon restored the practice of living off the land to maintain his huge armies, unable to supply them from France.

infiltration routes into Israel, the territories ceased to be a buffer against terrorists. Religious claims? But those are questionable in the modern world, where most Jews are secular. That claim brings everything to a dead end, as Israel would also have to fulfill the biblical obligation of eradicating all other religions in her territory[47] and blow up the Aqsa Mosque. Few zealots would suggest destroying Christian and Arab holy places. The Torah does not enjoin an obligation analogous to jihad of acquiring the Promised Land but rather of waiting for the divine command, as did Joshua. Historical right? There is none. Nations swap land around all the time. Hardly any nation today occupies precisely its original territory. States grow or shrink. The right to make Arabs speak Hebrew and elect delegates to Knesset? That is not desirable. The right of retribution, to make the Arabs pay for past Arab domination of Jews? Of all nations, Arabs were the most tolerant of Jews, and revenge is unwarranted. No one contests the right of Jews to settle wherever they like. Jewish communities flourished in Arab milieux for centuries. Had Jewish settlers asked only for cultural autonomy, the Palestinians would have granted it. Indeed, giving autonomy to *dhimmis* is a religious obligation, augmented by the centuries-old practice of *capitulation,* giving Westerners in Islamic countries immunity under various intergovernmental arrangements. Five million Jews settled throughout Eretz Israel would restore their pre-historic density, too low for economic, social, and security purposes. Whatever the choice, Israel must consider the economic consequences. Clinging to ancient Judea and Samaria has already cost Israel hundreds of billions in army maintenance and other economic losses over the decades. With that, they could buy a nice chunk of New York.

The possibility of ceding the territories

Holding only the territories, let alone the present network of settlements, is not feasible. Opposition and the force required to curb it are not very different whether Israel takes the West Bank or half of Lebanon as well. Indeed, the less territory remains in Israeli hands, the more Arabs will pressure to have it back, which relates to the issue of Jerusalem. Without resolving that question, there is no sense in returning any territory whatsoever, since the conflict and the need for a large standing army will

---

[47] Leviticus 19:34 requires the Jews to love strangers in their land as themselves. But since aliens were prohibited from practicing idolatry and had to observe the Sabbath and other Jewish rules, the only way to love them was to make them equal to Jews—through assimilation. Luckily, modern Arabs would not accept that option. Another possible sense of the commandment is not oppressing aliens, as Egypt did the Hebrews, but that does not imply religious toleration, as evident from numerous condemnations of places of pagan worship. Beside, many Israeli Arabs are not peaceful strangers but often dislike Jews and Israel and pose a real threat to Israel's survival as a Jewish country by exploiting democratic institutions through the swelling numbers of Arabs.

persist. On the contrary, the territories will be bargaining chips in the final settlement. Giving them away piecemeal diminishes Israeli bargaining power with no corresponding advantage and increases the cost of holding the rest, as the 1973 Golan battles demonstrated when 1,400 Syrian tanks massed on a tiny front.

There are no practical reasons why Israel should not return the territories on condition of long-term demilitarization. Any conventional military build-up would be seen at once, giving Israel sufficient time to strike pre-emptively. The current situation is nothing like it was fifty years ago. The territories would not likely turn into strongholds for foreign armies, and even in that worst-case scenario, Israel is not precluded from attacking an independent Palestine for violating a demilitarization treaty. The potential build-up of guerrilla units in a sovereign Palestine is a problem, but policing the territories directly is the only alternative and was not effective even in refugee camps. Except when carried out vigorously and regardless of human rights, that is not a sustainable policy.

Aviation and missiles nullify the strategic importance of small buffer zones. AWACS aircraft gather better intelligence than hilltop observatories. Computerized tracking systems spot missile launchers and return fire within seconds. An Israeli response with chemicals and napalm would discourage attacks on Israeli border towns from hills in enemy hands. Besides, the Palestinians can be brought to agree to some border adjustments, so some of the strategic ground would remain in Israeli hands. While they held the Palestinian mandate, the British imposed a similar border rectification on Egypt by inconspicuous cartographical tricks without the Egyptians ever knowing about it.

The argument that Israel's small territory imposes economic limitations is mistaken. That reasoning would have meant swapping Jewish lives for possible economic gain. That may or may not be acceptable but must be clearly stated, so people know they are dying for money, not principles. Further, there are valid arguments to the contrary, namely, that territorial limitations enhance competitiveness, witness Japan, South Korea, and Switzerland. A case in point is the Negev Desert in southern Israel, where a land shortage in the rest of Israel triggered irrigation and land development techniques.

Jerusalem is another matter. While it has been a focus of emotional attachment for Jews for millennia, its significance for Muslims is relatively recent, provoked by their humiliating loss of the city in 1967. The creation of the Christian Kingdom of Jerusalem in 1099 during the first crusade made little or no stir in the Islamic world. On the other hand, unless a radical Jewish group blows up the Dome of the Rock and other Muslim shrines,[48] there is no chance the Arabs will cede Jerusalem—and even then

---

[48] Not an option to disregard: medieval Arabs did not hesitate to build their temples on Jewish shrines. Going further, there is no shame in studying the option of

they could try to rebuild the place, as they have several times before. From the viewpoint of modern, nationalist Arabs, their holy places fell into the hands of religiously inferior people. Unless Israel resolves finally to thwart militant Arab aspirations, she cannot ignore the problem. She might offer the Muslim holy places to Jordan for its embassy with diplomatic immunity under Arab administrative sovereignty. Pilgrims would have to be driven from airports to places of worship and back. That would give Arab rulers a way out while saving their faces as defenders of Islamic values. It would also enhance the status of friendly, Westernizing Jordan in the Arab world and obviate any Iraqi claim to Jordan since annexation would mean breaking diplomatic relations between Jordan and Israel. Compare this to abuse of Jewish holy places by Arabs.[49]

Still another option is to offer Jerusalem's Islamic shrines to non-Arab but Muslim Bangladesh or Pakistan or Mali to foment inter-ethnic discord among Muslims. If they accepted such a Trojan horse, other Muslims could not object on religious grounds. Other possibilities include turning the Muslim shrines over to the Saudi *ulema* to set the conservative, state-aligned religious bureaucracy against the radical clergy. Egypt is not acceptable, since Israel does not want Egyptian involvement in Jerusalem; a weak partner is preferable. In any case, the Islamic landmarks in Jerusalem should not be transferred to Palestine, which would stir up religious feelings in secular Palestinian society and validate the Palestinians as the keepers of the holy places.

Giving major Islamic sites in Jerusalem up to Muslim jurisdiction would signal an end to Jewish religious aspirations. Pagan temples in the holiest place in the Promised Land strikes hard at Jewish consciousness. More important, such an arrangement would preclude the ultimate Jewish hope of rebuilding the Temple. Peace based on joint possession of Jerusalem would be a Pyrrhic victory for Jews.

Gaza is a special case. Transferring it to the Palestinian Authority was a mistake, predictably creating a springboard for terrorist operations and partitioning Israel to create a conduit from the West Bank to Gaza. What other country would accept a foreign road cutting it in half? Let the Palestinians access Gaza from the sea if they wish, not even by air. Israel cannot risk Palestinian planes in her airspace. Control of Gaza gives

---

destroying the Qaaba, the center of Islamic consciousness. Imagine a Shia group doing that in retribution for limiting Shiite access to the site, or fringe Christian, neo-crusader terrorists.

[49] Recent incidents include the destruction of the tomb of Joseph in 2000, the attempt to blow up the Cave of the Patriarchs in 2001 and the subsequent prohibition for Jews to pray there, firebomb attacks on the tomb of Rachel, numerous desecrations of synagogues and attacks on Jewish settlements, denial of access to many important sites in the Palestinian Authority. Unlike what any decent government would have done, the Israeli government generally tolerates such perpetrations.

Palestine large offshore gas reserves. Gaza is also agriculturally viable. Israel should close the corridor and relocate Gazans to the West Bank to the settlements the Jews left. A suitable and reasonable pretext is the large number of terrorist organizations thriving among the Gazans. Relocation is not an outdated, barbaric device. Only eighty years ago, relocation solved the centuries-old Greco-Turkish conflict, among others.

The Golan Heights are no real impediment to peace with Syria. If Syria could be made to overcome their ages-old hatred of Jews and sign a treaty with Israel, it could surely be made to forget the Golan. It makes military and economic sense for Israel to annex the heights.

Support for annexing the territories comes mostly from older and religious people, not subject to conscription, not likely to die in battle. Young people with the same view are usually radicals. Lack of fear and compassion is also common at this age. One wonders if, spared indoctrination, they would support all-out war. Are they ready to see their loved ones die, to die themselves, or even pay exorbitant taxes only to secure useless land for Israel?

Returning the territories might not lead to normalizing Arab-Israeli relations

Jews came to Palestine in the 19th century without incident. Almost without precedent, they tried to build a country by buying the land, not by driving out the indigenous population. For decades, they responded to Arab assaults, falling slowly into the spiral of violence only in the 1930s, after mass pogroms by marauding Palestinian villagers who wanted to sell the land but did not want Jews to settle on it. Muslims do not offer peace. Muslims conquer.

Arabs would take devolution as a sign of weakness, not goodwill. They will sooner cooperate with a stronger neighbor conducting policy detrimental to them than with a weaker neighbor surrendering assets to them. If Israel gives the land away, it must not look like yielding to guerrilla pressure, which would encourage further demands.

The return of the territories would not bring peace. A ludicrously small Palestinian state would be a worse and permanent insult than no state at all. Arabs are proud of the Palestinian conflict but would see a political settlement creating a non-viable state as a defeat. When they realized they had been fighting for a tiny strip of land to be settled by the Palestinians, whom they despise, they would demand further compensation: the partition of Jerusalem, the right of return for the descendants of refugees, and the restoration of their property. Israel drifts toward this scenario.

Ignoring facts makes expensive politics. Israel will leave the territories not out of goodwill but because she cannot bear the cost of guerrilla warfare. Seen thus, restitution is futile. Someone will always be ready to fight the Jews, whether in open war or as guerrillas.[50] The present fight stems from Arab xenophobia, not from the attachment to useless land to which no Arab attaches great significance. Land is a pretext for expelling an alien culture from the Islamic Middle East. Giving it to the Arabs will not solve the problem. Israel has to contain the threat militarily.

Western perceptions of Arab nationalism are exaggerated

Arab nationalism is often exaggerated. It is relatively weak and new, traceable only to the late 19th century, after the decline of the Ottoman Empire. Most Arab countries are recent creations by colonial powers, existing within artificial borders under rulers illegitimate by religious standards. Defying the notion of community, Arab states war with one another continuously. If not for the common enemy, Israel, the region would have likely plunged into border wars.

Even Egypt, the only Arab country with territorial and cultural integrity, is used to occupation and territorial predation. It acquiesced to its aggressors: the Turks, the French, and the British, the last two still respected there. The Japanese were aggressive and xenophobic. Western cultural expansion, started in 1852 when Commodore Perry sailed into Tokyo Bay, continued with Japan's World War II defeat in 1945, and culminated when Japan found a high-end economic outlet in the American market for their exports, siphoning nationalism from politics into economy.

The most important factor in cementing new territorial acquisitions and making the losers accept the loss is not overwhelming force. The realization that fighting over a minor territorial issue is not worth the trouble argues for peace. That happens now with Israel who returns land not from goodwill but grudgingly, neither willing nor able to bear the cost in lives, material, and reputation of holding it. Rather, that is how Israel's enemies must be made to think – and sue for peace.

Annexation will not necessarily impede peace

Seizing another's territory does not necessarily preclude a peace arrangement. Examples to the contrary abound. The French-German dispute over Alsace-Lorraine was not resolved but rather faded into insignificance. The United States took British, French, and Spanish territories. Saudi Arabia was born of conquest and annexation. Virtually no country occupies its original borders. Few borders survived the last century intact, and even

---

[50] Israel, with all her military might, behaves politically like a typical weak Jew: shrinking away from employing force, appealing to the U.S. for protection, importuning Arabs to grant her peace, willing to forsake her land acquisitions, and whining over her victims and morality. The importance of weakness in provoking anti-Semitism is evidenced by the fact that historically even slight opposition from authorities sufficed to quench pogroms.

core territories were established by force at the expense of some other country or an indigenous population.

If Israelis decide to annex the territories, not offering justifications is of paramount importance. Any justifications—legal, military, economic, or religious—can be disputed. The only valid argument for annexation is that Israel wants the land and can defend her acquisitions.

Formally annexing the territories would give Israel a freer hand to deal with the guerrillas and their supporters, since she would be defending her own territory. The legality of annexation would remain in dispute, but as the similar issue of Jerusalem demonstrated, the Western powers do not worry much about the legal details of acquiring land; they all acquired their land more or less illegally. They worry more about current depredations on another nation's (Palestine's) territory only while the Palestinians exist—or are perceived as—a nation. The West would object more to Israeli seizure of a few hilltops for Jewish settlements than about grabbing whole regions. They would tolerate Jewish seizure of the whole sooner than of some parts. Liberals, ignoring their countries' experience, would scream bloody murder, but the politicians at the helm are more realistic: Algeria, Tibet, the Falklands, Afghanistan, and Iraq are not the names from half-forgotten medieval books.

A culturally attractive Israel could annex the territories more easily

Becoming culturally attractive would facilitate Israeli annexation of the territories. A nation will hardly cede valuable territory people it deems inferior, though loss to someone it admires might sting less. Arabs do not admire Israel; they attribute her military victories to United States support,[51] and her economic situation is feeble, especially contrasted with the oil gluttony of Arab economies. Britain was culturally attractive even to Muslims who trust the ideological superiority of their final revelation. Jews, second-rate *dhimmis* in the Muslim world for centuries, will achieve that goal only with difficulty. Arabs will make peace only when Israel becomes a major economic power.

Israel as regional empire

Israel, possibly the fourth strongest military power in the world,[52] is wasting her military potential and paying for it without using it. It could,

---

[51] The Arab view is inconsistent with the facts. The U.S. first provided major aid to Israel in the closing days of the 1973 war to counter the massive Soviet aid to Egypt. The effect was largely psychological, since aircraft and tank reserves proved almost sufficient. Israel won her other wars without critical assistance of foreign powers.

[52] The second place is better justified. The ramshackle Russian army lacks fighting capability, unless resorting to nuclear option which is unlikely: even without

70

however, be put to profitable use. Israel could establish herself as a regional empire undergirded by military might. She can seize territory from the Arabs (and perhaps others) or convert it into tribute-paying protectorates, prohibited from arming or mobilizing. Hordes of *fellahin*, though armed, would be powerless against an Israel with secure borders.

Colonialism, suppression, and repression would impose a huge burden on Israeli morale. Using force for material gain does not set well on the modern conscience. To justify themselves, Israelis would treat their subjects as inferiors, as they do Palestinians now. But colonialism exists in other forms; it must be investigated and either accepted with full knowledge of the moral consequences or rejected with full understanding of the economic losses. Since the protection racket varies by degree, Israel may shrink from the extreme of direct colonialism for the milder option of protecting the existing regimes against their neighbors—for a fee.

The natural resources of failed African states are attractive. Israel need only occupy resource-rich areas, fence them off, and exploit them. The citizens there receive no benefits from their resources, which are plundered by corrupt politicians or tribal strongmen. To save face, Israel might use a part of the proceeds for humanitarian purposes among the local population that would be better off under such an arrangement than they are now. The West tries to suppress the black market of diamonds, ostensibly to suffocate the guerrillas financially—nicely protecting De Beers' monopoly. Israeli occupation, by this logic, would extinguish many tribal wars.

Israel might play the balance of power game, supporting or protecting weak Arab states against the stronger, as when she defused the Syrian-Jordanian conflict. Israel replicates the peculiar position of Britain *vis à vis* Europe: strong enough to influence any process yet not immediately part of it. Israel might play that role in Africa, whose countries bear her no prejudice. Latin America and Asia are also attractive, but Israel should placate local powers, the United States, and China, by assuring them that such involvement is mercenary without political ambitions.

Protecting small to mid-size nations would pay Israel and win her a place in the international arena. Because an army relies on the threat it poses and so does not have to jump into actual conflict, the job would not be unduly risky. The Israeli Defense Force, further, could hire infantry

---

American military reprisal, economic boycott would ruin Russian economy hinging on oil and gas exports. Chinese forces are not tried in any major confrontation, and fared badly against Vietnamese. Chinese crude infantry power is of limited value. Chinese-made sophisticated weapons are as unreliable as Soviet. Many bad planes are worthless against few great ones Israel possesses. Technological advantage of the American and Israeli armies over those of other countries is overwhelming. I.D.F. enjoys the same kind of advantage new high-tech factories have over the larger old ones: new is better than modernized. Financial restraints made I.D.F. relatively lean, much more cost-effective than mammoth U.S. Army burdened with Stealth bombers, aircraft carriers, and the like.

elsewhere and fight not for Jewish nationalism but for profit. Foreign mercenaries joining a strong I.D.F. would not despise Jews, since anti-Semitism is provoked by Jewish weakness. Mercenaries are suited for moderate conflicts, even preferable to distance principals from their allies' cruelty. Democratic, relatively open Israel cannot play the balance of power game, supporting regimes regardless of moral merits; mercenaries can do this job.

Legalizing private armies would bring armies of "military consultants" to Israel. The country has plenty of room for camps in the Negev, and the resulting competitive edge in warmongering would promote Israeli exports of military equipment.

Conquer only militarily weak, economically viable states

Still another option is to occupy several militarily weak but economically important countries, like the United Arab Emirates, Kuwait, Qatar, and Saudi Arabia except the religiously sensitive area around Mecca—or their oil fields. The few people living near the fields can be forced to resettle in nearby cities or driven back into the desert. These people roamed the Arabian peninsula a few decades ago, and talking of their cultural attachment to the land is ludicrous. Israel would keep control only so long as oil is valuable.

Sheikhdoms are easy prey. Machiavelli recognized that totalitarian states are hard to conquer, but easy to keep subjugated, since people are used to living without freedom. The I.D.F. will have no problem with conquest. Except for a few locals, most residents would be better off with Israel disbursing a fraction of the oil proceeds to them. Face-saving gestures would not help, however. Only cynical application of overwhelming power will make Arabs acquiesce to occupation.

A comparison of the British and Assyrian empires is instructive. The Assyrians dislocated indigenous peoples and eliminated patriotic attachments. Not even the Jews were eager to move back home. The empire settled the emptied lands with other foreigners who relied on them for protection, transforming colonies from sources of unrest into support bases. Machiavelli would have been proud of them. (Significantly, although the Assyrians often resettled only skilled workers, Israel cannot use that half measure, since Arab universities would continue inflaming the people against Israel. Anyone with the slightest claim to the land must be resettled, the universities and *madrassas* closed.) The British, on the contrary, did not change the demography of their vast colonies and had to employ huge forces to contain unrest. The Industrial Revolution devaluated colonial goods, raw materials in particular, and raised soldiers' wages, making military suppression of colonies unprofitable. Nationalism in the dependencies and liberalism at home finally meant giving up the colonies.

In the case of Saudi Arabia, Israel should incite strife between the dominant Sunni West and the suppressed Shia in the oil-rich East, possibly involving the Iraqi Shia majority, also repressed and yearning for its share of oil profits. Whether Israel would annex the oil fields later or not is another matter, but the enemy must be weakened. Israel could supply the fundamentalist Shiite sheikhs with weapons through Iran. Given the Iran-Contra experience,[53] there is no reason to doubt Iran would not comply. Israel could deliver through Russian and Azerbaijani agents. Other means could fuel the Iran-Saudi conflict, like inserting *agents provocateurs* among Iranian pilgrims to incite them against the Saudi *hajj* quota. If Israel succeeded only in causing an outcry against pilgrim quotas in the world media and forced Saudi Arabia to abandon them,[54] the Iranians would do the rest by sending Shiite hordes likely to cause trouble in Mecca. If a justification is needed, Saudi support for Palestinian suicide bombers provides it.

A similar approach should work with Nigeria. Israel could help the increasingly oppressed Nigerian Christians to cede from the country's Muslim North. That would both strip the Nigerian Muslims of oil revenues and win oil concessions from Israel's Christian clients.

As she preys on militarily insignificant states, Israel should not repeat German strategic errors in World War II, when the initial depredation roused England and France, countries sufficiently important that the United States was forced to follow. Should she choose this option, Israel must provide assurances that her ambitions do not encompass militarily significant and economically not viable states like Pakistan and Egypt.[55]

A clear statement that Israel has no designs upon it but only pursues economic goals, will go a long way to keep Egypt quiet. Saddam's incursion into Kuwait aroused no concern among Arab states, except Saudi Arabia, because they understood his objective: oil. On the contrary, unpredictable American military endeavors make the third world nervous. A country does not necessarily fear a strong, aggressive neighbor (*e.g.,* Mexico and the modern United States) but does one it suspects of hostile designs. The British accommodated German annexation of Austria and Czechoslovakia; only the acquisition of Poland made German imperial ambitions undeniable, and the United Kingdom declared war. Under reasonable and cynical leadership, Egypt hesitates to fight for its brethren at odds with Israel. Even apprehension about Israeli intentions would not make Egypt risk starting an all-out preemptive war with powerful Israel,

---

[53] Given this level of tacit cooperation with a hostile state, one wonders whether ways could be found to stop the Iranian nuclear program?

[54] An unlikely scenario. Saudi little responsiveness to the world opinion should be a model for Israel. An outcry is still good for Israeli public relations.

[55] Deuteronomy 23:7 enjoins respect for Egyptians which may be interpreted as not harming them. Though the ancient inhabitants were not Arabs, Jews should think twice before possibly violating the commandment.

which the international community would call aggression. The 1973 war was a defensive war of reconquest.

Lebanon and Jordan are tempting but dubious cases. There should be no problem dividing Lebanon with Syria, which would jump on the pretext to further its Greater Syria ambitions, but the immediate use of annexing southern Lebanon is not clear. Convert it into a Christian buffer enclave and relocate the Muslims to the Syrian sector? That could be justified on the grounds of stopping the perpetual civil war. The influx of Lebanese Christian citizens into an expanded Israel, however, would upset Israeli demography and voting patterns. In any conflict with Syria, a semi-independent Lebanon would be more valuable as a buffer zone than southern Lebanon incorporated into Israel proper. Perhaps, Israel should content herself with a thirty-mile-wide no-pass zone on her Lebanese border. Dividing the country with Syria makes more sense if all the Palestinians are moved to Syrian-controlled Lebanon. Syria would likely agree to assimilate a few million Palestinians in return for Israeli and American acquiescence in the partition of Lebanon—and France could not enforce its inevitable objections.

Jordan is a tougher case than Lebanon, since Israel would have no internal allies like the Lebanese Christians), and Syria is less likely to collaborate there than it might in Lebanon. Jordanians have no place to go, or rather Israel has no place to send them, unless to Iraq, should it fail as a state after the American invasion. Successful annexation requires eviction and dispersion of the population, and though that is militarily possible, Israel has no economic and little military interest in it.

Israel must not rule conquered people directly. That way lies either a war of national liberation or an anti-apartheid struggle or the unwelcome assimilation of aliens into the Israeli milieu. Some countries—Afghanistan, Lebanon, Palestine—are inherently ungovernable. The options include driving people away, installing a brutal local administration, or requiring them to refrain from supporting the guerrillas under the threat of harsh Israeli retaliation. But never, ever govern the foreigners![56]

Annexing foreign land

Israel is not a colony[57] whose borders are to be established by external powers; like any other state, she may establish her borders by force, expanding them as much as economically or ideologically feasible without overextending herself. Annexing territory to counter aggression is

---

[56] America made that error in Iraq. Boots on the ground are necessary to completely destroy the enemy's army—if no reliable local collaborators could be found—but not for policing and administration.

[57] Even in the time of the British Mandate, Jews largely administered their own affairs, had a semi-legal armed force, pursued foreign policy, and generally were close to independence.

74

de facto politically acceptable, even after the adoption of the United Nations Charter in 1945. The Soviets hold the Japanese Kuril Islands, the U.S. reshaped the Korean and Vietnamese borders, and Poland obtained disputed territories from Germany after WWII. In each case, the beneficiary had some legal basis for its claim, but the point is that other party did not fight over the reshaped borders. The United States' decision to make war on the sponsors of the guerilla attacks of 9/11 is a precedent[58] which establishes tolerance of or positive support of terrorists as aggression against any country the terrorists attack. Therefore, Syria, Iran, Iraq, and Saudi Arabia opened hostilities against Israel and are the quasi-legitimate objects of retributory land claims. Israel might use it against a Palestinian state, declaring war on the pretext of terrorist sponsorship and annexing land as restitution. The United States did this to Mexico.

Winning tolerance of foreigners to annexation

Israel's army today can stage a military confrontation in order to annex certain territory, which the superpowers would tolerate for a number of reasons. History shows that American tolerance knows no limits: Dresden and Hiroshima, the Vietnam defoliation campaign, standing by during Rwandan massacres, acquiescence in Russian atrocities in Chechnya and of Iraq in Kurdistan during the Anfal campaign, and disregarding unspeakably brutal suppression of the Muslim Brothers' insurgency by Syria, as well as many other shameful incidents which would have made Caligula blush. America accords still higher tolerance to its allies who brutalize non-white and ideologically alien populations: Japan was virtually acquitted for its WWII crimes, not incomparable with the German variety, and atrocities by anti-communist forces in Guatemala and Nicaragua propped by the United States made few headlines there. In even more relevant example, oil was a major reason for the United States annexation of a chunk of Mexico. No American politician offers now to return the supposedly illegally acquired land, nor does Mexico raise an outcry. The more brutal a regime is, less morality America demands of it, especially if the regime opposes a larger evil: Maoist China, which butchered millions of its people, was America's ally against the U.S.S.R., while the minuscule Tiananmen incident led to sanctions. Acting brutally but efficiently, Israel need not fear Western opposition. European powers are more cynical (or realistic) than the Americans and would not protest annexation if done quickly and cleanly. The West was unconcerned with a short war in

---

[58] What would be otherwise termed aggression against Afghanistan and Iraq is rationalized and made into international case law when perpetrated by a country sufficiently strong to establish its arbitrariness as law, and make scores of countries accept it. The precedent is useful for Israel regardless of whether the American actions were justified. The precedent also conforms to historical norm when even harboring hostile rulers in exile was often a cause of war.

irrelevant Afghanistan but protested protracted war in economically viable Iraq. After the occupation of Poland by the U.S.S.R. and Germany, Britain declared war on Germany but not on the Soviet Union; the powers care about stability, not losers like Poland or Palestine.

As recently as in 1972, the United States supported Israel's rebuff of Sadat's settlement plan, since after 1967 Israel seemed able to handle a military confrontation with Egypt easily. The Americans showed no concern about the Palestinian issue until the media made it prominent. There is no inherent opposition to annexation among Western powers. Israeli schizophrenic indecisiveness provokes their antagonism.

Israel should offer the West cheap oil and gas from the annexed land, perhaps even at cost. At the beginning, some resources could even be internationalized to reduce the price of gasoline to one-fiftieth its present level, winning Israel the goodwill of foreigners who care more about gas than Arabs. Expropriation can be rationalized: the tribal royalty of a handful of states should not control a resource so important to all humanity as oil at the expense of the rest of the world by the accident of being established by colonial powers in oil-rich places. Gambling winnings are generally heavily taxed, as are inheritances. Some people are lucky this way and unlucky that, so the odds are even. Many countries have mineral resources, yet they do not internationalize them; but wealth of the magnitude of the Arab oil reserves, which they could not even exploit by themselves without international corporations, should be heavily taxed. Instead, the world like a herd of lambs suffers from O.P.E.C.'s monopoly prices, a collusion illegal in any civilized country.[59] The common explanation of this defeatism,

---

[59] The oil-price hike cannot be meaningfully compared to embargo America instituted against its adversaries. Arabs employed embargo against Israel, but the oil-price increase affected every country regardless of its Middle East policy, disqualifying the move as a foreign-policy device. Arabs did not reduce the price even when the U.S. defended Saudi Arabia and Kuwait against Iraq; the American tolerance of such abuse for all its help is bizarre.

The U.S. Court of Appeals in San Francisco decided in 1981 it has no authority over the acts by foreign states, but non-sovereign oil companies effect price hikes. The Supreme Court's *Keeton vs. Hustler* established jurisdiction of a state where the product is intentionally sold. The U.S. prosecutes foreigners violating American laws without entering the country, such as heads of drug cartels and terrorists. O.P.E.C., which engages in market manipulation and other operations illegal in the U.S., should be treated similarly.

The U.S. applies anti-dumping sanctions to foreign companies exporting the goods to the American market below the cost. Exporting at monopolistically high prices should be similarly punishable.

O.P.E.C. could be also indicted on Racketeer-Influenced Corrupt Organizations (RICO) Act because its members include rogue states known for supporting terrorism and anti-American incitation. Oil proceeds conditioned on the O.P.E.C.'s monopolistic pricing are the major source of funding the activities illegal under the U.S. law.

76

namely that the U.S. feared confrontation with the Soviets, is irrelevant. America clashed with the Soviets in West Berlin, Greece, Korea, Vietnam, Cuba, and many other places—to the extent of nuclear alert. The Kennan doctrine of containment dictated firm opposition to O.P.E.C. policy, at least if it was Soviet-backed. The real reasons behind the West's acceptance are the Vietnam syndrome, liberal free markets, the nationalist concept of sovereignty over resources, and the lobbying oil corporations which profited enormously both through the increase in value of their reserves and the Arabs' ability to pay for their services.

The United States government gets royalty-in-kind payments from domestic oil producers unrelated to profits, and price raises drive profitability up. The same accounting system that let corporations fake profits in the 1990s boom lets them hide profits from taxation. Since America imports about half its oil, its domestic output only needs to double instead of unnecessary conservation. An alternative is to explore and promote other energy sources to eliminate dependence on the Middle East or O.P.E.C. altogether—which will require overcoming important vested interests of oil corporations relying on O.P.E.C. for price benchmarks and lucrative service contracts. American corporations collaborated with Nazi Germany; now they cooperate with Islamist governments. But when Israel offers them oil concessions and uninterrupted supplies and profits, they will lobby their governments to accept annexation. The countries and corporations that cooperated with fascists would not care about dispossessed Arabs.

A hundred years ago oil extortion would have been a *casus belli*. If the United States priced some scarce resource almost hundred times above the costs, there would be an outcry. Not so with the Arabs. Would the world sit silent if someone monopolized fresh water and jacked the price up? The Arabs not only practice extortion but also use oil for political pressure and fund terrorists and fundamentalists worldwide with the profit. They fund an anti-Western ideological and military campaign, and still have audacity to accept American foreign aid. Saudi Arabia and Kuwait, defended and directly fought for by the United States, steer the oil racket.

Breaking O.P.E.C. would lower monopolist prices. Whether the oil price is too high, or, as ecologists claim, too low, is unimportant. Absent price-fixing, the price would be lower.

Natural resources should not belong to a nation only because it owns the geography but rather to those who find them, which did the colonial powers. Socialists do not recognize unearned profit and should oppose Arab wealth. There are abundant grounds to challenge Arab claims to the oil. Islamists think plundering enemies is legitimate; Al Qaeda specifically called for it in a statement of February 1998. They should not complain if Israelis plunder them.

Ecologists should be mobilized to decry the irresponsible development of oil resources by the Arabs and their corporate partners. The

Antarctic is under international control; inter-government agencies regulate the use of rivers and lakes. Public control over oil is not inconceivable. Oil is one of the last resources that justifies a colonial foreign policy, and annexation would pay. Even if the West firmly opposes annexation, Israel would agree to internationalization to devastate the Arab economies, only 1% of which is not oil-related.

If the United States suspended arms shipments to Israel, she could still overcome her weak opponents with her existing arsenal. Yet why should the United States be upset if Israel takes control of the Saudi oilfields? The American government resents Saudi financing of fundamentalist Islam and terrorism. America supported dictatorial Iraq against Iran and authoritarian Saudi Arabia against Iraq to assure an uninterrupted oil supply. Why not let Israel do the job? The Americans will acquiesce if Israel provides stability, crushing Arab will to fight instead of protracted conflict and pitiful moralizing.

The current Saudi crackdown on fundamentalists is temporary. Monarchy has zero legitimacy with nationalists and democrats. Handing sovereignty over to a royal family undermines nationalism. Westernizers think monarchy is obsolete. Socialists also oppose it. Rank-and-file Arabs expect a bigger share of oil revenues in democracy and have no reason to support the ruling dynasty. The Saudi monarchy cannot disregard the clerics who support autocracy, which alone can shield them from religious competition. The Saudi theological monopoly trust fundamentalism to keep a firm grip on the population. Fundamentalism and monarchy reinforce one another. The crackdown has singled out only clerics who accuse the regime of atheism, insufficient promotion of Wahhabism, or accommodating heathen instead of declaring military jihad, and has not affected the scores of religious extremists preaching hatred of Jews and Christians alike. Claiming to counter the fundamentalists, the Saudi rulers have imprisoned many political liberals to avoid upsetting the clerics. Saudi politics drifts ineluctably to the right as the monarchy refuses to fade into insignificance.

To take over the Arab states, Israel could rely on the fifth column of resident aliens in those countries, people discontent with their low status and longing for Western-style equality and a share of the oil profits. Arab states prohibit naturalization even for people who have lived there for generations; compare this with Israel's treatment of her Arabs. Aliens, mostly Indians, but also Filipinos and other Asians, constitute close to 100% of the workforce—not government employees or foreign company sponsors[60]—in Saudi Arabia, Kuwait, and the United Arab Emirates. Socialist and nationalist propaganda among them would disrupt Arab economies.

---

[60] Those countries prohibit non-citizen ownership of domestic corporations, creating a bonanza for locals who "sponsor" foreign companies.

Annexation tactics, expansion from a security belt

Israel needs a morally acceptable way to annex the border territories. During previous occupations, casualties resulted mainly from policing areas crowded with hostile civilians, actions that raised most of the international concern. Instead, Israel should create a mile wide buffer zone. When there is guerrilla action on the enemy side of the buffer, clear the area of infiltrators, extend the buffer, and aim eventually at a thirty-mile wide belt around Israel. Regardless of its dubious military efficiency, foreign public opinion would understand a security belt, a diplomatic, not a strategic device. Drive the inhabitants away, leave their cities desolate. Permit no settlement and prohibit traffic to create a broad no-pass no-man's-land and cover it with land mines. Scorched earth can be controlled from the air without casualties. Without Jewish settlements or military installations, the land would be much easier to support diplomatically, since it would have a defensive role, a response to guerrilla actions. That is a long-term policy. Subsequent governments would need the patience to avoid annexing the land. Only after dozens of years could Israel matter-of-factly annex it when no other effective claim would exist.

The threat of expansion would bring peace

An active military policy is an effective peacemaking device. Faced with the threat of Israeli expansion, the Arabs would seek peace, as they did after 1967 but stopped after the Sinai retreat. Peace would call for Arabs to compromise, not demand the 1949 armistice borders. After the 1973 war, Israel retreated under American pressure from her forward positions in the Sinai and eventually gave the peninsula up under the Camp David agreement. That concession included the viable isthmus area, along with military infrastructure and the only oil wells in Israel. If she had instead expanded west from the Suez Canal, Egypt would have been forced to sign a different peace treaty, leaving the isthmus with Israel to get the rest of the peninsula back and stop further Israeli encroachment. The U.S. might not have pressured Israel into withdrawing from the Egyptian side of the channel, had it been clear that Israel intended to acquire more land as bargaining chips and to increase the tension to bring the enemy to the negotiating table. If Egypt or any other Arab country were in a situation where delaying the peace settlement was dangerous and expensive, it would compromise instead of insisting that victorious Israel withdraw. For example, Egypt agreed to settle its war with Sudan instead of clinging to her initial demands. But during negotiations, Israel lost sight of the objective. Instead of the gaining an important oil-producing territory, she went in search of a treaty, as easily violated as signed and producing no trade benefits.

Proper Military Strategy

Hiring foreign infantry

Israel could introduce mercenaries, perhaps anti-Muslim Indians who have suffered at Muslim hands or even Christians who feel some attachment to Israel. Other reasons, like racism or revenge for terrorism, could boost recruitment. The Russian hatred of Muslim Chechens and Serbian hatred of Bosnians, Albanians, and Turks should be exploited. Soldiers respect strength, and cannot be anti-Semitic while Israel is strong. Mercenaries could form most infantry units. Paying mercenaries mostly from underdeveloped countries would be cheaper than draining the economy of young, creative people. Other technically advanced branches of the army can fill their ranks with Jewish volunteers. Mercenaries fit the Israeli military psychology better than any other country's, since only Israel does not expect its soldiers to die like heroes, *en masse* and unnecessarily. Mercenaries tolerate low casualties. Mercenaries do not fight fiercely, but frequent clashes for minor readjustments of the balance of power are not fierce; they only become such when politicians stifle minor confrontations, and accumulated controversies reach major proportions.

The I.D.F. could attract some of the best soldiers of fortune, because it provides a possibility of relatively low danger action. The United States has recruited foreigners for a long time, though without attracting many volunteers. The use of non-conventional weapons during major confrontations obviates the need for a large infantry. As a last resort, Israelis must be ready to defend themselves, but in peacetime, privately managed mercenary armies are economically efficient.

The modern dislike of mercenaries recalls their poor performance in the late Renaissance, not an institutional failure but rather the consequence of too many emerging states hiring too many people too cheap. King Gustavus II Adolphus invented the modern conscripted army; previously, citizens were conscripted only for defense emergencies, a reasonable policy. Other cash-strapped powers accepted conscription, and military intellectuals propped the development up with theory.

The Israeli situation is crucially different from the Swedish. At the time, Swedes were among the poorest Europeans, and Gustavus II could not get any cheaper soldiers. Israel is reasonably well off, and would find soldiers from less developed nations much cheaper than wasting GDP input from the conscripted Jews.

Israel could create a security belt of Arab farmers, dependent on Israel not only for irrigation but also for technology and genetically modified seeds. Better, however, to settle Indian farmers there. The Arabs would not scare them; they have no quarrel with Israel and a lot with Muslims. Indians would demand neither Israeli citizenship nor government benefits. Indians have a record of loyalty to countries of temporary

80

immigration, and after decades have changed the demography of the territories irreversibly, Jewish farmers could replace them without severe conflict.

Western Christian radicals could be invited to police the territories. They would be happy to get a training ground for their militia. Western states' security agencies would infiltrate them, mitigating the potential threat to home countries, and Israel could be assured of less barbaric methods than SLA employed. The radicals or other ruthless foreigners, such as Russian *spetznaz*, might even be used for anti-Muslim terrorism, a proper retribution. If, however, Israel abandons or restricts them, they would embrace Islamic radicals. Playing with the devil is a game of skill.

Harsh measures, not limited victory

Arabs now commit aggression against Israel safely. In the worst case, they simply retreat to the *status quo ante*. Israel must counterattack. In 1967 and 1973, the Israeli army should have taken Cairo and Damascus and replaced the leadership with puppet rulers. The United States restrained Israel to prevent major destabilization in the region. If Israel had changed the regimes swiftly, the United States would have acquiesced, as when the Northern Alliance it cooperated with but did not welcome took Kabul in 2001.[61] The United States could have commanded Israel and her neighbors to sign a peace treaty long ago on terms agreeable to the Arabs' Russian sponsors; the United States effectively commanded Israel, Great Britain and France out of the Suez war in 1956. On the other hand, America wants no involvement in a major war. Low-intensity conflict suits its role of arbiter. Its aid lets both sides go on, though they would have settled otherwise from exhaustion. The United States would also accept regional stability under Israeli dominance, as American policy supports Japan against the rest of East Asia. Sensitive Jews, however, do not take hints and try to persuade the United States government of Israeli concern for human rights and Palestinian aspirations, as well as Israel's accommodation of other Arabs—

---

[61] Even if Soviets intervened, the U.S. could revenge the defeats in Korea and Vietnam. Absent the Soviet or American ground troops, the warfare would have been aerial, where America hold advantage. Both sides would not have used nuclear weapons, fearing reprisal. Soviets did not stand a chance in confrontation with the U.S. over Egypt because the Russian doctrine of overcoming qualitative deficiencies with quantity does not work with airlift.

Some explain Israeli restraint by Scud-B missiles with nuclear warheads which the U.S.S.R. reportedly deployed in Northern Egypt in the war last days. This argument works against Israeli politicians: if they considered the nuclear threat credible, they had to destroy the missiles or force Egypt to remove them by escalation Kennedy employed in Cuban missile crisis. Still earlier in the war, Israel must have shot Soviet supply planes flying to Egypt; not attacking supply lines is ludicrous.

things altogether not on the agenda of American administrations which support brutal dictators when expedient.

Limited victory is meaningless in war between comparable enemies. Carthage's recovery led Cato to proclaim, *Carthago delenda est*. Israel lacks the defensive logistical advantage America had in the War of Independence, and must finish off her enemies. Otherwise, Arab-Israeli conflict is nearing the span of the Seventy-Year War.

Can five million Jews overcome a billion Muslims? They surely can. Numerous empires achieved close to a 200:1 ratio of acquisitions to their own population: Babylon, the Greek federation, Rome, England, Spain, Portugal, and the Netherlands. Like start-up corporations with innovative products rise to dominate markets, countries with innovative strategies establish empires and sustain them at subjects' expense. In the end, quantity matters and empires dissolve, but they last for centuries before settling into a comfortable niche of respectable isolation.

Unlike governments, guerrillas and terrorists do not make peace. They do not fear retribution, even death. They must be destroyed. Their lives are so miserable that high purpose easily outstrips earthly benefits, and they are ready to die. Bettering Arab conditions would shrink the terrorists' conscription base, though it would take time. Ridiculing their ideology and religion is much easier and happened to the U.S.S.R. There, as in the Muslim world, people were dissatisfied with the governing ideology and their rulers and cynical about anti-Western propaganda. Ridiculing religion is insulting, but it registers and undermines clerical pronouncements. Advertising works if repeated enough. The U.S.S.R. debilitated deep-seated Orthodox Christianity in just a few years by offering a substitute ideology, and the West offers consumerism. Such policies would not eliminate terrorists altogether but would decrease their number.

Non-response to their aggression encourages Arabs. If Israel had carpet-bombed Cairo in 1968, there would have been no War of Attrition. If the I.D.F. had marched through it in 1973, the issue of returning the Sinai Peninsula would not have arisen. Overwhelming retribution does not always crush the will to fight and provokes a suicidal response in two situations. One is the will to die in the apocalyptic war with evil, hardly applicable to Arabs. Another is the hope of survival. Arbitrarily applied violence during the French revolutionary *Terreur* stirred people to revolt. It does not do so, however, when it is employed as cleverly as Stalin did, who assured the Soviet population that only *others* were threatened, not they themselves. Without mass media, the French revolutionaries could not tell that lie and were forced out. Israel must assure Arabs that only terrorists and their sponsors suffer and that good Arabs have nothing to fear. Like the United Arab Emirates, Muslim countries that do not support terrorists need not fear retribution.

Labeling such measures war crimes is tautology. War is a crime. If a country decides to go to war, it is pointless to try to humanize what is inhumane in the first place.

The necessity of using chemical, biological, and nuclear weapons

Israel could have saved thousands of lives in the Yom Kippur War by using non-conventional weapons. The available weapons must be used to the fullest extent possible, after which the victor may destroy the loser's ability to respond. In the Yom Kippur War, Israel should have used nuclear power and demilitarized Egypt to control its military development in the years to come. Harmful effects of chemical and nuclear weapons, especially micro-charges, would dissipate before reaching Israeli centers. Self-restraint has led Israel to face a highly dangerous situation in which a change of regime in Egypt may mean the use of non-conventional weapons against Israel. Regardless of her military prowess, Israel lacks depth of defense against such weapons. In a sense, even Russia and the U.S. lack nuclear depth of defense, since they find even the smallest losses from WMD intolerable. In reality, however, all military planners accept a certain percentage of military personnel and civilians killed, and contingency plans for major war assume some warheads will hit their targets. The probability is higher in border areas. Since Israel is but one border area, her depth of defense is nil.

The highly mechanized I.D.F. is better suited for chemical warfare than the Arabs, who rely on unprotected infantry. Chemical weapons are made to kill and make combatants hesitant to use them for fear of retaliation. Israel might develop more effective non-lethal chemical and biological weapons for inflicting long-term disability, insufficient to cause escalation against her cities.

The CBN threat must be credible; Israel's is discredited by her self-restraint in 1973. Dismantling the I.D.F. almost fully, except for air defense and small tank forces, will show the world that Israel will use the nuclear option in any large-scale confrontation. Only the doctrine of the first-response nuclear weapons could relieve Israeli of the devastating peacetime military expenditures.

Israel needs to publish a roster of CBN triggers. Should someone detonate an A-bomb in Tel Aviv, Israel would strike neither Egypt, Syria, Iran, nor Pakistan, immobilized by fear of escalation. Israel should legislate that a CBN attack against her from whatever source means immediate, simultaneous nuclear destruction of everything Muslim—capitals, temples, population centers—by the hundred or so nuclear weapons in her possession. Terrorists who plan to use nuclear weapon against Israel must understand that Tel Aviv will be commemorated with a really big bang. The Western powers, which has long discounted the nuclear threat, should realize that they would be passive observers and collateral victims of the Jewish-Muslim WWIII unless they eliminate third-world CBN arsenals completely. Everybody in the yellow submarine shares the fear and responsibility. The problem is not only Israel's.

Do not let potentially hostile regimes build Chemical Biological Nuclear arsenals

After World War I, the Allies humiliated Germany politically, supported it economically, and failed to insure permanent German demilitarization. When the Nazis came to power, they were ready to exploit the accumulated hatred and the military industrial capabilities, a situation much like that in the Middle East today. Germany started the war, even though the Allies outstripped it economically, in natural resources, and in manpower. How much more likely is heavily armed, fundamentalist, aggressive Iran to start a war? It does not matter that Arab armies cannot handle the Israeli Defense Force. A few missiles with non-conventional warheads or a sea container with a nuclear weapon unloaded at Ashdod or Haifa would wipe out the Israeli population crowded on the narrow coastal strip. Buffer zones are useful against guerrillas but not against aircraft or missiles. Preventing a CBN attack is hard but critical to Israeli survival. Neither anti-aircraft nor anti-missile defenses will provide total security; and nothing less than maximum security is acceptable to tiny Israel.

Any large, militarist country is a potential threat to others. Muslim countries in particular have "proven criminal intent," repeatedly warring on Israel. Israel can deal with war at her borders. She survived the 1948 war, fought deep in her territory. Israel did not counterattack when Iraqi Scuds penetrated her defenses. But the risk of a CBN attack is intolerable. Demilitarizing the Muslims is risky, but to do nothing is suicide, now or in the next generation.

It is hard for a democracy to gather support for pre-emption unless the threat is clear, as in 1967[62] or in the case of the Iraqi Osiraq reactor. Pinpoint preemptive strikes, however, do not ordinarily escalate into war. In the earliest years, Israel launched limited retaliatory attacks against her neighbors without inciting all-out war. Such tactics are inexpensive and let Israel keep the I.D.F. lean.

Israel must destroy not only CBN and medium- and long-range missile facilities but also the relevant infrastructure of scientists,

---

[62] In the events leading to the Six-Day War, Nasser deployed troops in demilitarized Sinai, likely a bluff to support his image as protector of Syrians, who suffered humiliating losses in air skirmishes with Israel they provoked. Not trusting Nasser's good intentions, Israel attacked ground installations before war was declared on her. That decisiveness gave Israel one of the most spectacular victories in military history.

84

laboratories,[63] launching pads, and airstrips, without exception, even at the risk of war, as in the case of Egypt. Israel lost a chance for a regional nuclear ban offered in 1976 by Egyptian Prime Minister Ismail Fahmy, but can still jump on the similar pronouncements by Egyptian leaders. Israel fooled the International Atomic Energy Agency inspections of her reactors before, sealing sections with false walls, and could have continued. In the worst case, Israel could simply conserve her facilities, or nominally convert them to civilian use, and rest assured by the considerable number of nuclear charges hidden. Egypt only needed a face-saving excuse to kill its expensive nuclear program, and Israel stupidly failed to provide that pretext.

If Egypt seems stable and peaceful, consider how peaceful Lebanon, Libya, Iran, Iraq, Pakistan, Sudan, and many other states were just before a political *volte-face*, something that happens in autocracies. Egypt went through various stages and rulers in only half a century. Radicals often attempted takeovers.

Israel should at least prepare to strike automatically at Egyptian CBN facilities the minute a hostile regime comes to power. But keep in mind that many good Egyptian presidents accumulate CBN for a single bad one. How likely is a mad ruler? Most likely, given enough time; one crackpot per century is plausible, and will annihilate Israel.

Delay would cost Israel dearly. The Egyptian army is no match for the I.D.F. and strong only compared to other Arab armies. Napoleon conquered Egypt with a small expeditionary force, and Sharon was posed to do the same in 1973, had Israel not yielded to United States pressure. Economically, militarily, and psychologically, it is better to suffer a confrontation now than to bear the cost of defensive readiness into the distant future. The West tolerates Chinese CBN destined for use in Asia; but Egypt has no enemy besides Israel, and Israel cannot let Arabs detonate nuclear bombs, even in their own conflicts, near her. What, besides political cowardice, prevents Israel from confronting the issue sooner rather than later? Kennedy responded to the deployment of Soviet missiles in Cuba with immediate confrontation to defuse the threat. The world closes its eyes to Muslim countries arming with WMD, much as it trusted Germany until the outbreak of WWII. Islam is as aggressive as Nazism, with as little reverence for human life, theirs or their enemies'.

Another option is to agree to mutual destruction of CBN arsenals and then re-arm secretly, which is how Israel acquired nuclear capability. Discovering a rearmament program in Egypt would be a legitimate reason to strike its CBN facilities. National security is no arena for mythical knightly honesty.

---

[63] An attack on bio-warfare facilities with vacuum bombs and napalm, perhaps nuclear micro-charges, runs no risk of releasing germs. The radius of radioactive pollution does not threaten Israel.

When the threat of CBN development becomes credible, Israel should strike. Right now Israel is heading into a problem with Iran: should America succeed in changing the regime there, it would be next to impossible for Israel to attack a United States-sponsored country. Egypt similarly developed its nuclear capability under the umbrella of American military guarantees. Destroying the Iranian nuclear program now is wiser than hoping the United States will keep Iran from acquiring WMD. It is not that Iran would use CBN against Israel: *mullahs* are not so sure of Ibn Kathir's seventy virgins that they would rush to paradise through Israeli retaliation. They would pass the WMDs to terrorists. Iran would not even need to make the transfer; the threat alone would increase Iran's bargaining power dramatically. The United States could do nothing if Iran threatened to supply chemical, biological, nuclear weapons to Al Qaeda: a preemptive strike would not eliminate all the weapon stocks and would invite nuclear reprisal from Iran. Nuclear weapons became the ultimate equalizer of power. How much can the owner of CBN bargain for? Quite a lot: North Korea won political and economic concessions by threatening to develop a bomb—and is developing it. Ransom is inadmissible: American accommodation of North Korea sets bad precedents for rogue regimes to extort American cooperation. Someone with several nuclear bombs could force the evacuation of Jews from the Middle East without serious casualties by detonating one bomb in the Negev and another on a ship fifty miles from New York harbor, and claiming to have others hidden in Tel Aviv, Jerusalem, and Washington, programmed to detonate in forty-eight hours. Suppose a radical Muslim regime threatened distributing CBN to buyers or colleagues and offered to relent if the United States abandoned Israel. Or imagine if terrorists spread biohazard in New York and withheld the antidote until the United States left the Middle East. Acquiescence to such demands is likely. Israel should not let Iran have nuclear weapons, even to be used against Saudi Arabia. Having used CBN once, Iran would eventually target Israel. The United States does not punish Pakistan for its support of Al Qaeda because Pakistan has nuclear bombs but rather pretends to believe that Pakistan is not involved in terrorism. CBN provide next-to-perfect immunity for sponsoring terror. A nuclear Iran could carry on conventional warfare without much fear of reprisal. Owning CBN pays, and Israel must not let her enemies have them. Israel would gain politically if someone exploded a nuclear bomb in the United States, the likely destiny of the first bomb the terrorists get their hands on. A unique weapon goes against the Great Satan, not its Israeli affiliate. Americans would see that the consequences, though horrible, are statistically slight and mostly psychological. Small CBN stocks would no longer deter anything, and CBN would remain the major tactical weapon of terrorists, even used for commercial extortion, but of limited political use. Such an attack, though aimed at pushing America to isolationism, would likely lead it to harsher retaliation and pre-emption. The ultimate aim is to get the United States to disarm rogue nuclear states at any cost. Faced with a real ultimatum, hostile nations would open their nuclear facilities to verification and interrogation to uncover all stockpiles. This policy could bring on a nuclear showdown.

That fear of retaliation stopped the use of poison gas in WWII is doubtful. The Soviets in 1941 and the Germans in 1945 were sufficiently suicidal to disregard the threat. Rather, chemical weapons are inefficient in the open air, especially if the wind changes. The means of production were vulnerable, and transportation was precarious. Weapons once made are used, and human nature has not changed in the nuclear era. At least some of Israel's enemies do not fear retaliation and will use CBN as soon as they get them, not at all implausible with Russia, China, India, Pakistan, Egypt, North Korea, and Iran in the club.

Does forced CBN disarmament bring on an otherwise unlikely confrontation? Only confrontation between states is unlikely. The guerrillas mean to attack Jews, are not afraid, and do not care about Muslim collateral damage, as Osama's African bombing demonstrated. The question is not if confrontation is likely but if the terrorists are likely to get CBN. The A-bomb is based on technology everyone, including Muslims, understands. Its important parts are available from private firms for civilian purposes. Underpaid servicemen guard the nuclear stockpiles of irresponsible regimes with a proven record of supporting terrorists. Who in his right mind can say the terrorists will not get nuclear weapons and fairly soon? Tackling the problem now offers advantages. Some nuclear states might be coerced or bribed into cooperation, but once terrorists use nuclear weapons, countries will be reluctant to give those practical weapons up. Forced disarmament is risky, but it eliminates loose nuclear arsenals. Leaving things to their own devices accumulates the risk perpetually: after the first nuclear incident, more are probable.

Procrastination aggravates the threat. Better force North Korea to get rid of a few nuclear warheads than dozens. Better annihilate the reactor in Algerian desert now than resist nuclear blackmail when the reactor goes hot. The urgency is greater with nuclear aspirants like Iran, which has the facilities but not yet the weapons. Any war, any pressure, involves the probability of reprisal, as would a demand for nuclear disarmament. Why keep a huge army, then shrink from using it against credible threats?

A nuclear strike against the United States or Israel in response to a demand for the disarmament of a minor nuclear power is unlikely, since one or two bombs would not wound America critically but would elicit an overwhelming response. The best bet is a pre-emptive strike against all possible nuclear storage facilities and a simultaneous airborne assault to capture the enemy leader and military officials, torturing them to reveal loose stocks swiftly.

Non-military measures might affect nuclear disarmament. Bribes, threats, face-saving treaties could do the job. India and Pakistan would happily succumb to international pressure to dismantle nuclear facilities and destroy stockpiles, with a NATO guarantee of intervention in case of major conflict. North Korea would make concessions to buy international respect and aid which would push it toward integration with South Korea. Egypt could agree to regional nuclear demilitarization. The political options are numerous, but the West does not want to exploit them relentlessly. Buy-out programs should offer immunity and exorbitant payments for fissile material to black market operators, raising the tag beyond terrorists' abilities. Even a billion dollars per nuclear head is a price to pay to clean up stolen weapons.

The Israeli security belt is not limited to the neighboring Muslim states but also includes other countries likely to engage in nuclear proliferation, like Pakistan and North Korea who might sell nuclear arms to terrorists, and actually sent combat aircraft to Syria and Egypt, respectively, during the 1973 war. Pakistan does not even need to sell the bomb: the Islamic fundamentalists in its nuclear programs will get the know-how out soon enough. Israel should return to assassinating research fellows in hostile countries' nuclear laboratories. They are enemy soldiers on duty and should be treated as such. Scientists are formally military in all rogue nuclear states. Israel should advertise her objectives, pursuing inimical nuclear scientists everywhere and offering rewards for their heads. Other countries concerned about proliferation would tacitly support Israel. Israel could persuade India to attack Pakistan's nuclear facilities and stockpiles. After superficial objections, the West would applaud the elimination of any rogue menace. Except for world opinion the United States would have long since done away with the North Korean, Pakistani, and Iranian nuclear programs. Seeing the Israelis doing the job for their benefit would only strengthen the American attachment to Israel.

Confusing the unfamiliar with the improbable, politicians doubt that Arab states or terrorists will use CBN. They even say the Iranian program is less than some suspect, as if Israel cares whether Iran has five nuclear warheads or fifty. Israel's rulers will not try to disarm her enemies absent imminent threat, letting them accumulate or develop weapons. That absence of policy correlates with Israeli public opinion which is to take harsh action only when absolutely necessary—and too late, too difficult, or too costly. Israel should not let the natural weakness of a peaceful democracy mask the need for pre-emption to stop the proliferation of CBN.

The case of China and Russia is difficult. Both are certain to engage in proliferation eventually. Russia's politicians and military are corrupt, and Russian nuclear warheads will eventually wind up in Muslim hands. They will use the first one or two against the United States for maximum effect, but Israel is next. Israel can hardly attack China or Russia at this point, nor would the United States government take pre-emptive action against either. Israel should use public opinion to pressure America into buying up Soviet nuclear stockpiles and requiring the destruction of biological agents without compensation. Though the United States paid for the destruction of some Soviet weapons, many remain. Russia would probably insist on retaining some warheads to preserve her superpower status, though they are virtually useless without modern aircraft. Russia would probably give up her mobile intercontinental ballistic missile launchers, which are not very accurate and are suitable only for large civilian targets. America may let Russia retain some silo-based missiles, which are relatively open to control.

Luring China and her weapons into NATO and under central command is possibly the best option, though the pragmatic Chinese would likely hide a few bombs. Economic sanctions would not help, as the aftermath of Tiananmen showed. Generally, Communists care more about ideology than people or the economy. That underscores the importance of undermining communism in China, fomenting democracy, and breaking the country up into reasonably sized states dependent upon America and the West. A boycott aimed at establishing international control over Chinese CBN would be effective only if important Western countries participate. China needs many concessions from the international community, and every request should be used to gain further control over Chinese non-conventional weapons. The United States could set an example by accepting international control of its weapons.

Any country with pieces of nuclear technology is a danger to Israel, even without overtly threatening her. A host of unscrupulous proliferators—China, India, North Korea, Russia, Pakistan, Iraq, France, Switzerland, Argentina, even Morocco—helped Egypt mount a nuclear program. Some of them participated directly in what was clearly a military program. China enriched Egyptian uranium on its Russian-built centrifuges. Israel cannot control all those countries, but the rest of the world has the responsibility. Anyone would worry about a neighbor storing dynamite; a postman would worry about delivering a book on bomb making; ex-criminals may not buy firearms—so why does the public accept the dissemination of military nuclear technology and let rogues stockpile CBN? Americans accepted the inviolability of borders, a self-serving doctrine of European nation-states, as an excuse for not punishing proliferators. A country like Pakistan threatens the whole world with proliferation, protected by the fiction of sovereignty. No one who stores dynamite can expect to be left alone; a country building nuclear weapons may not claim sovereign immunity.

Proliferation through private companies acting as proxies for various governments is commonly ignored. After the United States pushed France out of the arrangement to build a nuclear fuel plant in Egypt in 1976, the private French company Robotel gave Egypt the hot cells essential for its plutonium extraction complex in 1980. Punishing private entities is simple even for Israel alone. Similarly, she should have pressed or bribed Niger not to sell uranium to Egypt.

To make things go more smoothly in war, Israel should force her neighbors to demobilize, citing fear of nuclear weapons falling into the hands of religious fanatics. While the United Nations would doubtless condemn such attacks, aiming to destroy the strategic weapons of sovereign Arab states, the United States and its allies would support Israel's establishing regional stability under American control. That kind of imposed peace kept the Roman Empire relatively safe for centuries.

Humane war is costly and ineffective

Israel's large army is unwarranted and results from the government's reluctance to use effective non-conventional weapons, a policy which only increases casualties. In a protracted struggle, not only more Israeli soldiers but also more foreign civilians die. Unrestricted force crushes the people's and the army's will to fight; skirmishes encourage them when public opinion demands further "humane" restrictions to scale the war down to a level where they can fight the Israeli Defense Force on equal terms, thereby prolonging suffering and defeating Israeli objectives. Heavy losses in continuous minor encounters turned Israeli public opinion against the Lebanese war. Even worse, after taking Beirut, Israel let the P.L.O. slip away to Tunisia instead of bombing them along with the remaining civilians they used as cover. In 1973, Egyptian Minister of War Ismail Ali was ready to bomb his own troops stuck in the pocket alongside Israeli forces pushing to Cairo. Only stupidity prompted Israel to honor its agreement with the P.L.O. instead of sinking their ships with fighters using the Christian South Lebanon Army[64] as a proxy, thus preventing thousands of subsequent P.L.O. murders. Further low-intensity warfare would be a mistake; slowly increasing the violence would be even worse, as people grow used to terror. A deterrent is effective only while unused: afterward it becomes tolerable. The enemy devises counter-measures, spiraling devastation incrementally, and the population grows accustomed and less afraid. To succeed, violence should be immediately overwhelming. Israel should show itself a bloodthirsty monster to scare the Arabs into submission. Israel should control casualties by preventing counter-attacks, destroying the enemy's military capabilities, and extinguishing his financial supply. Second best to overwhelming destruction is pinpoint destruction, devastating a skyscraper in Riyadh on the background of others untouched. Violence must be exceptional to succeed.

Both Dresden and Guernica were moderately effective militarily. Both were exceedingly inhumane – though perhaps all too human. The perceptions of the two differ because history is written and shaped by

---

[64] South Lebanon Army, a Christian militia supported by Israel against the P.L.O., generally unconcerned with human rights, though mild by local standards. Muslim factions committed atrocities exceeding trumpeted Sabra and Shatila by order of magnitude.

winners. Israel should concentrate on winning, and the historians will acquit her.

Make retaliation personal

Enemy rulers must suffer on a par with soldiers. Israeli leaders must feel some unconscious bond with their Arab counterparts, even with Arafat. Whether he sponsored terrorism or was just politically unable to contain it, Palestine would have been better off without him; yet Israel gave him royal treatment while his soldiers killed Jews.[65] National leaders today are immune even when their countries are attacked. The Allies hanged only a handful of Nazi bosses, and the United States turned Saddam over to Iraqi prosecutors instead of convicting him of crimes against humanity and executing him publicly at once or extraditing him to the Kurds. Any attempt to get at national leaders would reveal the arbitrariness of current policies. The Americans are ready to kill bin Laden. The only reason for not eliminating some leaders promptly is the reverence of diplomatic immunity. Why wage a war on Iraq to remove Saddam, instead of assassinating him with a missile? That was a problem in Afghanistan where it took hours for missiles to reach the target, but not in Iraq with the U.S. Navy nearby. Retaliation should be personal, bombing their residences and the companies they own, forcing banks to freeze their assets, killing them and their relatives.

While murdering a family is condemnable in peace, war justifies it. Endangering a foreign dictator's dear ones would go some way to prevent the war or finish it sooner, thus save lives. Relatives often influence dictators and could dissuade them from escalation. This measure is not a panacea—ancient wars saw royal families exterminated—but worth trying, considering the statistically low civilian losses it involves. Besides, the families of Arab dictators are almost always deeply involved in government business. Stalin's refusal to ransom his captured son from the Nazis is unique.

The personal approach would improve international policing. Waging no more than two wars at a time limits the American ability to fight evil, provoking accusations of the arbitrariness of prosecution: Iraq was arbitrarily chosen out of many dangerous dictatorships. But why all the tremendously expensive[66] wars? Aerial strikes eliminating Milosevic, Saddam, and their like would do the job, destroying a few dozen houses and killing few hundred people—fewer than a war. The next rulers would mind

---

[65] In WWI, the Tsar, the Kaiser and the King of England were cousins and maintained a friendly correspondence during the war while their subjects died on the battlefields. Compare that to meetings with Arafat and Israeli remittances to the Palestinian Administration during the guerrilla war of attrition against Israel.

[66] Iraq war cost in excess of $300 billion translates into a million dollars for each of 300,000 people whose murder is attributed to Saddam

human rights and American interests, if they did not want to hide in bunkers. If they did not, another inexpensive air strike would bring their case to trial in Hades. Pinpoint attacks could punish offenders quickly, cheaply, and efficiently, and free the world.

Israeli and American leaders oppose such measures because of reciprocal danger. Saddam's plot against Bush Sr. and the 9/11 attempt against the White House signaled a return to the historical norm. Decent rulers led their troops until the 18th century, and reputations hinged on battlefield performance. Now rulers are shielded from the wars they launch. Public opinion should press for change so rulers face danger before common citizens.

Israel should minimize the security of her rulers, and at any rate remove government protection from their family members. Let the top officials fear for their loved ones. Then the government would deal with Intifada more efficiently.

Deterrence does not work

The threat of violence should not replace its actual use. Threat is never absolutely effective. Unless one state is clearly stronger, there is no example among nuclear powers and certainly not among others of permanent peace based on mutual deterrence. Mutual deterrence means keeping arms levels approximately the same; any change, however minor, real or perceived, can lead one party to believe it has the advantage—and initiate hostilities. Deterrence creates a delicate balance of power, periodically reevaluated by wars and border clashes. Little Israel cannot tolerate even limited war on her territory, nor can she use chemical, biological, or nuclear weapons near her own people.

Deterrence presumes an unwarlike enemy. Rome and Carthage, the strongest powers of their time, did not deter each other. Germany defied American and Soviet deterrence. Authoritarian rulers often care little about casualties and are not deterred. Deterrence raises the barrier of decision for opening hostilities but hardly eliminates war. The United States and the Soviet Union did not attack each other during the Cold War, not out of fear but because neither wanted to conquer the other. The I.D.F.'s power in 1967 did not deter Egypt in 1973. An army should rely on surprise, not saber rattling.

The U.S., the U.S.S.R., and to a lesser extent the P.R.C. learned that mutual deterrence between comparable enemies means an economically unsustainable arms race: not tit-for-tat but over-reaction that bankrupts the economy. Israel does not want to know if she could survive such a race. Sustained over time, deterrence costs more than defeat. Deterrence, if any, should be one-way to discourage attempts to close the gap. That requires disarming the enemy. Not only does Israel ignore the obvious need to reduce the threat to her, but she also shreds the credibility of her own threat by avoiding cruelty. Deterrence does not work, if the enemy knows you do not mean it.[67] Who would expect a nuclear counter-attack from the Israel who drug her feet in Beirut to save a few civilians in the targeted districts?

Use large forces for conquest

Forced demilitarization supported by pre-emptive strikes is the only feasible option. Otherwise Israel must maintain her expensive air force, anti-missile defenses, satellite early warning systems, tanks—all in peacetime. She cannot do without them, since treaties are worthless. IDF grew after the treaty with Egypt. So why does Israel need peace? For the same money, she could conquer. Therefore, the real choice, at least until the Middle East settles down, is not between war and peace but between using the army for conquest or for disarming the Arabs and maintaining only the smallest possible pre-emptive strike force.

Inaction stultifies an army. The adventurous miss the action and lose interest. Accustomed to a bloodless life, soldiers lose the taste for fighting, though their job is to fight and kill. An overwhelming technical or manpower advantage masks unpreparedness, and losses are called victories.[68]An army should go from one conflict to the next to stay focused and efficient.

Force Arab disarmament and turn Arab states into protectorates

Letting Israel supervise Arab state military matters would give her hegemony over the region, a *pax iudaica*, in which she protects some Arab states against their Arab adversaries, a Monroe Doctrine for the Middle East. Under that arrangement, Israel would not interfere in the internal affairs of her dependents, only make sure they do not prepare to war against her and do not fight much among themselves. The surprise opening of the Yom Kippur War showed that Israel cannot read the Arab rulers' minds; she should instead forbid them to stockpile modern weapons. If Israel dominated the region, the United States would no longer have to police it.

America harbors some reservations about Israel. They stem, however, from problems Israel should overcome. Israel does not always submit to the wishes of American presidents, but she backs down about as

---

[67] Kennedy got the Soviet generals attention by mobilizing. Soviet plans generally did not consider demobilization, and they took Kennedy's move as preparation for war.

[68] It took twenty million Soviet corpses and the comparable American industrial damage to crush the relatively small German army in WWII. Both "victories" over Iraq are defeats considering the astronomical costs of killing Iraqi soldiers: over a million dollars per head even in the initial campaign, with more by an order of magnitude later. Iraqi soldiers would have committed suicide for a fraction of this money, and Saddam would have changed his policy and embraced America for a bribe perhaps less than monthly cost of the war.

often she can without losing the last trace of sovereignty. She "disobeys" usually on humanitarian issues, the Palestinian problem. Should Israel force Jordan and Lebanon to naturalize Palestinians, America's malaise would eventually vanish. Israeli dominance would also stop border skirmishes with Arab countries, another point Americans fuss about. By pursuing a policy of economic self-interest, Israel would quash complaints about her unpredictability. Americans have been happy to see their clients—Japan, South Africa, Germany—become regional hegemons elsewhere. America invited Israel to take that role when she opposed the Syrian invasion of Jordan. Traditionally anti-imperialist, the United States objects to formal hegemony, though the essence of American policy always allows *de facto* dominance, as the Monroe Doctrine prescribes. Israel should word her policy acceptably for the Western public.

The objective is two-fold. One option would be to threaten Egypt into neutrality, Egypt's legal obligation under the peace treaty, and dominate the rest of the Middle East. The more ambitious project of turning Egypt into a protectorate is possible but would require considerable national determination. As long as Egypt has stable, reasonable leaders and does not spike its stockpiles of weapons of mass destruction, the notion is questionable; but with Egyptian neutrality secured either way, Israel could turn on Iran, Iraq, and Syria. The years to come will be apt for such moves, since the world considers those countries terrorist havens. The Egyptian army, without its Russian sponsors, is weaker than the I.D.F. American assistance to Egypt slowly closes the gap. If Israeli intelligence can identify all the Egyptian nuclear facilities, she has a rare chance to demilitarize Egypt.

Israel should contain the most important states first by disarming or reassuring them, before turning to smaller oil-producing Arab entities. Israel is much stronger than any Arab state[69] and can face any of them right now.

Minimize the involvement of I.D.F. infantry

To avoid repeating the error of getting mixed up in the Lebanese civil war in 1982, Israel should not send ground troops to Arab countries but rather bomb them into submission and install puppet governments as a temporary solution. Rebellion could be punished by mid-scale military operations. A sufficiently cruel and militarily effective administration usually eliminates opposition, though such a policy failed in Lebanon because the South Lebanon Army did not handle the job. Controlled territory should be combed for guerrillas and isolated from intrusion. As the Soviet Union showed, border control can be effective even over an immense perimeter.

---

[69] Arab GDP figures are misleading, consisting largely of oil revenues—almost 100%, in the case of Saudi Arabia.

94

Non-military harassment of Arabs

Israel should go after Arab wealth, conscripting the best lawyers to entangle wealthy Arabs and Arab countries everywhere in lawsuits and put pressure on their interests with the aim of taking away their income. The Arab O.P.E.C. countries are obvious targets due to price collusion.[70] Islamic charities that support terrorists are also candidates for civil prosecution. They have significant assets, and the prosecution would pay for itself.

Families of terrorists' victims have a good case against Saudi Arabia and Iran, as well as against individual donors for their support of terrorists. The options range from civil lawsuits to criminal indictment under the RICO act.

The descendants of Israelis who left property in Iraq and Egypt have a reasonable claim for those assets, either nationalized or pillaged by mobs. To be fair, Israel should hear Palestinian property claims: the balance will favor the Israelis, many of whom left documented assets in Arab countries while most Palestinians were peasants without title to the land. Hearing Arab property claims does not mean letting their descendants return: citizenship is personal. Once abrogated, descendents cannot inherit it. The Jews returned after 1,900 years, not by right but by force, which Arabs can resist and Israel can defend. The Arab refugees in 1948 were not Israeli citizens. They fled the invasion and sided with Israel's enemy.

Further claims could be entertained, like suing the Arabs for the cost of Israel's defensive military build-up, necessitated by Arab violation of United Nations resolutions.[71] Israeli casualties in the clearly defensive 1948 war, and of civilians, qualify for wrongful death compensation. It may be possible to invoke the concept of crimes against humanity retroactively and implicate the Arabs in earlier crimes—like the Palestinian pogroms of

---

[70] The U.S. Court of Appeals in San Francisco decided in 1981 it has no authority over the acts by foreign states, but non-sovereign oil companies effect price hikes. The Supreme Court's *Keeton vs. Hustler* established jurisdiction of a state where the product is intentionally sold. The U.S. prosecutes foreigners violating American laws without entering the country, such as heads of drug cartels and terrorists. O.P.E.C., which engages in operations illegal in the U.S., should be treated similarly.

O.P.E.C. could be also indicted on Racketeer-Influenced Corrupt Organizations (RICO) Act because its members include rogue states known for supporting terrorism and anti-American incitation.

[71] The legal basis for Israeli claims would not be the U.N. resolution *per se*, which is only a recommendation, but rather Arab acceptance of the terms the resolution laid down. Arabs could not counterclaim for Israeli violations of the U.N. resolutions on withdrawal, since Israel never agreed to the resolutions. The fact that they were never enforced by U.N. military intervention testifies that Israeli actions did not substantially violate the peace.

the late 1920s[72] and 1930s; the atrocities against Jewish civilians in the 1948 war; the Iraqi massacre of 1941, led by the Palestinian Nazi sympathizers, and persecution for the ensuing decade; the devastation of Egyptian Jewish communities by followers of Al Banna[73] in 1945; and many other past acts, beginning when Mohammed exiled two Jewish tribes from Yathrib (Medina) and killed all the males of a third tribe and enslaved the women and children.[74]

Libel suits are also potentially fruitful. The Egyptian government-controlled mass media openly incite in violation of the peace treaty.[75] European law, unlike the American, defines defamation broadly. The mosques in Paris and Lyon sued novelist Michel Houllebecq for calling Islam the stupidest religion. Jews would find enough defamatory material in Muslim appeals to sue the publishers into bankruptcy. Israelis, however, must formulate the suits carefully, since Jewish religious schools, though not the media, do the same, and the Basic Law includes the goal of Greater Israel, much as the P.L.O. Charter did for Palestine. Arabs could sue the *yeshivas* and various Jewish fringe groups on the same ground, not without benefit.

Even Arab mainstream newspapers in Egypt and Qatar preach hatred of Jews and often call on their readers to kill Jews. Hostile mass media outlets could be shut down not only legally but by subverting their publishing and transmitting facilities and closing, not just censoring, the hostile Palestinian media. It is even easier to shut down internet sites on which fringe groups like Al Qaeda depend for appeal. Rather than engaging in cyber-warfare, Israel should file civil or criminal charges against the internet providers hosting such sites. The targets should include insurgent groups' official websites but also forums, chat rooms, secondary Islamic support sites, and so on. Security services should log the IP addresses of everyone who visits those sites and track them down, even subpoena them through the local police. Better monitor their e-mail accounts than shut

---

[72] Hundreds of Jews were killed after they tried to put benches near the Western Wall and pray there, and Jews were massacred in Hebron in 1929.

[73] The Egyptian fundamentalist cleric who provided a religious basis for modern terrorism by reinventing *jihad*. Al Banna was affiliated with the Nazis and instigated attacks on Jews in the previously very tolerant Egyptian milieu.

[74] The murky details came to us only through Islamic sources. The Jewish tribes of Medina welcomed Mohammed, supposedly signed a treaty providing for peaceful coexistence and defense. According to Islamic scholars, the Jews violated the treaty by deriding Mohammed and refusing to fight for him. Jews say they had every reason to be skeptical of Mohammed's prophecy and refused to fight both because his people started the conflict ambushing caravans and because his army, deserted even by many of his own, stood no chance against the Meccans. The forged treaty text has the Jews acknowledging Mohammed as a prophet and a judge on the treaty he is a party to.

[75] Summarized at www.memri.org

them down, especially when they are a gold mine of intelligence, such as when terrorists appeal to Muslims for small-time intelligence on vulnerable assets. The anonymous free mail accounts terrorists usually use let investigators log the IPs and track the owner's movements. Horror stories of police brutally interrogating Islamic chat participants would discourage use of those sites the governments did not block yet, especially by the fifth column of Muslim immigrants in the West. The F.B.I. did the same thing on a smaller scale to combat child pornography where curious onlookers are presumed guilty. Since most people in Muslim countries access the internet from cyber cafés, local governments should be told as a condition of their connection to the American-controlled internet to require fingerprint access to public computers and install security cameras in the cafés, already mandatory in some countries. The decision to shut down or monitor any particular site is arbitrary: grassroots forums that attract people who might support terrorists politically or financially should be closed, while major terrorist group sites visited by hardcore adherents should be monitored. Freedom of expression on the internet does not include inciting people to murder. People should be scared away from terrorism.

Terrorist charges of violation of freedom of speech are ridiculous. Muslims suppress that freedom wherever they come to power. Enemies should be dealt with reciprocally, not liberally. Israel does not need to suppress freedom to achieve her ends. Theoretically, there are no absolute freedoms. If Islamic aims are unacceptable to the West and worth fighting, then propaganda supporting them is unacceptable. Calling for murder is not a problem: America publicized bloodthirsty appeals from the allied South Vietnamese officials. Western political thinking tolerates collateral damage: American troops killed seven to twelve hundred rioting civilians in Mogadishu in 1993. The Iranian verdict on Salman Rushdie for desecrating their supranational symbol, the prophet of Islam, is of the same legal stock as the American criminal penalty for burning the flag, enforced forty years ago. The problem is the Islamic radicals' intent to murder civilians in the West. Neither the Israeli nor the American government would care if Shiites published a newspaper in London calling for overturning the Sunni regime in Afghanistan in the name of Islam, even at the risk of a civilian bloodbath, but they do care when the attack is aimed at them. There is no obligation to protect an enemy's freedom of expression. Speech is a tool of war, no different from mobilization centers. Incitement is more immediate than ordinary radical rhetoric. Radicalism is acceptable so long as it stays non-violent and urges only the force needed to overthrow an egregiously rotten regime. Islamic radicals incite people to violence against anyone who disagrees with them.

Theoretically, only actions should be punished, not thoughts or value judgments. That is the essence of Judaism. Each person is endowed with free will and must decide for himself between Western liberal propaganda and Islamic fundamentalist propaganda. Israel should suppress the radical mouthpieces specifically because they are mouthpieces and part of the enemy organization. They are immune from prosecution for what they say, but they are responsible for what they do—and they act for Israel's enemies. They should be prosecuted not as criminals but as enemies in time of war. America suppressed Nazi propaganda during World War II, but today news outlets air Bin Laden videos.

The same is true for non-media incitement, such as Muslim leaders in Europe use to stir up attacks on Jews; the same kind of propaganda that led to the pogroms and set the stage for the Holocaust. European governments tolerate them, since the large, unassimilated Muslim communities vote and pander to European interests in the Arab world. Nevertheless, nobody likes the meddling and would be content so see Israel eliminate the masterminds. Europeans care little when Muslims attack Jews in their countries and will not worry if Jews give the Muslims as good as they get. Israel might recruit European right-wing xenophobes to make common cause to curtail the influx of Muslims into Europe. They are not inherently anti-Semitic but rather anti-alien. Jews are more assimilated to Europe than are the Muslims who outnumber them. Xenophobia can be focused. Visibly alien Muslim immigrants make an easy target for European nationalists, a welcome shift of hatred from Jews. Israel should seek tactical *rapprochement* with right-wing radicals before Islamic guerrillas and rogue states do. Israel has a stake in curtailing Muslim immigration to America and Europe and the resulting changes in voting patterns and political affiliations.

Alienating immigrants to the West from mainstream Muslims is important. Muslims are prohibited from living under heathen rule. Israel could hoax a kind of Lavon affair[76] for Arabs: radical Muslim group bombing the places frequented by European Muslims to drive them to Dar al-Islam. Measures from the times of anti-communist witch hunts could prove useful, such as requiring Muslims during immigration or job interviews to sign a statement dissociating themselves from terrorists. The oath will not preclude terrorists from acting but will create public intolerance of Islamism. Disgraceful as McCarthyism was, it succeeded in making communist allegiance indecent. Forceful secularization, as in France, could help to assimilate Muslims. No one prohibits veils in public—just in the public schools. These attributes thus cannot enjoy attraction of prohibited items, yet children are taught that veils are indecent. Picturing terrorists and their leaders in the media as stupid, backward folk

---

[76] Israel facilitated Jewish exodus from Arab countries—unnecessarily, since negative attitudes to Israel would have soon forced Jews from Arab countries, anyway. Israelis extended provocations and bombed the U.S. Embassy in Cairo to set up the Americans against Arabs. Inexperienced Israeli operatives blew the operation, which resulted in major scandal, and discredited claims of Arab terrorism for years to come.

would make the immigrants ashamed of them. Being a Wahhabite Muslim should become as bizarre as practicing shamanism. There is every reason to foster an Islamic reform movement with equal rights for women, including female imams, peaceful coexistence with other religions and renouncing jihad as an old barbaric habit, secular education, Quranic textual analysis, and critical evaluation of rulings issued by religious authorities.

Touching on freedom of expression, consider the leaking of military secrets. Long a national sport among the American bureaucracy, it happens in Israel. Leaking military secrets when they abet the enemy and endanger troops should be called treason. Identifying a culprit from the small circle of those in the know is not a problem; the political will to prosecute high-ranking officials is lacking. Journalists should be dealt with the same way. Public interest even in exposing typically classified wrongdoings of military is small. In democracies, such incidents are relatively minor, but unearthing them greatly harms the state's credibility.[77]

Western media trumpet every Palestinian casualty from Israeli retaliatory strikes while scarcely mentioning mass atrocities by a Muslim regime. Many, perhaps most, Westerners do not know about the wars and riots which lasted years and took thousands and even millions of Muslim lives, though everyone knows that Israel somehow persecutes Palestinians. This attitude stems from two factors: Israel is considered civilized and thus accountable, unlike the barbaric regimes, and shooting documentaries in Palestine is easy and safe.

Freedom of reporting terrorist acts needs reevaluation.[78] The actual damage from terror is small. Guerrillas seek to frighten the people brainwashed with images of bloodshed. No one, repeat, no one assists terrorists in their aim like the media. The media damage national security to please the mob and commit high treason in the war on terror. Picturesque reporting on terrorist acts must be prohibited, and only short notices allowed, with no photos or video feed, except censored images in drastic cases, like the W.T.C. attacks. Nothing would impair low-level terrorist efforts as much as such a ban. The policy is not misinformation, as did the Japanese throughout the war and the Soviets throughout their existence. It rather prevents misinformation, distortion, and exaggeration. People get true information, with facts and figures. The mind is non-linear; it does not, like a computer, ignore repetitive or superfluous data but registers it as

---

[77] The world media made a great deal of sentencing the American sergeant for shooting a terminally wounded Iraqi fighter. The fact that the sergeant tried to save the Iraqi from a burning truck was lost in the chorus of condemnation. The news' consumers are disproportionably interested in accidents. Compare a huge coverage of American soldiers mildly pressuring interrogated enemies, and next-to-no coverage of everyday mass tortures in Russian, Chinese, Egyptian jails and that of perhaps all but handful of countries.

[78] In the era of Internet and satellite broadcasting, censorship is unsustainable and is only useful during short wars.

more important. Vivid pictures cause excessive anger and anxiety in people who have never seen blood. No network shows blown buses along with reports from surgery rooms in the American Midwest; that would discount the sentimental effect. Give the people figures instead of photos or news anchors' faces wrought in fake compassion. Most people in the West do not realize that casualties during the much-trumpeted *intifada* favorably compare to loss of life in car accidents, or that statistically Israeli Arabs prefer living in the "oppressive" Jewish state to moving to Dar al-Islam. Many people cannot objectively evaluate tobacco ads — thus mandatory health warnings. Reports on terrorism must be similarly accompanied with cautionary notices.

Making people used to reports of violence is a half-measure. People see cruelty mostly in connection with Israel and Iraq. Showing the bloodshed happening daily around the world would divert attention from Israeli actions and from the terrorists. Media audiences are not interested in atrocities in Rwanda or Syria or Yugoslavia perpetrated by black, Islamic, or Orthodox barbarians. Keeping these aliens on television would make them familiar, and Westerners might then apply to them the stringent moral standards, dissipating the reproach concentrated on Israel.

Western media often trumpets jihadist quotes of Islamic leaders, and pumps fear into the people who do not know how common is empty rhetoric in Muslim world. The leaders, proud of the effect, escalate the spiral of hateful rhetoric. Ignoring such speeches is the best way to finish them.

Western governments should stop granting asylum to Muslim dissidents, most of whom belong to aggressive fundamentalist groups. France harbored Khomeini and got a hostile Iran to deal with. America refused to extradite blind Sheikh Omar to Egypt, where he was under sentence for terrorism, and he bombed the World Trade Center.

Financial scams, phony banks and mutual funds, and Ponzi schemes may be as useful against the enemy as conventional weapons; uneducated rich Arabs are perfect prey. In the early 1990s, many swindlers pretended to sell uranium, red mercury, and other radioactive materials. Some say national security services fishing for terrorists orchestrated the frauds. The business should be extended not only to identify terrorist groups but also to seize their resources and destabilize the black market in weapons.

Blackmail as a source of funds and influence has huge potential in the Muslim world entangled with unnatural prohibitions, hypocritically moral though rotten.

Another way to discredit Arab leaders is to feign Israeli support for them, praising them in government press releases or asking the United States to make minor but well-publicized concessions to them.

Trade sanctions, popular in effete unwarlike societies, are useless. They did not prevent Japan from getting ready for World War II. Iraq circumvented them with ease after the 1991 war. Administered by corrupt bureaucracies, they are worse than nothing at all. Iraq played American, Russian, and French lobbyists against one another to embezzle chunks of profitable sanctioned trade. Sanctions do not work in economies[79] where every product, including most military equipment, is available on the gray market, and even such a supposedly easily controlled product as oil was extensively smuggled out of Iraq. Conflicts between states cannot be solved by palliatives but require the credible threat of force.

What justice could Israel expect from the United Nations, where Muslim-dominated countries have sixty votes? Or for how long will the West be able to refuse the sixty countries and over a billion people a seat on the Security Council? Israel could not accept the U.N. with a Muslim veto and corresponding bargaining power. She cannot but laugh at the institution whose Human Rights Commission has Saudi Arabia, Syria, and Libya on board. The United Nations where America and Zimbabwe have similar votes is dysfunctional; its decisions are implemented only when they conform to the balance of power.

Discrediting the hostile United Nations and exploiting its weaknesses make sense. Votes of negligible countries like Tuvalu could be bought and obtained through blackmail and bribery. Israel could set up bogus jurisdictions by buying minor islands and registering them with the United Nations as countries of the Israeli commonwealth, increasing her voting power.

Sun Tzu and Machiavelli advocated such war, and Bismarck created such a peace: finish wars before they begin; seek and exploit the enemy's weaknesses not only in the military sphere but in finances, logistics, diplomacy; do not risk battles but devise unorthodox strategies. Could not the Jews do this?

Cruelty to prisoners

Giving the Palestine Liberation Organization permission to leave Beirut and releasing Egyptian prisoners of war in 1973 were mistakes. Americans, Australians in the Pacific and Russians routinely did not take prisoners in WWII. Short of annihilation, enemy soldiers could be sent to forced-labor camps. Releasing them would have made sense as part of a peace treaty, but no such treaty was in sight. Many P.L.O. members returned to Palestine to fight again, and the Egyptian POWs joined the reserves and remained a potential threat at least until the normalization in 1979. Releasing POWs without *de facto* peace is without precedent.

Israel could have entrusted annihilation of the P.L.O. in Beirut to her Lebanese allies. The prisoners could be lashed, released naked, smeared

---

[79] Restrictive sanctions do not work. Protective sanctions, like refusing to import beef possibly affected by mad-cow decease, are easier to implement. Governments can control their own borders but not their enemies'.

with tar, and covered with feathers, laughed at and humiliated. Such treatment of guerrillas and their supporters will bring peace closer.

Arabs take releases of prisoners as an encouraging sign of Jewish weakness and lack of manly cruelty. Small Arab boys slaughter sheep during festivals. Israelis should consider the events from the Arab viewpoint, not the world's. The enemy must understand and fear Israel, not laugh at her morality. Iraqi doctors cut ears off deserters. The Taliban castrated the Afghan ex-ruler Najibullah. The *mujahedin* elaborately tortured Russian prisoners and executed them by skinning or shoving snakes into their rectums. Even American soldiers in Vietnam sometimes mutilated prisoners. Palestinian collaborators of Israel could do the same. To oppose the monsters with their methods is terrible but efficiently crushes their will to fight. War is not a competition in moral values. If we are speaking to the enemy in his language, why not treat him according to his ethics?[80] Clemency for POWs is questionable. Burglars caught in the act are not sent back home but tried and sentenced for breaking and entering. Courts require restitution for damages caused. The same logic applies to POWs, who should be put to hard labor for killing and destroying property. Soldiers are the armed extension of political policies someone opposes, and the killing they do in war is by definition illegal—murder—in the eyes of their opponents. Enemy soldiers are always criminals.

On the pragmatic side, leniency with POWs can be used to induce the enemy to surrender. Given, however, the alternative of being killed in action, especially if Israel uses weapons of mass destruction, many would prefer fairly harsh treatment—and survival.

If warfare were more brutal, people would go to war less enthusiastically and oppose their rulers' bloody ambitions more vigorously. A citizenry that expects war to mean high casualties or slave labor for citizen soldiers is likely to oppose policies likely to lead to war.

Israelis are lenient with POWs because they do not tolerate their own soldiers' suffering well and fear escalation and retaliation. Terrorists, however, rarely take hostages and do not treat them humanely when they do.

The Sinai treaty was misguided

Peace treaties are not necessarily beneficial. The Arabs saw Israel's peace with Egypt as a sign not of goodwill but rather of Israel's weakness and folly. Israel swapped land for paper. The Arabs may be right. Before World War II, the Entente guaranteed France's security but did nothing when a German army reoccupied the demilitarized the Rhineland. It was German territory, after all. If some radical Egyptian leader moved troops into the Sinai just for show, Israel would still be one-on-one with her

---

[80] Preempting the obvious retort: yes, with Nazis, too. I could have found no objections if the Allies delivered SS troops to the vacated death camps.

enemy. In 1967, Israel's allies did not agree that military maneuvers justified war and refused to support what they considered an Israeli pre-emptive strike.

Holding the Sinai Peninsula—unlike the West Bank—increased the depth of Israel's defenses significantly, and Israel should declare war automatically any time the Egyptians militarize the Sinai. The peninsula and the Red Sea contain deposits of fissile materials which can be used in an Egyptian nuclear-weapons program.

Following the peace treaty, Egypt started receiving massive American aid and became a *de facto* arbiter of Israeli-Arab relations. Its nuclear program was tolerated.

To say Egypt had no reason to go to war is silly. The existence of Israel is cause enough for many, notably Muslim radicals and those who fear Western values and democracy. Egypt is ripe for such people to come to power. To say Egypt would not have given up territory is equally mistaken. Egypt's territory was not fixed in antiquity, nor is it now. Egyptians are used to occupation—the Turks, the French, the British—and occupying powers do not ordinarily excuse themselves and offer to retreat, as Israel did. Most absurd is the argument that a peace treaty guarantees peace. Wars always break legal peace, and treaties signed under duress do not usually last long.

The Sinai treaty was wasted. Israel failed to exploit the opportunity the United States gave her, by guaranteeing Egyptian non-involvement, to annex the Palestinian territories at once and relocate the Palestinians to Lebanon and Jordan.

Ideological warfare

To say that Arab hostility to the United States is a result of American foreign policy rationalizes Arab xenophobia and jealousy. Arabs observe the West on satellite TV channels, the internet, and movies, and cannot fail to see the contrasts to their own world. Arab hatred of the West is not related to religion. When Indian Hindus and Indian Muslims quarrel, they burn each other's temples and mosques. The Arabs, however, attacked not the Vatican but New York, not New York churches but two skyscrapers devoted to international trade, the essence of the new world order.

The 9/11 attacks offered a rationalization for anti-Semitism: the evil Jews, Arabs suggested, arranged the attack and blamed it on Osama bin Laden. Yet Arabs lauded bin Laden after the event, giving that *quasi*-official line the lie. Muslims know he masterminded the attack, not Israelis. Arabs always rationalize their hatred of everything foreign, typical of ambitious but lagging nations. Whatever Israel or the West do, Muslims take as a new reason to hate the rest of the world. Not that the Western world should care what Arabs think. How did anyone think Arabs would respond to the American invasion of Iraq? Islam resents foreign intrusion. So what? International police action does not require Arab consent. With vested and conflicting interests, Arabs would certainly prefer dominating a war-torn, isolated region of tribal entities to being pushed around by a more advanced civilization, even if it does get rid of one of their worst tyrants.

The antidote to the problem of anti-Western sentiment is clear: Arabs must be converted to Western secular ideology. The American invasion of Iraq in 2003 was ostensibly an attempt to introduce democracy, but Saddam was elected more or less democratically, and so was Hitler. The West has no business promoting democracy that could bring fundamentalists, socialists, nationalists, or other troublesome elements to power. Theodore Roosevelt said, "If a nation shows that it knows how to act with reasonable efficiency and decency in social and political matters, if it keeps order and pays its obligations, it need fear no interference from the United States." Democracy in the undeveloped Arab countries would come nowhere near that goal. When the communist bloc threatened, the West used every propaganda tool, from radio broadcasts and open support of dissidents to jazz and jeans, to seed its ideology and undermine the will to fight instead of risking open conflict. The same must be done in the Arab countries. Not nuclear bombs but culture is the ultimate weapon. Western political machines engineer popular consent to get their way; those skills should be used on the Arabs. Atatürk forced secularization on Turkey and marginalized religious leaders. Sadat exterminated subversive elements with police methods developed societies recently declared off-limits but which are unavoidable in lawless societies—societies which do not obey the kind of law the West wants.

Westernizing ideological pressure must be constant. The Turks made the mistake of resting on the laurels of Atatürk's reforms, believing secularization was irreversible. That proved wrong. An influx of rural people into the cities, an increase of the population with the least education, and toleration of religious propaganda (deemed to have been suppressed too vigorously) came to fruition in the 1990s and brought Islamist parties to power with 34% of the vote in 2002—a higher percentage even than in Pakistan.

To beat her enemies without war, Israel must discredit Muslim culture, much as was done with communist culture, by making selected superficial aspects of Western culture—from jeans to CDs to TV programming to offshore ship-based nightlife and gambling facilities—available. To Arabs those are symbols of foreign pleasure, glimpses of the other world's attractions, entirely unlike the dull world of the hypocritically austere Islamic *ulema*. The Islamic world means fruitless exhaustive work which does not buy the equivalent of a house in California with a Cadillac in the garage and a Hollywood blonde in the bedroom. As icons represent religion, consumer symbols represent capitalism. Theological and ideological theories are irrelevant; external attributes matter. Ideological battles are a quest for fancier idols. Many Russians and Arabs in the 1990s rejected Western capitalism but longed for the consumer perks it offered.

The idols and ceremonies of the free market—commodities and shopping *vs.* statues and demonstrations—won the Leninists over and would also outperform mosques and *jihad*-inspired suicide. Muslim scorn of Western culture is posturing. Muslims watch Western TV, read Western magazines, and listen to Western music, envious and admiring. People are mildly contemptuous of those they do not join, and hate those whom they want to join but cannot, thus reversing an old saying into, "If you can't join 'em, beat 'em." To stop the Islamic insurrection, they should be allowed to join, if only superficially. The most importantly, it should not be done as a weak tributary bribing the strong. Rather, as Reagan did to the Soviets, the West must set itself as the ultimately strongest side, and allow no infringements on its interests and punish any violations. The idea is to besiege the Muslims economically and militarily, and only then give them a way out of the besieged fortress of Islam, the way of joining the strong culturally.

Dismal support in Muslim countries for American actions points out no problem in ideological warfare. Polls are biased because people indulge in radicalism when questioned about their attitude to a *pro forma* enemy, especially after crises, like 9/11. This bias misrepresents envy as animosity. Soviet people also had a love-hate relationship with America, loved jazz and Coke and hated imperialist warmongers. Coke won. In mass religions, idols always win.

Atatürk converted the world's most Islamic country to relatively tolerant secularism in just about fifteen years. The West should identify and support Muslim leadership looking to open Muslim countries to cosmopolitan ideas. Such leaders, however, often replace religion with nationalism, equally intolerable to the West. The cultural modification of Dar al-Islam cannot be left to the locals.

The West cannot reach an agreement with Muslims because they believe differently. To Muslims, freedom and economic well-being are insignificant compared to ideology; Europeans had a similar outlook not long ago. Muslims must be induced to accept Western values.

Islamic culture is, like all cultures, neither completely rational nor irrational but both. Muslims often dress real grievances in hatred by demonizing the perpetrators and attributing evil intentions to them. Popular leaders consciously exploit that hatred, setting irrational goals and settling for realistic ones, threatening irrational war while adhering to rational military tactics. They must be rational to come to terms with their enemies or be exterminated. Islamic civilization's inferiority to the West is real and rational. Blaming its failures on some Zionist conspiracy is irrational, but terrorists channel that belief cynically and rationally. The *jihad's* proclaimed objective is irrational. The nationalist agenda is rational. Weapons are no good against unreason unless they crush it. The West should use propaganda to give Muslims rational concerns, which can be discussed and settled, not fought over. If a fight is necessary, it need not be apocalyptic. Rational terrorists can be persuaded by military means.

Osama is neither pragmatic nor an apocalyptic terrorist but rather something in between. His goals are pragmatic: getting the United States out of the Muslim world, as his colleagues drove the U.S.S.R. from Afghanistan. But Osama faces a problem he did not have with Russia: even if it withdraws militarily, America will be present through economic and cultural ties. Therefore, he must change American habits, an undertaking of apocalyptic scale. Osama would likely settle for something tangible, like military withdrawal and withholding Western support for Israel and the most autocratic Arab regimes. That he could rein the other fanatics in is unlikely.

A coherent, aggressive ideology is powerful and can hardly be overcome except by eliminating its followers or discrediting it. Modern communication-based societies might find the latter more attractive.

Islamic communalism, typical of poor societies urges all Muslims to oppose Israel. Promoting a more individualist culture among Arabs would help Israel. Individualism comes with increased wealth and consumerism. Education also promotes diversity. Fostering Islamic protestantism would reduce the role of mosques, a major communal institution in Dar al-Islam. Groups need enemies; individuals fear them.

Sex is the most potent ingredient of pop culture for young Muslims. They would eagerly accept pornography and sex culture. Worldly desires would divert them from Islam and Arab nationalism. Israel should set up enclaves *à la* Las Vegas in permissive Lebanon and Israeli-controlled West Bank areas. Muslims who visited them would tell others immensely attractive stories. If Israel transfers the territories to the Palestinians, she may set up the prostitution-gambling-drinking enclave in Israel proper, just across the border. It could be the only entry point from Palestine to Israel, a visa-free zone, both for Arabs and prostitutes, with no tax or restrictions on selling liquor. Talmud says, "Everyone wishing to defile himself with sin will find all gates open before him, and everyone wishing to attain the highest degree of purity will find all good forces ready to help him." Israel must open the gates of sin before Muslims at least as wide as they are open in the West.

The more than half of Muslim populations under twenty are perfect targets for internet propaganda promoting Western culture. Proxy access from legitimate sites of Western governments and media will bypass Muslim governments' blocking of hostile sites. More sensitive receivers and small, indoor satellite dishes would beat restrictions on viewing satellite broadcasting in place in Muslim countries.

Israel could ask America to fund Western cultural expansionism, subsidizing such ideologically charged items as DVDs and tickets to Hollywood movies, supporting Arab dissidents and publishing their books, distributing free Western magazines, all means employed during the Cold War. They would be war expenses and so should be measured on the scale of military expenditures and should run into the billions. Yet spending the money that way would more likely pacify Dar al-Islam than buying new weapons.

Western propagandists should learn to address Muslims in their language. Foreign values like freedom and democracy must be packaged in Islamic terms. Even style is important: the concise Western style offends Muslims used to wordy eloquence.

Israel should take control of Palestinian education. Instead of tolerating violently anti-Semitic texts, she should monitor Palestinian education programs, hire and fire the teachers, or substitute Israeli designed systems. The Western powers would do well to keep an eye on the dissemination of Islamist hatred under the umbrella of religious freedom under their own noses. Freedom of religion does not extend to urging massacring people who do not share the faith. The *madrassas* should be sued for defamation and insurrection to stop radical Islamic propaganda. Israel need not tolerate hostile propaganda in Palestine, or censor or forbid local media, but blow up the offices of hostile outlets.

Islam is only a thin shell on the surface of Arab society. The *umma* is overregulated with unnatural prohibitions. Arabs abroad enjoy alcohol, gambling, and pornography. They used legal legerdemain to reintroduce usury. A small wedge of Westernization in the 1920s broke up the Islamic Ottoman Empire, which had endured for almost over six centuries, brought down secular Communism decades later, and can slip past the taboos restraining the hopes of modern Arabs to engage Western culture.

An opportunity not to be overlooked is the Prophet's explicit encouragement of trade. The least the West should do is to establish complicated economic contacts with Muslims by circumventing the current monopolistic arrangements in most Islamic countries, giving direct access to major foreign suppliers to very few companies. Western governments should urge, even subsidize, Western firms to find and deal with small businesses in Muslim countries. China supplies more consumer goods to Muslims than the West. Since the profit margin on wholesale in low-end items is minuscule, incentives could induce Muslims to deal with Western agents of Chinese factories. The goal should be to engage as many businesses in Islamic countries in economic relations with the West as possible.

Atheism disguised as liberal interpretation of Islam might prevent right-wing, extremist religious groups from assuming community leadership, as happens in an ideological vacuum. Ridiculing both Islam and the uneducated *mullahs* will also promote atheism. Publish compilations of opinions that contradict Muslim scholars on important subjects to bewilder intellectual Muslims.

Atheism will remove the otherworldly incentive for suicide terrorism, though it does not depend only on belief in the afterlife. In World War II, Soviet soldiers carried out suicide missions regardless of religious convictions. *Kamikazes* need only the belief in some high ideal worth dying for. For Palestinians, that ideal is political. Israel must either crush her enemies or discredit the political ideas behind them—in particular, by discrediting the leaders of *jihad*.

Soldiers go to war because people habitually obey governments. De-legitimizing Arab rulers is therefore important. Publicize solid facts about the illegitimacy and corruption of unfriendly Arab leaders, especially their private lives, their departure from Islamic values, their violation of *sharia* point by point, with many examples.[81] Not only do they violate *sharia*, but Arab leaders also lack the status of caliphs. That and their un-Islamic behavior could drive a wedge between them and the devoted Muslims. Appealing to the old Islamic view that working for a government is indecent would also undermine its authority. Islamist radicals criticize their governments. Usurping that critique and flooding the media with it, the West would turn radicals into copycats who echo the popular line.

Exposing corruption would make Arab governments more transparent and distribute wealth more evenly, making ordinary citizens better off and averse to fighting. Leading policy-making families would depend for income less on transparent governments and more on market activities, and support free-market policies and, eventually, democratization, reducing the power and militancy of states.

Arabs are extraverted. Their religious consciousness is communal with little emphasis on personal piety. They are prone to seek praise and rewards. The Arab boycott of Naguib Mahfouz of Egypt for his subtle overtures to Israel turned into a wave of acclaim and fame after he won the 1988 Nobel Prize for literature. Arabs envy the West and perceive themselves as despised. The hatred is a kind of psychological score settling. But what if the West seems to respect Arabs and Muslims in general? What if their *mullahs* are invited to theological conferences with Christians, Jews, Buddhists, Hindus, and others, if their journalists publish irenic articles in the *New York Times,* if their scientists are invited to work overseas, if their military participate in joint maneuvers, if their politicians are received in frock coats? Arabs would look to the West for the respect they know they cannot get otherwise. Showering Muslims with international honors would be a source of pride other than the *jihad*. Corrupt Arab opinion-makers. Invite them to the world's capitals, let them meet high-ranking officials, give them mass-media attention, especially young Palestinian activists and intelligentsia who should be offered good jobs in Israeli companies and abroad. That worked with most American hippies and would work with Arab nationalists. They would sell their countries for perks.

The same approach could work against terrorist organizations. If Israel cannot root them out or get Arafat's successors to do so, legitimizing

---

[81] Bin Laden, whose simple way of life is touted by Islamist propaganda, had villa in Khartoum luxurious enough that the owner of the "pharmaceutical" factory the U.S. destroyed bought it.

them is the next best option. Force the Palestinians and other Arabs to admit the radical factions to their parliaments, where they would be bureaucratized, corrupted, and discredited. The game is dangerous: if the West stops showing them respect, they would turn for respect to their citizens and force. Nazis subverted the parliament because other countries made Germany a political incubator, neither providing incentives nor punishing misconduct. Palestine is not viable, depends on other countries for sustenance and protection, and is thus necessarily open. Flirting with Muslim rulers, the West should use any opportunity and concessions to further its cultural influence in Dar al-Islam.

Radicals often lose their zeal when they come to power; fiery revolutionaries become impotent functionaries. Hamas and its ilk are mostly rural types whom the red-carpet welcome, cocktail parties, and photo opportunities would corrupt. Step by step, they would drop the disgusting violence, unfashionable with their new colleagues, and change the traditional dress for Versace suits. Do not negotiate with them as militant commanders; turn them first into inefficient politicians.

Israel should divide and corrupt Arabs by bestowing honors on them, apparently unrelated to politics. Provide scholarships and grants for foreign study, publish their scholarly works through Israeli foundations, and support their charities. Awards should be arbitrary, so that all will aspire, and losers will suspect beneficiaries of collaboration.

Fundamentalism, the desperate claim to esteem in societies lacking other achievements, brings only scorn. Muslims, unable to claim esteem on their own culture, will bandwagon Western or Asian civilization. By approaching them with a show of respect, America will draw Muslims into its orbit.

When the Soviets attacked religion, they offered communist ideology instead. Israel should offer the Arabs Western culture: music and movies, emancipation and sexual revolution. Clandestine operations should distribute DVDs and adult magazines. Offer women education in Western proxy schools. Ostensibly charitable agencies in traditionally Arab-friendly countries like France could promote Western values through education and various cultural programs. Saudi Arabia disseminates Wahhabism through free education. To that should be opposed both alternative education and pressure on other governments to close Saudi-sponsored fundamentalist schools. The West could invite poor Muslim families to send their children to Western-sponsored schools with free tuition and a small stipend. Perhaps it would be best to stick to technical education, though Palestinian universities and colleges flourishing under Israeli oppression teach mostly liberal arts and sciences, the breeding ground of radicalism. People with technical education but without good jobs lead the *jihad*, so it is important to teach no more students than the economies accommodate. Education is not an end but a means to indoctrinate young Muslims with Western values.

Another form of ideological warfare is disinformation. Websites, e-mail lists, and online chat rooms let terrorists show their ideas to the public. Israel could do the same. The options are numerous: setting up bogus terrorist websites, spreading phony news, subtly defaming terrorist leaders (the Saudi government puts Osama's friends on television to speak of him as a gentle, unwarlike person), and collecting the e-mail addresses of people who visit terrorist and fundamentalist sites or support bogus Islamist charities.

Uneducated Muslims trust their politicians and the guerrilla leaders. Turn their credulity around: for example, the United States wants to help, but the corrupt local regimes oppose the help to continue their autocratic rule. The *Shared Values* commercials assumed the Muslim masses have analytical skills and did not bring *rapprochement*. Shower Muslims with assertions, true or not; persistent lies are believable. Massive advertising sells products far worse than Western goodwill to Muslims.

Terrorist leaders should be systematically assassinated to shorten the queue of willing successors. There were few ancient Christian martyrs, and modern people are averse to suffering. If eliminating them as soon as they take office is troublesome or prohibitively expensive, grant them public immunity and go after the rank-and-file and other supporters who will resent their bosses' immunity.

Attributing the 9/11 attacks to Al Qaeda tremendously increased the obscure group's prestige. Osama learned about the operation days before it occurred. Even if he masterminded the attack, it would have made every sense to rob him of his laurels, attributing the operation to an imaginary group.[82]

---

[82] Al Qaeda's authorship of 9/11 is not evident. Terrorists claim responsibility for the acts. Al Qaeda's extensively bragged after it bombed the USS *Cole*, but the perpetrators of 9/11 attacks remained silent. Osama could not be afraid to announce that he organized 9/11; such operation is a crowning jewel of any terrorist's career, worth dying for. The 9/11 plot differed qualitatively from primitive bombings Al Qaeda had staged both before and after 9/11. The much-circulated video of bin Laden taking responsibility is suspicious because an Islamic fundamentalist speaks of "Western civilization under the leadership of America" and "awesome symbolic towers that speak of liberty, human rights and humanity."

The 2003 Riyadh bombing was originally attributed to Osama, though he accommodates his home regime, which in turn tolerates his financiers. In a statement published in February, 1998, Osama relieved the Saudi royals of responsibility for anti-Islamic policies because America subjugated them. Then, Iran was designated the culprit, though new Iranian government was timidly approaching America. A new version suggested that Iranian fundamentalists organized the bombing to frame the Iranian government. But they would have left clear traces implicating Iranian government; why frame it without leaving traces? Other forces could stage the Riyadh bombing to show the Muslims they should join America's anti-terrorist fight.

Arab and Islamic civilizations should be held up to judgment before world opinion. Many mistakenly believe that Arabs built the pyramids, that science flourished under Islam, that Muslim empires were peaceful and tolerant. In fact they were generally cruel, religiously intolerant, xenophobic, culturally vapid, and economically irrelevant. Protest the way Egypt handles archeological remains which belong to all humanity, drilling tunnels in pyramids, flooding relics at Aswan, damaging artifacts. Jews might rethink their rejection of the likely roots of Judaism with Akhenaton and the heritage of Heliopolis.

The shoe-bomber also smells of a show: evidently insane person with enough explosives to make headlines but not damage the plane, setting a shoe on fire in the cabin. Public got a much-needed foiled plot.

Western governments show too many plots discovered for a few realized. The success ratio could not be that large. Terrorist acts are surprisingly isolated: after a simple bombing of trains in Spain resonated in media, and brought concessions on Iraq, why terrorists not continued in Spain and elsewhere?

Russian government staged the bombings attributed to Chechens to stir popular opinion for the war. American administration might be no less cynical.

During the first U.S.-Iraq war, why Saddam kept his army in Kuwait after American buildup exceeded show-of-force level, instead of retreating with dignity in face of overwhelming enemy? Saddam must have expected the coalition to pursue him into Baghdad and overthrow; it made every sense to retreat without fighting. He was concerned with American reaction, since asked the U.S. ambassador for acquiescence to invasion of Kuwait; and the ambassador acquiesced, though American government opposed the invasion post factum. Saddam's objections to weapons inspections are odd because Iraq had no weapons to hide. Having captured Saddam, the Americans promptly released him for mock trial. American cooperation with Saddam, active for years, might continue beyond 1991 to threaten Saudi Arabia into the American protection.

Counteracting Guerrilla Warfare

Terrorism is a war like any other

Terrorism is a form of war. It is wrong to treat it like a riot, calling only for police action. Effective warfare can be neither limited (in terms of scale, weapons, targets) nor humane. It allows no armistice between unequal enemies, since armistice benefits the weaker. The enemy must be destroyed, either in his person or his will to fight, and his popular, industrial, and financial support crushed.

Terrorists justifiably target civilians

Nor is terrorism especially immoral. Every war involves civilian casualties. Rear-guard and home front attacks are important military tactics, designed not only to destroy supply and communication lines but also to erode popular support for the war. Only recent centuries have seen futile attempts to control civilian losses, concentrating instead on defeating the fighting units. Terrorism, moreover, is the best strategy against a much stronger enemy; that is why countries that spend fortunes on traditional armies, ineffective against asymmetric threat, object to it. Asymmetric warfare is not an aberration but a historical norm; the ancient Chinese called it "unorthodox strategy." Military historians distinguish low-intensity guerrilla warfare, like the Franco-Russian war of 1812 and the United States-Vietnam war, when the population organizes paramilitary units to strike the aggressor's military forces, and terrorism directed mostly at civilians. The distinction is artificial. The Israeli population is enlisted in the military reserve. It supports the war politically by voting, economically by paying taxes and working at military factories, and demographically and morally by encouraging their children to do likewise. Israeli civilian life is not very different from Israeli army life; some victims who were actively pro-Palestinian are collateral damage serving the war purpose.[83] Civilians are not defenseless: their taxes maintain a huge army and police force. Israeli civilians also have the option of voting for an anti-war government ready to give in to terrorist demands.

Terrorism is a less murderous means of achieving political ends than normal war. About a thousand Israelis have died in the four years of the second *intifada*. That number is less than a traditional war with Arab armies would have claimed to achieve the same political results. Unlike traditional war, where only those in hot action feel threatened, terrorism

---

[83] This is not to say that some terrorists would not engage in murder for its own sake, though even Aum Shinriko pursued political objectives. Terrorism is not suitable for mass murders, but structured to threaten its victim (population, government, corporations) into acquiescence to certain demands by notable and well-publicized blows. That is a military tactic, not a crime.

holds everyone hostage. It is extremely economical in terms of the lives needed to achieve war's major goal, destroying the enemy's will to fight.

The Palestinian attack upon the Jewish population to push it toward ending the war is not like the Nazi murder of Jews for its own sake. Murder is the means in the first case, the end in the second. While suffering Israeli civilians look like innocent victims to other Jews, Arabs see them as part of the enemy establishment. Popular vote legitimizes the Israeli government, so each citizen is legally and morally responsible for the state's action, and unconditional doves are relatively few. Some Germans fought the Nazis, but no Israelis fight for the Palestinians. Palestinians repeatedly kill children and others with little connection to the conflict whatsoever, but no war is entirely just. Solzhenitsyn wrote that the Soviet regime could not have committed its atrocities if citizens met the police coming to arrest them with axes. Gandhi's followers were few but sufficiently resolute to overthrow the government. Martin Luther King had fewer followers than the white racists, yet succeeded in changing fundamental policy. Democracy is not rule by the majority but by the largest coherent and determined group. German civilians who tacitly supported the Nazis or did not oppose it are culpable. Presuming Israeli guilt, Palestinians are justified in attacking Jewish civilians. Israelis should spend less time moralizing and more getting ready for war.

Terrorism is historically common, normal. During the War of Independence, Americans targeted British non-combatants, whose descendants two centuries later were targets of Jewish terrorism in the Mandate period. In 1937-39, the Jews repeatedly bombed Arab marketplaces. Civilians were targeted in almost all wars.

Arabs did not invent kidnapping. Even before the young Ariel Sharon kicked off the hostage-taking spiral by kidnapping Jordanian officers to exchange them for Israeli MIAs, the Jewish militia kidnapped the British judge Windham in Tel Aviv to exchange him for Jewish detainees in British prison. In 1947, they killed two British hostages after the British did not give in to their demand to cancel the death sentences of two Jews convicted of guerrilla activity in Akko.[84] In 1954, Israelis released the genie by inventing airplane hijacking: they captured a Syrian civilian plane to obtain hostages to exchange for captured Israeli Defense Force soldiers. It is hard to see any difference between that and the terrorists taking hostages to bail their captured comrades out of Israeli jails.

The claim that the terrorists' ugly means predetermine the ugliness of the ends is wrong. American settlers killed Indian civilians, yet unrepentant Americans produced the most liberal large society on the planet. Israel benefited in practical ways from the Stern group's murder of

---

[84] Jews did not learn their lesson, and not only keep terrorists in jail instead of executing them, but also instituted numerous exchanges.

Arabs to drive them from the land, but Israel is the most democratic country in the Middle East.

Jews have historically engaged in terrorism

The world's first terrorist was Moses. He forced a major political concession from the Egyptian state by attacking its population with plagues—biological warfare—and killing the firstborn civilians. Whether the details are true or not, most Jews and many Christians praise the act.

Arab terrorism today is not unlike the terrorism of Jewish organizations in Palestine, like the Irgun, though the Irgun adopted the military approach of the Enlightenment, attacking military and paramilitary targets. Not only the fringe Irgun Zvai Leumi and the Stern group but also the semi-official Palmach sometimes attacked British non-military administrators and Arab villages. Spiraling violence blurred the difference between attack and reprisal, and what Jewish militia called revenge, Arab historians call aggression. The Arabs, facing an overwhelming enemy, could not afford moral restraint and attacked civilians, tactics not unknown to Jews, namely the *Sicarii* (Dagger Men) before the War of 66 C.E. Like them, the Arabs resorted to repeated low-intensity attacks to terrify Jewish civilians and erode popular support for military measures. Like the Jews, they have a specific objective, to form a Palestinian state. Whether their approach is reasonable or whether discussion could have resolved matters sooner is open to question. Jews did not negotiate with Arabs when they founded Israel, nor did they seriously talk to the Palestinians before the *intifada*.

Nor are the suicide bombers anything new. Fighting with no chance of survival is as ancient as warfare itself. Sun Tzu writes of expendable spies, certain to be discovered and killed. Greeks ostensibly killed messengers who brought bad news, and yet the messengers volunteered. Dying killing an evil ruler is putatively noble. Modern warfare has seen efficient and dignified kamikaze pilots, and Soviet soldiers conducted suicide missions against hopeless Nazi odds. The Arab media claim that the *shahedeen* (martyrs to *jihad*) die with the assurance of a virgin-laden paradise is a myth. Many Arab martyrs are women, whose fate in paradise the Koran hardly discusses, and the opinion that women, too, are awarded *houris* contradicts the tradition. Women are inferior in Dar al-Islam. The suicide bombers are mostly too young for religiosity but driven by nationalist ideology. Because death in war is acceptable to poor Arabs, who lack the Jewish extensive sense of self-worth, nationalism creates suicide bombers. Palestinian parents often seem proud and resigned to lose their children in suicide bombings. In the Book of Maccabees, a mother urges her seven sons to die before violating Judaic law, and Jewish teenage fighters refused to beg the British for clemency. Some people readily accept death for higher purposes.

Terrorists should be respected as warriors

To condemn Arab fighters as terrorists mistakenly represents the conflict in moral terms,[85] while it is a question of warfare where the moral dimension is inapplicable. It takes courage or faith, religious or ideological, to be a suicide bomber; their morals may be deplorable but not despicable. While Jews see Israeli civilians as innocent victims, Arabs see them as enemies. Votes create and sustain Israel, so each citizen is legally and morally responsible for the state's actions. Civilians are often targets in war. Palestinians see Israeli civilians that way and are entitled to attack them.

Criminals inflict damage on victims who never harmed them; terrorists attack the population which ostensibly wronged the Arabs. The claim of rectifying the damages made Robin Hood a popular fighter rather than criminal. Muslim guerrillas, unlike criminals, share with Jews much of the ethics; they differ in axioms – each side prefers its national goals over its enemies'.

Terrorists are not cowards;[86] rather terror is the only kind of war possible against a much stronger enemy. Calling them warriors gives them the right to be treated with the respect due to soldiers but also the liability of being dealt with as soldiers—military means, not moralizing, negotiation, and police action.

The same approach should be extended to Arab civilians: Jews support their government, and Arabs support the militants and, as the enemy's home front, are responsible for their actions and can expect to be attacked.

Attack terrorist bases

Water can put out small fires but not big ones. That takes another fire. Medieval towns used ditching and counter-fire, as did prairie pioneers. Israel should fight fire with fire.

The Nazis swiftly cornered a large and entrenched German communist party by killing them without due process.[87] The trials resulted in few reported wrong "convictions." The Nazi had informants among the

---

[85] When labeling their opponents to turn popular opinion against them, Jews should not believe the labels. Many call the Egyptian attack on Yom Kippur treacherous though Egypt betrayed no one, and Israelis were similarly ready to preempt, violating armistice. Neither the attack on the holiest day was blasphemous without precedent: Jews disregard prayer times and other religious concerns of Arabs. One lesson of the Yom Kippur war is to strike Arabs at final days of Ramadan, when Muslims are wear from long fast.

[86] I actually read a report calling a Palestinian guerrilla, who crossed Israeli border by glider at night and shot six Israeli soldiers, a coward.

[87] Due process for communists and terrorists is an oxymoron. No judicial process is due those who refuse it to their enemies.

communists, and more appeared when the communists realized that informing was the only way to stay alive. Their mass conversion to Nazism took place later when the Nazis were strong enough to admit them without fear of subversion. Since terrorists sneer at relatively comfortable Israeli prisons, killing during arrest is the ticket. Milder tactics only arouse the opposition and help recruit terrorists. Israel should shoot enough Hamas, PIJ, Hezbollah, and other terrorists to create panic.

Classic military theory teaches that a passive defense is useless against a resolved, resourceful assailant—and the Arab guerrillas are operating in ideal circumstances. They have strong ideological and religious beliefs, the support of a friendly population and abundant resources, perfect logistics secured by the Arab states right up to Israel's borders, tolerant treatment if captured, and glory if killed. Under those conditions, even a big war could drag on for years, as in ancient Greece or feudal Germany. Low-profile conflict can be sustained forever. Attrition works only against Israel. The Palestinians have no economy.

Passive security, like fences or land mines, will not solve the problem. The answer to terrorists is attack them. They are not just hostile elements but enemies at war. Their bases are like airfields to which enemy aircraft repair to re-arm for maintenance after every mission. Israel, however, tolerates even the training camps in the Lebanese Bekaa Valley which should have been scorched with napalm and vacuum bombs long ago. Government forces eliminated the medieval Assassins by systematically overrunning their strongholds. Even if they did not get all the camps, raids might stop the stream of volunteers. Terrorists do not stop being terrorists when they can get together in Iran or Syria or Saudi Arabia or Belgium to plot against Israel in the safety of sovereign borders. Belgium, France, Sweden, and some others provide safe haven for the terrorist high command, tantamount to Switzerland letting Nazi troops reorganize there in 1945. Israel should not limit herself to killing terrorists only when they cross her borders, only in Palestine. They are enemies wherever they are, and Israel should let other governments know that if they harbor terrorists, she will attack them where she finds them. That is not outrageous. What if Israel sheltered German terrorists who blew up French cathedrals and demanded the return of Alsace-Lorraine to Germany? Imagined? This is how Israel should behave in her case.

Attack governments and civilians who support terrorists

The terrorists are few, but they depend on many. With American and Arab support, the Afghan *mujahedin* defeated the Soviets. Without such support the Afghan Taliban lost, if temporarily, in three weeks. Hezbollah, Hamas, and PIJ are relatively inexpensive ventures, though their budgets run into tens of millions annually. Not only much of their income but also some of their expenses are traceable, such as annuities paid the families of suicide bombers. Terrorists need a large pool of followers to

116

troll for suicide bombers, for hideouts, for funds. Their supporters are not innocent civilians; they are the home front. Newspapers that incite people to kill Jews, anti-Israeli demonstrations, American and European Islamic fundamentalist charities that collect and donate to militant Muslim causes, and hate-mongering Muslim politicians should not be tolerated. Freedom of speech stops when it costs lives. Identified supporters' offices and businesses should be blown up right along with them. Wherever possible, Israel should seek cooperation from governments, friendly or hostile, by persuasion, assistance, threat, or blackmail. Failing that, she should not shy from confrontation. Western governments rarely protest when someone does a dirty job they want to do but can't. Offering rewards would invite criminals to do the job. Offering the incentives from Israel is useless. A requirement to betray their dearest principles would reduce the number of volunteers. Instead, such offers should come from organizations ostensibly connected to the Egyptian or Saudi government; Shiites might seek to eliminate bin Laden. The disguise need not be believable to reasonable people and should only provide an excuse for treason. Muslims' loyalty to their leaders is not unqualified: a two million dollar bounty for Abdul Basit (Ramzi Yousef), who organized the 1993 World Trade Center bombing, generated a flood of leads. The rewards should be kept realistic: the tens of millions offered for senior Al Qaeda staff look fantastic and are unconsciously disregarded. A hundred thousand would snare a poor Arab or a gang of them as quickly as twenty-five million. Smaller amounts could be paid for non-crucial information. People might be more ready to betray the terrorists in seemingly unimportant ways, such as details of recent actions or bin Laden's location yesterday. Eventually, collaborators would agree to provide critical information for a jackpot reward.

Israel should expel all Israeli Arabs who support the enemy. Muslims who participate in a pro-Palestinian demonstration should be loaded onto buses and driven straight to Jordan. Donors to Islamic charities should be identified and, where possible, expelled, jailed—or demonstratively assassinated to offer an example to others compassionate with Islamist causes. Most self-styled Islamic charities are connected with terrorists.

Muslims who support terrorists safely from afar are a greater threat than the weary Palestinians. Few Muslims respond to appeals for *jihad,* but they are supporters and donors. That irritating crowd of spectators is fertile soil for grassroots terrorists. Retaliation would scare most away before they become participants. Some might join the terrorists in retaliation, but the objective is not to prevent recruitment but rather to eradicate the terrorists' indispensable support base.

The ancient Assassins, some of the earliest known terrorists, held out for centuries in mountainous regions; fighting terrorists on their own turf is futile. Urban warfare is even more complicated than war in the mountains. The same was true of the Sicarii. There are not many ways to isolate terrorists who hide out among the population. Fences or land mines stop some. Turncoats finger some. Most vanish in retaliation raids, along with peaceful people unlucky enough to reside nearby. Some unlucky Jews boarded the buses subsequently blown up.

Attacking terrorist bases, their sponsors, or bystanders among the Arab population may generate support for them and intensify their actions, unless Israel shows she means to root them all out.[88] People tolerate casualties in wartime so long as they believe victory is possible but lose resolve if those casualties are not answered. The will to fight deteriorates over time, so the conflict should be escalated and resolved. The side that shows greatest resolve wins.

Calling the war a conflict or any other euphemism weakens Israeli resolve. War is about the will to fight. Advantages in arms, population, and strategic depth overcome will power. Yet Israel enjoys none of them. The Arabs are more populous, indoctrinated, and ready to die than are the Jews. Arabs have more weapons and could re-supply from Russia and China on demand. The superior will to fight is indispensable for Israel. At their current pace, Israelis would likely accept the partition of Jerusalem and the right of return for Arabs. A weak economy and political turmoil further sap resolve. Israel must gird her loins for war if she hopes to achieve lasting peace.

Egypt and Syria, which fight terrorists with torture and execution, laugh at Israel's impotence. In a notable example: Egypt rooted out radicals by combing the neighborhood with thousands of troops, searching every house for people, literature, and weapons, arresting and interrogating a multitude. After the 9/11 attacks, some Arab governments dealt harshly with local terrorists, quietly destroyed terrorist infrastructure, and extradited many to the United States.

Israel's centralized security agencies are hard put to detect tiny terrorist groups. A better idea would be to create a vertical organization like the F.B.I. with agents in the state police, local police departments, on the beat in every precinct. To this end, Israel needs to seek cooperation from other governments to comb their territories for terrorists. Local citizens are more likely to betray terrorists to their own police than to Israeli agents.

American protection did not prevent Saudi Arabia from fomenting anti-American groups until they threatened the Saudi establishment. Sanctions did not stop Iran from supporting the terrorists. The carrot of statehood did not induce Arafat to corner Hamas and PIJ. Bureaucrats taking bribes do not feel obliged by them, but to preserve self-esteem take

---

[88] The Soviet population in the occupied territories was submissive, because the Nazis carried out summary executions. People often turned partisans in. Too soft policy encourages rebels; extremely harsh treatment causes bravery of desperation. People must understand the enemy is not bent on extermination, yet will cruelly punish prohibited behavior.

118

them as a favor to the suborner, feeling no gratitude and goodwill. Unless America wants to bribe the Arabs with ever-increasing sops, paying for their every move against terrorists and expecting the cooperation to cease when the bribes are reduced, only force will make Arabs cooperate. People could forgo possible profits, like assistance, but not lose their assets in retaliation.

Attack Arab countries in response to terrorist acts

In 1948, Arabs realized they could not defeat Israel in war and turned to attrition through border shelling, skirmishes, and guerrilla raids. Their support of terrorists is a continuation of the attritional warfare.

Although annexation will not work unless the population is expelled or assimilated into the invading population, punitive expeditions designed to stop Arab support for terrorists would work. The question is stopping support of guerrillas, a dispensable issue for Muslims, not regime change or any other critical matter. As Commodore Perry showed with Japan, countries can be threatened into changing policies and opening doors. The doors are sufficiently open even in fundamentalist Saudi Arabia that warfare is not necessary. Israel should concentrate on forcing the Arabs to abandon the terrorists without reference to other matters.

Quick strikes would shock wealthy Arabs who think they are safe while their governments pursue anti-Israeli policies. The Saudi rich fund martyrs but are themselves no martyrs. Violence can and should disillusion them and shock them into getting rid of terrorists. When Arabs want peace, the negotiations will move right along.

Every terrorist attack is a loss for Israel. But small tactical victories over Israel could be Pyrrhic for the Arabs if Israel made them pay for them. Immense, disproportional retaliation would position Israel as a monster and allow the Muslim countries to withdraw from the conflict. The deaths of eighteen American combatants against a thousand Somalis encouraged guerrillas worldwide. Terrorists receive support while they deliver headlines at no loss to their sponsors. Had the United States flattened Mogadishu, people in other conflict zones would be more cautious about supporting guerrillas. Israel made a similar error withdrawing from Lebanon: she won the war but lost the media battle. Poor, uneducated, numerous, ideologically inspired Muslims don't see things the way Westerners do and take anything less than total defeat as victory, regardless of the cost. Israel must inflict clear-cut, devastating, humiliating defeat. The number of casualties is irrelevant to Muslims. Israel must show cruelty greater than the Arabs' and overwhelming power. The Arabs did not soon forget Dir Yassin. Razing another settlement and slaughtering the population would pacify the region for years, saving many more lives than it cost when Arabs realize it was not an isolated incident and could be repeated.

The Torah teaches "an eye for an eye," so how can Israel react so disproportionably? The idea behind the commandment is, *half of the offender's eyes for half of the victim's eyes*, the relative equality of damages. Since Muslims outnumber the Israeli Jews 300:1, killing three hundred Muslims for every Jew dead in the terrorist attacks fits the biblical concept of reciprocity. "An eye for an eye" is not a doctrine of compensation but a prescription for inflicting equable damage on culprits to discourage repetition.

The doctrine of equal reciprocity covers only situations involving simple offenses where a culprit is likely to be identified and punished, like a fistfight. When, however, multiple offenses are likely to go unpunished, Torah requires penalties double the immediate damage. The idea is plain: a thief is unlikely to get caught every time he steals, so when he is caught, the punishment should cover his undetected crimes as well. Major offenses, like stealing an ox, are punished at a 5:1 ratio. Similarly, the terrorists' relatives or direct supporters are not likely to suffer from Israeli retaliation. When terrorist sponsors hide behind other Muslims, Israel should give back better than she gets.

Arabs rich and poor share a weak spot, the oil infrastructure. Everyday Iraqis, Iranians, and Egyptians get very little oil revenue, though enough to worry them, if only because interruptions in the oil supply disrupt their economies. The least threat will force major concessions.[89] Would that make Arabs more hostile? Surely—unless they see that further hostility means further retribution. The parties to the vendetta persist because, the clans being about equal, each hopes to prevail. The case of Iran under Ayatollah Khomeini is instructive: actively involved in terrorism almost everywhere, Iran felt the burden of retaliatory sanctions, not even very effective ones, and limited its support for terrorism to Lebanon, Palestine, Sudan, and Bosnia, places unlikely to trigger additional sanctions. Muslims are not about to sacrifice their oil infrastructure for the Palestinians. The Saudis are too rich and too lazy to risk all-out war with Israel and would use Israeli threats as an excuse for cutting aid to terrorists. Arabs have no reason to stand up to Israeli strikes; it is not their war. Few Arabs worry about Palestinian nationalism and will not support governments that incur Israeli reprisals. Although the international community would pressure Israel not to attack oil-producing facilities, it would just as quickly pressure the Arabs to stop supporting terrorists if they threatened the West's oil supply.

Beside oil-related targets, Israel can attack military installations, airfields first, which would cost Arabs both financially and morally and

---

[89] That does not work in Iraq, where terrorists target oil facilities, because they see that as the best strategy to run the Americans off and build dissatisfaction with occupiers who don't deliver the promised welfare without oil. Iraqi guerrillas do not profit from oil, and thus do not value it.

120

would destroy their arsenals. That policy would rule out annexing Arab territory beyond Palestine. Unless they are disabled completely, the Arabs will fear escalation and might strike back with the large weaponry that remains. An overwhelming initial strike must precede annexation. Anything less could be used only to stop the support for terrorists.

Automatic retaliation should not be confused with hostility toward the particular Arab regime affected. Islamic radicals hoped the Khobar bombing would spoil the efforts of the Iranian government to normalize relations with the West. Israel should punish Muslim countries cautiously for attacks originating on their soil to avoid ruining relations with potentially friendly governments.

International law prohibits revenge, but harsh retaliation prevents escalation. To improve public relations, Israel should retaliate within minutes after terrorist attacks to avoid cause-and-effect disputes.

Retaliate against civilians for terrorist attacks

Tit-for-tat is a proper response to any harm, terrorism included. A bus blown in Ramallah is an answer to the bus blown in Tel Aviv. Swift retaliation will make the cause-and-effect relation evident and prevent escalation. Announce towns targeted for reprisal beforehand, so that people in fear would press the terrorists to abstain. Living the countdown will cause anxiety, unattainable if Arabs everywhere see themselves as improbable target. Media will aggravate fear with reportages from doomed towns. Israel should target cities with offices of terrorist organizations and where demonstrations in support of terrorists took place recently. This will make the inhabitants cautious of tolerating guerrillas. Many Israeli soldiers will shy from intentionally harming civilians, even if militarily sound; few takers will always be found. Or Jewish guerrillas could answer in kind, formally relieving the government of responsibility for acts questioned by world opinion. Israel could invite Indians or Russians who served in commando units to do the job, though Lehi proves that moral Jews can do that as well.

Reciprocal violence critically differs from initiated violence, as in the case of criminals and the police pursuing them. Jews have no problem with reciprocal violence; indeed, the Torah mandates that witnesses— common citizens, not specialized and despised executioners—carry out the sentences. Enforcing justice, even violently, is an obligation incumbent on every Jew, and carries no moral stigma. But note the condemnation of Baruch Goldstein who erred on technicality, and will likely be praised fifty years from now; Avraham Stern became an official hero only after the decades blurred the events. While Stern tailored reprisals to offenses, Goldstein's killing of Muslims in a mosque exceeded the limits of reciprocity: Muslims did not murder praying Jews for decades. Jews who lost their dear ones in Islamic suicidal bombings may legitimately blow themselves up at crowded bus stops in Nablus. Vengeance will reestablish the respect to Jews, and curtail the bombings; Lehi achieved just that. Exacting vengeance on other nations, however, is a communal affair of Jews and Israeli government should undertake it.

Arabs are not inherently bad or antagonistic to Jews. The Israeli Arabs are reasonably loyal, though hardly fervent citizens. They have not become a fifth column in any war Israel has fought, not so much because Israel is good to them but rather because they value the high quality of life they have compared to their brethren in other Middle East countries. Only nationalist propaganda and troublemaking prevent a similar *rapprochement* in the territories. Local administrators cannot crack down on the militants for fear of endangering their financial and political support from Arab countries. The only way to stop terrorism is to turn Palestinians against the radicals. Financial aid will not accomplish that end and is largely stolen or diverted anyway. External power cannot make people rich and happy. Only fear will make Palestinians root out the militants. The ways to instill fear are many, from summary executions to large-firepower strikes to razing neighborhoods of suicide bombers to pervasive police work and spying. The latter options are less cruel, and a reasonable Palestinian administration should use them. Sharon used them to keep Gaza quiet, but the West Bank is too large for Israel to police. She can, however, hit the Arabs often enough and hard enough to make them clean up their act and deal with their radicals. People whose children are blown in school buses need not be nice. The statehood the Palestinians aspire to imposes obligations. A householder who negligently rented to someone who stocked TNT to blow up the neighbors would be sued. Similarly, as would-be citizens, the Palestinians must deal with the terrorists among them, unless they think terrorism an acceptable means to a legitimate end, in which case they are the home front. When Colombia could not whip the drug dealers, it enlisted American help and things improved—though scores of civilians died in the process. The Palestinian Authority should deal with the terrorists by all possible means instead of refusing international military help. If the Palestinian Authority cannot or does not want to do away with the terrorists, then it cannot be a state, and Israel is justified in taking it over it, just as the United States annexed chunks of Mexico to stop the criminal anarchy on its border. Germans who disagreed with Nazi military policies still suffered in the war. The principle of collective responsibility means a state must be coherent in its relations with others. When people give up their individuality to form a state, they can no longer expect to be treated by outsiders as individuals with varying opinions. When a government signs a peace treaty, it must assure the other party has dealt with the home opposition, if there be any. When a country undertakes to phase out the production of CFCs, the other affected parties cannot worry if the producing factories suffer. When a country goes to war, it conscripts citizens regardless of the way they vote. A state exists as long as almost all its citizens agree to act as a single body, whether they agree with particular decisions or not; when the Chechens or the Bosnians stopped seeing themselves as a part of larger entity, they opted for independence. Many Americans protested the Vietnam War, making retaliation against the mainland unjustified and counterproductive. Not a single demonstration in Palestine has protested the Authority's tolerance and support of terrorists; no protests in other Muslim countries; no votes against the rulers and factions who attack Israel; no conscientious objectors; no conscripts preferring to run away than to kill Israelis; no one refusing to pay taxes to finance the war. Though a duty to fight evil may be disputed, not supporting it is obligatory. The Arabs consort with and encourage terrorists and their families instead of turning them in. Justice is statistical: collateral damage is inevitable in fighting criminals, from sentencing innocent people to killing hostages during rescue operations. The more heinous the crime, the higher the tolerance of collateral damage. Fighting terrorism, the most damaging crime, causes the highest collateral damage.

Muslims suffer, not because Israel wants to kill innocent civilians but because terrorists hide behind them. The population is a live shield held hostage by terrorists. If the people turned on the terrorists, they could not hide, and there would be no need for reprisals. Arabs in general and Palestinians in particular are responsible for the terrorist war. An individual's contribution to the war effort might be slight, but his chances of getting hurt in a reprisal attack are minor as well: reciprocal accountability is statistically equitable. Soldiers in conscripted armies are a representative sampling of civilians; as many soldiers oppose the war as civilians. Punishment based on responsibility should be logically extended to the enemy's soldiers, killing only those who credibly tried to kill Israelis; judging by Israeli losses, those are a small minority. Singling out soldiers or civilians directly responsible for Israeli deaths is impractical.

The term *collective responsibility* is misleading. Even with many pinpoint strikes, Israel cannot kill more than a fraction of 1% of the hostile Muslims. No punishment is applied with such exceedingly low probability. One is not really held responsible if his chance to suffer is one thousandth. Instead of resisting the war or changing their government or even asking the United States or the United Nations to help round up anti-Israeli organizations, civilians provide safe haven and financial and moral support for terrorists and conscripts for Arab armies whose primary target is Israel. They encourage terrorists to murder Israeli civilians. Whether the Arab means or ends are just is irrelevant. They are unacceptable to Israel. The notion that Arabs are ruled by tyrants who sneer at popular opinion is wrong—and impossible in the world of mass media and interconnectedness. Autocrats today rely on popular support. Stalin, Hitler, Nasser, Khomeini, Saddam, Assad enjoyed majority support and repressed only a few dissidents. The reasons people support rulers are irrelevant; but in undeveloped countries where differences of opinion are slight, the support is often overwhelming.

The distaste for warring on civilians comes from fear of retaliation and the notion that it is better to let the guilty go unpunished than to punish the innocent. That is wrong, since the guilty always turn on the innocent so in the end more innocent people suffer than would if the judicial system punished the innocent now and then. The media cry out at the occasional unjust sentence but say nothing about the criminals who escape punishment because some juror had reasonable doubt. Right and wrong judgments balance each other, and attempts to reduce the number of wrong ones upsets that balance and reduces right judgments as well. In a just society any tightening of the requirements to prove criminal guilt would more likely hamper right judgments than prevent mistakes. In most societies, people are rarely brought to trial for nothing, and the ratio of unjust judgments is small. The absolute number is very important; even a single innocent person wronged by the jury is a liability to society. The system of justice, however, is not guilty for convicting a statistically minor percentage of innocent people, since absolute righteousness is unattainable, and the cost of attempting it is enormous. The law of marginal utility fully applies to justice. Formalizing the rules of evidence away from a common-sense approach makes society less just and frees criminals more than it protects the innocent. The same is true of civilian casualties in anti-terrorist strikes. If societies allow the equivalent of 10% collateral damage judging common criminals, we should tolerate more when punishing terrorists, since each unpunished terrorist will inflict much more damage than any unpunished common criminal. Innocent Israeli civilians die in the terrorist attacks and innocent soldiers die hunting the terrorists; why protect Muslim civilians? Innocent hostages are routinely killed during the rescue operations; killing civilians alongside terrorists is similarly unavoidable.

Terrorists target civilians not as collateral damage but as a primary targets, military objectives to advance a political goal. Terrorists do not shrink from killing even friendly civilians, as in the U.S. embassy bombings which inflicted far heavier losses on bystanders than on the targeted personnel. Radical clerics try to justify using weapons of mass destruction against civilians with references to the Koran and *sharia*. Common Muslims support the terrorists by a large margin. Their support for the 9/11 attacks was nearly universal in various countries. Germans who supported the Nazi *Wehrmacht* could not dissociate themselves from its actions, nor can Muslims object to attacks on Muslim civilians while they favor attacking "infidels."

To accustom public opinion to reprisals against civilians, Israel should target active terrorist supporters like demonstrators. Every donor to Hezbollah and the like, from Egyptian janitors to Saudi princes, must fear. Once they are known to Israel, they should be dead men walking. It is one thing to support terror from the safety of your house and quite another when every malicious donation puts your life in danger. Donors finance terror and kill Jews. No need to go after all of them: a few dozen publicized cases would dissuade most people from supporting terror actively. Pinpoint targeting would be too expensive; rather, accept inevitable errors and collateral damage.

Implicit anti-escalation arrangement between Israel and the terrorists in place since late 1970s must cease. Violence should be decisive. Israel already lost many more people in low-profile terrorist acts than in the period when terrorists targeted Israeli embassies and people abroad. Terrorists, burdened with the political responsibilities of the Palestinian government, are now much more cautious about foreign public opinion than in the 1970s, and would hesitate to escalate anti-Israeli bombings in other countries. Not wasting resources on expensive pinpoint attacks, but rather accepting inevitable errors and collateral damage, targeting enemy's training camps and buildings with air strikes, Israel can inflict unbearable losses on terrorists and prevent escalation.

Terrorist warfare is not cheap—weapons, hideouts, training camps, payments to families, all add up—and terrorist leaders do not work for free. Cutting the money supply is an important counter-terror measure. Eliminating a handful of Saudi financiers and Iranian *mullahs* would choke off important terrorist resources.

Some say finding terrorists is almost impossible, since there are so few. That is wrong for at least two reasons. Even if they are few, they still have to talk: ground, cellular, and satellite phones, e-mail. More information comes with physical pressure or drugging imprisoned terrorists. The issue is not collecting data but rather the political will to use it. Small cells are usually unprofessional and easily detected. The experience of Al Qaeda shows the impossibility of building an army from scratch. Short training courses did not make Al Qaeda professional, nor was it professional until it built training camps in Afghanistan. The properly trained Hezbollah is the only Arab terrorist group remotely resembling an army unit—therefore it cannot hide underground and is sufficiently visible for Israel to attack it repeatedly.

Since the Arabs who support terror are accessories to terrorist crime, there is no reason to handle them with kid gloves. Both captured terrorists and the civilians who support them in any way whatsoever are liable to imprisonment and restitution of damaged Israeli property by confiscation or hard labor. Some wonder if terrorists and their supporters are criminals or soldiers, but the upshot is the same: they should be held responsible, their punishment should be sufficiently harsh to discourage others, and there is no need to prove guilt beyond participation in illegal activity or war.

Soldiers are trained to kill efficiently. On the battlefield, they don't just shoot people who shoot at them and let everybody else—tank drivers, for example—go. Warfare is no time for deliberation but rather for killing. The standard of reasonable doubt is much lower during war than in peacetime. Errors of judgment under extreme stress are inevitably many, and the resultant deaths, though wrong, are not wrongful.

Limiting attacks upon civilians to predictable levels puts the attacking army at a disadvantage. The Soviet instructors in Vietnam noted a puzzling American habit: American troops warned villages before they attacked, and most raids destroyed only empty huts. The population survived to fight on. Attacking civilians has been effective in many wars, notably in World War II but also in civil wars against dictators. The long Iran-Iraq war ended only when the United States downed Iranian civilian aircraft—and that by mistake. People support remote wars in another country but are less enthusiastic when *they* are the front and at risk.

Destroy oil infrastructure in retaliation

Israeli reaction must be fierce and translate into a high ratio of losses: for example, a hundred million dollars worth of civil infrastructure for every Israeli killed in a terrorist assault. Such an approach would extinguish Israeli losses or Arab property. Instead of tearing down a few ramshackle houses, Israel should strike at Arab universities, factories, and police stations. Pass a law that Israel will destroy the Aqsa and the Dome of the Rock—the perfect hostages—if a regular Arab army attacks or terrorists kill hundreds in a single attack. Arabs must see a connection between events in Israel and in their countries. When Arab states realize they will lose oil wells as a consequence of Palestinian mischief, they will oppose terrorism, at least politically and financially. Muslims, like anyone else, will turn on their own when they see the fight is lost. Muslims have a long history of murdering other Muslims when they pose a problem for the state. Recall the janissaries[90] or the Palestinians butchered in Jordan.

Since Arab countries export nothing besides oil, only going after the oil wells can succeed, regardless of foreign public opinion. Even if the Saudis and Iranians stand by the Palestinians to the end, the end would come soon as those governments, starved of cash, fell to internal insurrection. No oil means no foreign support, and they would have to face Israel alone.

In the Iran-Iraq war, the United States implicitly approved Iraqi attacks on Iranian oil shipments that quickly drained the Iranian resources. The hike in oil prices that stifled the oil supply in 1974 was a function of Egyptian military strategy, and the Arabs left no doubt they were using oil as a weapon. So if a weapon, oil should be a target.

Israeli assaults on Arab oil facilities would intensify the war briefly, but soon support for terror would vanish and put the guerrillas out of work—as has happened in virtually every war against them. With the present balance of power, there is no chance Muslims would launch an all-

---

[90] The Turkish government murdered many janissaries, on whom it had relied for centuries, to rid itself from their grip.

out war. Faced with escalation, they would have to settle. If the Israeli population knows a war is going on, a war conducted with clear purpose and resolution, it will tolerate casualties if they bring victory closer. The government need not treat Israelis like fools, terming a deep invasion of Lebanon or occupation of the West Bank "defensive." Propaganda stems from the misconceptions of liberal democracies unsupportive of aggressive wars, which are therefore redefined as defense. People generally support short, victorious wars, regardless of the long-term consequences or moral concerns, *e.g.,* the Six-Day War or the American campaign in Afghanistan. Popular opinion turns against war when it becomes protracted, bloody, and fruitless, as in Vietnam, Lebanon, or Iraq.

Propaganda can soften Arab reaction to Israeli assaults, especially in Lebanon and Palestine, which do not support terrorists willingly but are powerless to oppose them. Israel must create terror in the Arab states, like the terrorist bombings in Saudi Arabia and Iraq.[91] Eliminating the terrorists' financial support would provoke exactly that reaction and make Arab governments more amenable to Israeli anti-terror campaigns, possibly even induce tacit cooperation by local authorities, who will rely on Israel to solve their terror problems for them.

Harsh actions are less painful

In war, harsh actions are often the most humane. The sooner a people's will to fight and support fighters is crushed, the sooner the war and the suffering end. There have been periods of relative reduction of Arab resistance to Israel. Dir Yassin frightened Israeli Arabs, and Ariel Sharon's police operations in Gaza worked.[92] On the contrary, when Israel was tolerant and negotiated peacefully, the Palestinians rose in revolt, seeing that Israel is unable to sustain the conflict. Contrast the way the Arabs fled amateur Jewish soldiers in 1948 to the way they stood up to the Israeli Defense Force in 2003. They dare, not because they are brave but because they have nothing to fear. The Israeli army postures but does not kill. Palestinians, fearing ejection, did not participate in the 1973 war. That changed in the 1980s, when Israel was content to demolish a few houses that were soon rebuilt. Germans burned villages to eliminate support for Soviet partisans. Weak responses have an adverse effect. Palestinians cringe before fire barrages; but if all they face is a demolition crew, they are bold. Leniency only provokes more crime. Israel makes a fool of herself,

---

[91] Islamic militants killed and harmed many Muslim civilians in attacks against Western forces and their local supporters. The population surely doubts the *fatwas* establishing the legality of such murders by declaring the victims as *jihad* warriors.
[92] Sharon employed a network of Arab and Arab-speaking Jewish informers in the settlements to gather information on terrorist suspects who were dealt with in no-nonsense terms: killed some, arrested others, and expelled their families to Jordan. Historically, that has been the only effective policy.

using helicopter gunships, tanks, and artillery in massive assaults to wound a few people. NATO's civilian-casualty-free bombing of Yugoslavia did nothing to stop the massacre of the Albanians. If Israel wants to frighten her neighbor into compliance, she must be ready to inflict casualties. A good army kills well. Using the army for police operations like checkpoints, house searches, crowd control, and the like is demoralizing.

The attempt to fight an ethical war is futile. *War crime* is a tautology. *Civilized war* is an oxymoron. More people die in Syrian jails than Israel kills in the Palestinian war, where she only defends the status quo and does not infringe on Arab life and property *per se*. If a state must take morally objectionable action, then at least make it effective.

Strike the general population to quash terrorists

Israel's response to terrorism should be sufficiently cruel to discourage repetition and dry up support. A weak response provokes further escalation by turning aggression into no-risk heroics.

People are usually willing to die only for a winning cause. Israel must either crush Arab hopes for success with overwhelming retaliation or succumb to terror. Sixty years of compromise have taken Israel nowhere, while human and economic losses have skyrocketed, international prestige has vanished, and immigration has dwindled.

Producing ideologically motivated kamikazes requires persistent indoctrination. At the dawn of suicide operations, the Muslim Brothers had a hard time finding someone to kill Nasser. Indoctrination is a large-scale operation, vulnerable to countermeasures. Remarkably few scoundrels committed the atrocities in WWII Germany, Rwanda, Yugoslavia, but they depended on the tacit support and acquiescence of the general population. Israel should retaliate against the supporters of terrorism, rather than sifting out a handful of active participants who are immediately replaced by others. Terrorists must be killed, but destroying housing and infrastructure will stifle their supporters. Napoleon stopped a rebellion with a "whiff of grapeshot." A minor show of force can stop a mob; large groups rarely commit crimes unless immunity is assured. Small but persistent pressure on the groups and towns that support terrorists would soon extinguish that support.

The Nazis crushed Russian guerrilla resistance by punishing civilians who supported the partisans systematically and ruthlessly. The Arabs have twice routed terrorists out effectively: in Jordan, where an estimated eight thousand died in a matter of days, and in Syria, where about twenty thousand Muslims died in a few weeks. By contrast, Egypt's attempt to prosecute terror with judicial procedures is futile. Though we may not like the harsh way, no other way works.

Israel must use force and spend money and lives to preserve the State of Israel. Otherwise, her policies will vacillate and provoke angry Arab response to exploit Israel's internal weakness.

Define acceptable cruelty formally

Israel must determine what constitutes an adequate response. How many Arabs must die to prevent a terrorist attack? How many should die in reprisal? The calculations are important, since only ruthless cruelty will kill popular support for terrorists. Israel could have got rid of the grassroots violence long ago with time-tested measures. Protesters do not return if many were killed during the last demonstration. And why not? They support the terrorists who kill Israeli civilians.

Should Israel execute for shouting and waving flags? Organizing similar demonstrations in Israel in support of the I.D.F. is irrelevant. Breaking up demonstrations with water cannons would only be fun for the Palestinians, a cheerful deviation from the dull lives of unemployed welfare recipients. Rounding the demonstrators up in Israeli jails is tremendously expensive and creates a basis for long-term international condemnation for suppressing a political liberty to fight against Israel. Killing many demonstrators would make repetitions less likely. Many civilized countries killed demonstrators even in peacetime.

A less violent solution than killing vast numbers of Arab civilians and hardening the rest for a desperate fight against Israel is retaliation against Arab officials. Israel should destroy an office and the personnel of some hostile Arab country after every terrorist attack against Israel. A short reaction time is possible if Israel chooses the targets beforehand. That would mean civilian casualties but would worry the world media less than an Israeli attack on an Arab village. Government officials would stop associating openly with terrorists. Israel could target Arab government personnel and minimize or avoid strikes against population entirely. She could pretend to liberate Muslims from corrupt governments whose secret services nurture the terrorists.

Killing a few terrorist leaders would not be enough. To shift Arab attention from the supposed honor of martyrdom to the assurance of imminent death, inconspicuous and unmemorable, Israel needs to kill scores of leading terrorists. Her public relations will also benefit from replacing murder with statistics: people accept many deaths easier than a few.

If Israel could not find a particular terrorist, she might abandon the search, and wait until he surrenders or commits suicide—and systematically destroy villages and infrastructure with unavoidable civilian casualties until he does. That proven tactic would turn Arab populations against terrorists. Arabs will understand Israeli vengefulness.

Persecute the families of suicide bombers

Suicide bombers will not volunteer if their families are persecuted and their neighbors driven into exile. *Shahedeen*, righteous martyrs— suicide bombers—believe the Saudis will take care of their families and everyone will respect them. Destroy that belief by destroying the homes their families build, even in the future, or jail them. They are not innocent. Incitement is a crime. Even if they do not incite the *shahedeen,* they are nevertheless an important part of the bombers' decision and should be prosecuted regardless of their guilt. That approach would affect the dangerous solitary bombers and other hard-to-detect small groups. They would die knowing they subjected their relatives to punishment, even if they themselves do not fear death. Recruiting orphans for suicide missions is not easy in the Muslim environment of large families. People who fear exile or prison are more likely to inform on terrorists and suspicious activity in general.

Truth serum will show if the family is ignorant, but it is still should be persecuted to discourage the bombers. Israel should certainly not allow the families to receive benefits.

Invaders lost Lebanon and Afghanistan because of restraint toward civilians

Israel's failure in Lebanon and the Soviet Union's in Afghanistan,[93] the two cases of successful defensive *jihad* after centuries of Muslim impotence have the same cause: the unwillingness of the stronger power to wage normal war, which let defenders hide among the civilians and strike at leisure. The only way to fight a war is brutally. The choice is not between humaneness and cruelty but between waging war and surrender. Starting a war without being prepared to fight it is a recipe for failure, emboldening *jihadi.*

Destroy the terrorists' support base

In war, commanders often aim to destroy not enemy troops but their support: logistics and industry. When they do, enemy armies disintegrate without a bloody frontal assault. Likewise, successful anti-guerrilla campaigns aim at eradicating support: drug cartels in Latin America, Communists in Greece and Malaysia, partisans in World War II Russia. Sharon's tactics in Gaza, a rare example of proper policy, relied on stamping out popular support for terrorists, but Israel now mistakenly fights the terrorists themselves. That tactic is valid in the worst-case scenario, where independent terrorists appear. To overcome them is almost impossible: most terrorists acts require only a few agents, and there are always newcomers. But luckily Israel today deals with extended organizations, relying heavily on various forms of support. Even in the case of small or secretive groups, amateurish but not easily detected, an active policy makes terrorists nervous, and they err, letting the security services at

---

[93] The Afghan *mujahedeen* troops were peasants, serving part-time. Even though the Soviet Army was cruel in many cases, it refrained from attacking villages filled with decommissioned fighters.

them. They must be transformed from folk heroes into fugitives on the run with nowhere to go because no one dares offer them shelter and support.

The availability of suicide bombers depends on unflagging trust in the leaders and the cause. Flood media with presentations of bin Laden as an uneducated simpleton under the heel of Al-Zawahiri. Disseminate jokes about him. Claim him as an Israeli agent-provocateur. Subtle techniques of neurolinguistic programming can seed distrust, in many respects the most effective anti-terror measure. Once the coherence of the guerrillas' support base is ruptured, nothing would preclude Arab cynicism from encompassing the terrorists.

Hamas in Palestine, like Hezbollah in Lebanon, fields a large network of social services to assure popular support. Israel should destroy their camps and facilities. Their clients hate Israel anyway. They would not be grateful to Hamas either.

Abandon formalities; rely on suspicion and preemption

Israel at war mistakenly uses peacetime legislation to deal with hostile Arabs. They are not loyal citizens but enemies, killing Jews or supporting people who do. Not only should the penalties for disloyalty be harsher but also the burden of proof should be lightened, doing away with the presumption of innocence and allowing indefinite detention or expulsion without charge. The world did not object to the British summarily exiling Jewish guerrilla suspects to Eritrea. Terrorists' neighbors and people who demonstrate against the government should be dealt with by wartime standards. An anti-terrorist task force should not have to petition a judge to search a house or detain a suspect. The changes should not affect Jews. If Arabs object to the policy, they are free to leave, and Palestinians are not obliged to come into Israel.

The unintended consequence of "suspicion justice" could be crowded Israeli jails. To avoid the costs, Israel must exile suspects and their families and imprison only proven terrorists and their supporters—though even they cannot be jailed forever without formal trial. Israel has a habit of releasing inmates at political turns. One way to cut costs is to keep them on short rations in the kind of prisons common in the Arab world. Jails are to break criminals, not to feed and encourage them. Israeli jails have little deterrent effect. When Saudi Arabia mutilates convicts, Israel need not refrain. Executing terrorists is cheaper and more efficient. Israel should deduct prison costs from remittances to the Palestinian administration.

Common justice does not apply to international relations. Inside a state, police may search anywhere and interrogate anyone according to due process, letting courts establish truth beyond doubt, though one state may not do so in another state's territory in peacetime.[94] Consider the brouhaha

---

[94] The extraction and trial of Eichmann was an unnecessary, expensive show, since his guilt was beyond doubt. Attempting to repeat the experience with Mengele,

over whether Iraq did or did not have weapons of mass destruction. Even if Iraq had chemical and biological weapons, the United States could not intervene, because the inspectors found no laboratories, though there was reason to believe Saddam had them, since he repeatedly blocked inspections.

Every theory becomes inoperative on the fringes of data range. Formal justice, essential for well-being of peaceful societies, is counterproductive during wars or crises.

Formal justice is inappropriate for terrorists and their supporters, because hard proof often cannot be found and if found, sources cannot be revealed. In the wake of the Sudanese "pharmaceutical" factory bombing scandal, the press alleged that the soil samples with VX gas ingredients the CIA presented as evidence were inadmissible because the operative who delivered them could have tampered with them. Presumably, the alternative was to subpoena the terrorists. People usually trust governments on significant issues, such as monetary policy, without going into the details but are prone to question intelligence matters, asking for the proof behind the allegations on which limited strikes are predicated. It is impossible to reveal the sources, and incomplete information invites contempt. Intelligence matters should be kept secret, even at the risk of offending public opinion.

Police operations aim to solve crimes committed. Israel needs an agency dedicated to preventing terrorist attacks, which could hardly work in a courtroom, since it would target people not proven guilty, whose guilt is known or suspected only by a few. Indeed, they may not yet have committed a crime, but only be planning an attack. The agency should operate much like the early Mossad, neither plagued by bureaucracy nor burdened with political responsibility. Its head should be answerable only to the prime minister and even then only from a distance, to prevent politicians from leaking information. The head should hold office for a long term, possibly for life, to insulate him from political change and indecision. Alternatively, their tenure could be limited by fifteen years with full salary afterwards. White-collar criminals are apt for secret service work; organizations working outside the law need people with relevant experience. It should operate like a commando unit, raiding the enemy camps in other countries, assassinating supporters and encouraging dissenters. Israel might establish several such independent units, keeping them small and not bureaucratic. Information sharing, such as could have prevented the 9/11 attacks, is not joint planning and operations. The security organizations would still be constrained, allowed to kill only a narrowly defined category of enemies: terrorists and their supporters. One or three judges of the Israeli Supreme Court could investigate the most

---

Israel abandoned the operation instead of simply—or elaborately—killing him where they found him.

volatile cases in closed session. There is little reason to fear domestic abuses from agencies that operate abroad. Private security agencies, more flexible and unhampered by government hiring policies, might be considered. The government could subscribe to their briefings or put out contracts on certain targets. Private spies could sell information to the state.

A citizen alone has little power compared to a whole society and can harm it little. That allows the state to wait for crimes to happen or almost happen before punishing the culprit. Governments rely on more or less substantiated conjectures in foreign relations, almost never established facts. Relations with other countries more resemble police prosecuting a citizen for looking at illegal rifles on the internet, though he has neither bought one nor killed anyone.

That is the only practical approach, since nations want at all costs to avoid a first strike against themselves and must take pre-emptive action before aggression occurs if there is credible threat. Arab aggression against Israelis is ongoing. Civilized countries can let some guilty go unpunished to avoid punishing the innocent, and prosecute only committed crimes, but nations cannot wait for an attack and only *then* retaliate. If Israel attacked Arab state-owned assets, she would not punish the innocent, since Arab regimes support terrorists. People who decry bypassing standard judicial procedures and common law in international military relations do not understand the basic issues. Even the lip service Israel pays to international justice is too much: it hinders required state actions and erodes public support for extraordinary military actions. Since Israel already controls the territories, she could ask an international police force to prevent violence on both sides.

Syria, Saudi Arabia, and Iran openly support terrorists, and most Arab countries incite militant groups and ordinary Arabs against Israel, all the while proclaiming their readiness for accommodation, though the extent of their meddling is difficult to prove. Even when facts are available, they cannot be revealed for security reasons. Evidence obtained illegally is inadmissible in any case. Israel, therefore, should drop the pretense of legality and act efficiently instead. A war against terror means striking people who support terror without hesitation and formalities, wherever they are, not only in defenseless Palestine but anywhere. That idea is not altogether new, since Israel chased the P.L.O. all the way to Tunisia. The innovation would be to attack not only weak states but rich ones as well. Such action might not lead to reprisals or prolonged conflicts; no Arab army would stand a chance in a confrontation with Israel. Israel may even benefit from war since her army is stronger than her enemies' and could demilitarize them. Arab countries would likely be glad to retract their support, financial or otherwise, for terrorists who are a headache for their hosts. If some bin Laden outfit blackmailed Saudi Arabia into paying ransom instead of cracking down on the terrorists, the Israeli Defense Force should be able to terrorize the Saudis into standing up to them. Arab countries which support terrorists infringe on Israeli sovereignty, and Israel should reciprocate.

Pre-emptive or arbitrary military actions are not out of line today. Though in Korea and Vietnam the United States established a precedent for defining *enemy* within the legal framework of the United Nations, only after the American invasion of Iraq did the notion of pre-emptive aggression based on less than hard evidence come into play. Whether the invasion was justified is moot. The point is that a country strong enough to establish precedent by its actions did it. Should Israel adopt the strategy she can expect American support, if only to cover its fault in Iraq by similar incidents. Israel would not be long alone in preempting terrorists; other countries will do likewise. Unlike the United States in Iraq, Israel has positive evidence of Arab sabotage.

Pre-emptive or retaliatory strikes, especially at rich countries like Saudi Arabia, may elicit negative reactions, but the objections would be disingenuous. Destabilization and threat in the Middle East push Arab countries toward the West for protection and arbitrage. Isolated terrorist actions are hard to trace to any particular place. The actively anti-Israel Arab countries can be blamed for incitement and held responsible. Muslims talk about unity, and here is a chance to suffer for it.

Collective liability

Collective liability often means executing members of a persecuted group for real or imagined crimes. Summary executions are ugly, because they are usually the premeditated end for which the executioners invent hollow justifications. In the Middle East, collective liability is different. The primary subjects are states, not people, and punishment might include destroying buildings, oil wells, and irrigation, electric power, and military infrastructure. Individual civilians should be killed only for supporting terrorists actively or through malicious neglect. Enforcing collective liability would encourage pacification inhumanely but efficiently.

The Israeli-Arab "cold" war differs from other military actions only by degree. Every war involves civilian casualties, whether they support the war or not. During a declared war, civilian casualties can be minimized, since the location of the armies is well known. But in a popular war, as distinct from a war waged by military professionals, many civilians actively participate, supplying the army or sabotaging the invaders. The combination nationalist/peasant war—Algeria, Vietnam, Palestine—pits an alien army against guerrillas hiding among civilians and dependent on them for financing and supply. There is no way to fight such a war without considerable civilian casualties. Israel is engaged in exactly such a war and must acknowledge the inevitability of large civilian losses.

Punishing collective responsibility recalls dictators massacring multitudes for peccadilloes. In the Middle East, however, collective responsibility touches only countries which engage in anti-Israeli activity and deserve retribution. Israeli reprisals could aim at destroying government and civic targets, not civilians.

Collective responsibility is indispensable to military operations where careful individual judgments are impossible. America attacked all of Iraq for Saddam's crimes. The Syrians severely restricted all Jews to vex Israel and razed the city of Hama to stop the Muslim Brothers insurrection. The Russians interned German soldiers in labor camps after World War II. The French were not picky about killing Vietnamese and Algerians. And so on. Actions against civilians are only as wrong as war itself.

Is this Israeli terrorism? In a sense, yes, though the civilian casualties from Israeli reprisals are collateral damage, while they are the Arabs' primary weapon. Arab terrorists do not target Israeli infrastructure but rather civilians. Fighting a problem with the like means is reasonable. Police use force to stop criminals; people accept violence that mitigates another violence. Terrorists do not bring their civilian victims to trial before murdering them. Why should Israel observe legal niceties to identify and execute terrorists and their supporters?

The term *collective responsibility* is misleading. Civilians killed in retaliatory strikes are not responsible in any legal or moral sense. Israel rather holds them hostage. The policy is not just, but war is rarely just; the policy may, however, contain the terrorists and minimize suffering in the long run.

Collective responsibility is a biblical concept: whole nations are judged. The idea does not ignore the innocent but rather, as Lot's story demonstrates, finds societies more or less morally egalitarian, and righteous (or tolerant, in this case) people are free to leave an evil land—the option offered in Sodom, Dir Yassin, and Beirut.[95]

Arabs allege collective responsibility when they attack Israeli civilians or cheer such attacks. The Arabs see terrorism against the Israeli population as an acceptable military tactic to force Israel to make political concessions. The Israelis have every right to deal with Arabs likewise.

Act by stealth

Another approach may be taken with enemies who are not combatants but engage in subversive activity. The *lex talionis* is the best policy here. Countries like Saudi Arabia and Iran support anti-Israeli terror openly, though not at the government level. Similarly, Israel should encourage Israeli non-government paramilitary organizations, preferably based in the West Bank, to make retributive attacks on the economic infrastructure of states that support Arab terrorists. Radical Jewish groups

---

[95] Lebanese do not need visas to travel to many countries and could relocate instead of being bombed in Beirut along with entrenched P.L.O. fighters. Palestinians, more restricted, could have moved to not conflicted parts of the city or elsewhere in Lebanon.

related to fringe political or religious beliefs and located out of Israel proper, in the desert or in the territories, can operate despite nominal state opposition, just as the Arabs do. Developments in robotic weaponry have made warfare available to small groups. Israel might consider deploying heavy UAVs[96] of the Predator class with self-targeted Hellfire missiles if they could procure them unofficially; or GPS-guided[97] light aircraft adapted for unmanned flight and armed with ICM[98] explosives and chemical weapons preventing fire-fighting. More traditional armaments, like speedboat-launched Stinger missiles, are still useful. The Jewish radical groups need not take responsibility for their acts. Keep the Arabs guessing. Jews need their own Osama.

Suicide missions by Israelis are dubious, but gentiles could be hired. Incidents like *Achille Lauro*[99] are very useful. Similar actions may be used to compromise terrorist groups. Terrorists have already begun to threaten Arab states, notably Egypt and Saudi Arabia. The Saudi refusal to bow to bin Laden's political demands resulted in several bombings. Israel might simulate Islamic terrorists attacks in both places, targeting foreigners and local officials. Finding some poor Arab willing to carry out a suicide attack to enrich his family should not be a problem. In the face of frequent "terrorists," the Saudis would have no reason to placate Al Qaeda and would rather have to resist all terrorists, Al Qaeda included. Real or simulated terrorist attacks in Europe could force a crackdown on Islamists.

Is such deceit morally reprehensible? Not at all. The Israeli government has a single fiduciary obligation, and that is to Jews—not even to Arab Israelis whose citizenship is only a nod to world public opinion. There is no reason to care what the *international community* thinks, mostly hereditary anti-Semites, descendants of people who murdered and persecuted Jews, people with no stake in Israel's security. Since when are deceit and stealth wrong in war?[100] Israel is in fact at war with most Arab countries.

Israel would do well to learn Sadat's kind of deceit. Unlike Israel who boasts of military prowess she lacks the resolve to use, Egypt in 1973

---

[96] Unmanned Aerial Vehicle, a pilotless plane, relatively inexpensive and not easily destroyed because of its smaller size.

[97] Global Positioning System, satellite tracking device used for reconnaissance and targeting.

[98] Improved Conventional Munitions, expensive but of much higher explosive power than ordinary weapons, allowing for effective employment of light UAVs.

[99] PLFP-GC guerrillas captured the ship in 1985, taking four hundred hostages. The odd part is murder of a 69-year-old Jewish-American cripple which predictably created a flood of condemnation and estranged the world opinion from P.L.O. Italian police released Mahmoud Abbas, the chief of terrorists, immediately, and two other members shortly after. Israel did not punish Abbas who openly lived in Gaza since 1996, and Americans recently captured him near Baghdad.

[100] To Mohammed is attributed the saying, "War is deceit."

136

feigned weakness, then struck as hard as it could, turning the tables and getting the settlement it wanted.

Get the Arabs to fight for Israeli objectives

To achieve minimal direct involvement, some Arabs must be induced to take Israel's side. That is not impossible. Bedouins regularly attacked their settled brethren. Arabs in one country regularly fight Arabs in another. So do clans within a single country. Psychological warfare professionals will provide suitable smokescreens. Although it will be hard to get Arabs to fight for Israel, they will not hesitate to act against the Palestinians or Iran-supported fundamentalists or any kind of intra-Arab antagonist. Sunni-Shiite strife flares easily. The murder of peace-seeking imams would provoke protracted conflicts. Wealthy Arabs could wage a vendetta against a terrorist group which killed their relatives.

It is hard to recruit people from ideologically motivated intelligence services and terrorist groups. The solution is to induce potential traitors to infiltrate those organizations on their own. Advertising rewards for sabotage or intelligence and killing terrorist leaders would help. Infiltration takes years but can earn big rewards in the end. Individual rewards in the millions are not high compared to the reductions in military expenses they buy.[101] The operation should be easily accessible, a website where collaborators can contact Israeli intelligence services[102] or Arab organizations opposed to particular terrorist groups. Big pay can buy sabotage from mercenaries – even Jews, mostly criminals, cooperate with hostile Arab groups. Israel should learn to get others to wage war for her. The efforts to conquer without war should be financed on military scale.

Acceding to terrorist demands does not lead to peace

Muslim terrorists tempt Israel with an attractive way out: give up some non-essential land. The temptation to end the war expeditiously undermines Israeli resolve, already leaning toward the dead-end of concessions.

Hamas is driving Israel from the territories the way Hezbollah pushed her out of Lebanon: a step at a time. Giving way to their demands is an embarrassing option. But the demands are elastic: withdraw from Sinai, then from Lebanon, then from the Golan Heights, then from Judea and Samaria, leaving Israel with her 1948 borders. Such territorial losses in fewer than forty years show that a policy of accommodation is wrong—and

---

[101] Big rewards are due only to valuable spies who spend years or decades positioning themselves and know the price of their services. Rank-and-file traitors are inexpensive.

[102] While this book was being written, Mossad finally opened a Web site inviting recruits and tips. Mossad still needs to plant proxies to offer Arabs undetectable access to the site.

endless. If Israel gave back all the territories, a demand for the partition of Jerusalem would be next—and not just for administrative autonomy for Muslim shrines. After that, Israel would have to deal with the refugees' right to return—with reparations. Nothing precludes Arab terrorists from fighting until Israel vanishes; indeed, they admit that every agreement is an intermediary step to that end. Acceding to their demands presumes they will stop after the Arabs meet their reasonable goals. Not so, not the least because they understand reasonable objectives differently from the Israelis.

Formal peace might not end terrorism

Peace with Arab countries would not necessarily solve the terror problem for Israel, at least not for many years. Many will remain who do not accept Israel's existence. Terrorism will become more sporadic as Arabs become wealthier and less prone to aggression, but it will remain and grow deadlier.

There is no possibility of rooting out all the terrorists. Terrorism is an effective political and military tool. Arabs are predisposed to it by a long history of Bedouin hit-and-run tactics. Even with peace in the Middle East, fringe groups and others will engage in terrorism, and Israel will always be an attractive target for anti-Semites. So peace will not necessarily end terrorism. Unlike other countries, tiny Israel with a crowded population cannot tolerate even a single large-scale terrorist act, like hit the World Trade Center and the Pentagon in 2001. Israel cannot avoid terrorism absolutely, so she must find pre-emptive countermeasures to nip it in the bud.

No tactical negotiations with terrorists

Israel must return to the policy of no negotiations with terrorists, refusing even to exchange hostages. Released terrorists kill more Jews than an exchange might save. Israel is at war, and all Israelis are at the front; people will die, no matter before or after negotiations, before or after terrorists are released. Only their number, statistics, matters. Giving in to terrorist demands provokes more terrorism. The problem is two-fold: not only is hostage-taking profitable, it also is safe. Kidnappers know they will be ransomed if they are caught. Israel should issue an ultimatum to any country holding hostages or POWs, warning it of an impeding assault. That might turn Arabs against taking hostages. Israel should also return to the declared but never consistently practiced[103] policy of hunting down every perpetrator. Repress terrorists' families and neighbors, take Arab hostages by rounding up villagers, and blow up a couple of Muslim universities. Not fair? Neither is any war means. Suffice it be efficient.

---

[103] Not even all the terrorists who participated in the Munich affair were killed. The search at least for one of them was at some point abandoned, and at least one planner, Amin al Hindi, now officially works in the P.A. government.

138

Kidnapping has become a business: there is risk involved, but the profit is also there. By refusing to negotiate, Israel would cut out the profit. Kidnapping will be like murdering civilians: terrible but with no particular benefit, like getting other terrorists released.[104] A *no-negotiations with terrorists* policy prevents escalation and reduces the fighting.

Compromise means something to states, and stable political groups, inclined to keep their word for the sake of credibility. It means nothing to loose entities like the P.L.O. that sprout new radical branches as soon as the main body moderates. Compromise works as a tactical device in ordinary warfare; for example, cease-fires often prevent huge losses. Casualties from terrorism are statistically insignificant, and the political and military damage of tactical disengagement outweighs the importance of lives saved.

The charge that a no-negotiation policy is like marching a 19th century army straight into withering cannon fire is superficial. Terrorist acts usually have little material effect, more psychological than otherwise. Acts of terror kill fewer people than car accidents. The terrorists will run out of suicide recruits before society collapses—until the guerrillas start using WMD or strike expensive infrastructure. The enemy must see the futility of his actions and must be resisted psychologically by refusing to make concessions, even if that means small losses in life and material. If terrorism inflicts significant losses, it is conventional warfare, has more trouble maneuvering, and is vulnerable.

A logical extension of a no-ransom policy is the demand that other countries, mainly Saudi Arabia, not pay ransom. It is well known that terrorist groups extort semi-official donations from some. Whoever abets crime out of fear is culpable. Any payment to terrorists prejudices Israeli interests and should cease.

Ransom is nothing new. The ancient law obliges Jews to ransom their compatriots if captured. The Vatican ransomed three hundred Roman Jews in World War II with thirty pounds of gold—down payment on a hundred-pound payoff to the Nazis—though twelve thousand more were extradited and murdered. Trucks and gasoline bought other Jewish lives from the Nazis, a policy some say benefited mostly rich, well-connected families. All Jews are equally important for the Israeli government. Saving some by giving in to terrorist demands at the expense of others in the future makes sense only in politics where shortsighted governments mortgage the future to present expedience.

Political negotiations with terrorist groups are possible

Since terrorism is a form of war, hostilities need not cease before negotiations begin. There are no moderates in terrorist organizations like Hamas or Hezbollah, and their "political wings" are designed to lure Israel

---

[104] Israel's miscalculation culminated in the Tannenbaum exchange, when more than a hundred Arabs—many of them guerrillas—were freed for one Jew

into dialogue. They should therefore be talked to like any other political structure that pursues its ends by military means. Negotiations are both tactical and strategic. On the tactical level—hostage exchanges, for example—no compromise is possible. Prisoners are not exchanged during a battle, and opposing commanders do not negotiate partial withdrawal for ammunition. The case against tactical compromise is even stronger in guerrilla warfare, since militants can gain the edge in negotiations by taking a few civilian hostages. On the strategic level, there is no reason to avoid political negotiations, even with militants. If the distinction between the two kinds of negotiation seems blurred, it is in fact. That happens because political considerations skew tactical calculations. Compromise is possible in a terrorist war, where actions or demands are paced to the response they elicit, but then compromise must be approached from an offensive perspective. Negotiating for hostages, Israel should offer not an exchange but rather a pledge not to take out enemy bases or civilian targets. As things are now, the terrorists stay one step ahead: for every action Israel takes (like holding prisoners), they threaten new action unless the previous act is rectified (prisoners released). Negotiating offensively, Israel would take the lead: no compromise on repairing the past or on future plans but possibly on escalation and retaliation for concomitant adjustments. Israel should trade action for action; violent reaction is not negotiable. That policy would signal a return to military reality, where the stronger and the more resolute wins.

Israel has not benefited from a single settlement in her modern history. The armistice of 1948 was concluded after she drove the enemy out. The Sinai treaty won no significant economic benefits in return for a surrender to Egyptian demands. Israel should negotiate only to enforce her terms. She should not seek to stop the aggression; rather she should leave the Arabs desperate to negotiate. She might well escalate her own demands annually and actualize them *de facto* until the Arabs give in to mitigate further damage. She could start by carving out one square mile of Palestinian territory for every Israeli terrorists kill.

Terrorism's future is bright

Compared to the sophistication of contemporary military and political networks, terrorism is simple. The 1993 bombing of the World Trade Center was carried out by idiots, snagged when they tried to collect the deposit on a rental van they had just blown up. The miscues in the 2001 attacks did not spell failure only because American security was lax. Terrorists are often uneducated and pathologically aggressive people, and plenty more are being brainwashed daily by the *mullahs* and nationalists.

Terrorism will become more pervasive, ranging from commercial extortion to minor powers taking on militarily superior ones. That will bring many more players into the military enterprise. Little countries or sociopath freelancers, traditionally counted out, will use terrorism to extort a place at the table. Suicide bombers are either ideological freaks or stupid and don't mean much by global standards of war. Eventually, however, the world's geeks may consider asymmetrical warfare, disaffected biologists stockpiling viruses in university laboratories. The legendary evil geniuses will appear and elevate terrorism to a point where the damage it causes approaches that of open war. With governments ready to counterattack and to accept civilian casualties, terrorists will concentrate on private targets, that is, extortion, not only gangsters and Robin Hoods but also revolutionary zealots with few scruples for funding their shining path. Wealthy expatriate Arabs will be targeted to fund needy *jihadists;* then Western corporations and the oil-rich Arab states are due a systematic milking. Huge transnational corporations see no percentage in opposing terrorist demands and have shown themselves prone to play the ransom card, appeasing labor movements, bribing foreign officials, and cutting Israel loose to placate Arab clients. Given the chicanery in accounting practices, the corporations will be important terrorist targets. What corporation will risk a large factory when it can ransom it without anybody knowing?

The 9/11 attacks created a vast market for anti-terrorist services in the United States. The next obvious target in the United States is Las Vegas, the epicenter of American decadence, though bombing provincial targets is easier and more terrifying, showing that no place is immune. Terrorists will concentrate on Spain[105] which Muslims consider a part of Dar al-Islam. The burgeoning French Muslim population will clash with nationalists, tempting the terrorists to join. Countries like India, the Philippines, Indonesia, and Russia will need help defending themselves against terrorists as well. With the American army an inept colossus,[106] Israel could offer outsourcing of anti-terrorist services. Though the press exacerbates and exaggerates the real global security dilemma, there is no shortage of people ready to try terrorism, including Christian radicals in the United States. Israel should sponsor her security-related companies, which may become a big chunk of her economy, soaking up the money now spent on conventional warfare worldwide. Private funding will appear when people realize that the government cannot protect them and they turn to close-up hired security.

Conventional weapons and large armies are useless against terrorism. Experience and specialized electronic devices replace them. States that spend money on antiquated forms of warfare will likely never use them. If they do, there may be no victors left anyway. Israel must prepare for the new kind of war, CBN developed in small labs and

---

[105] The lecture from which this abstract is taken was given in October 2001, before the train bombings in Spain.

[106] Few countries entered defensive wars prepared. Military readiness in time of peace is too expensive.

delivered by suicide bombers—and Israel must learn to counter that threat. Israeli experience in controlling terror will be useful to other states faced with the necessity of an immediate wholesale change in military doctrine. Besides economic gain, Israel could achieve military dominance in asymmetric warfare, both defensive and offensive. A small country can be powerful in the age of technological warfare and mobility, when even the remotest corners of the globe are accessible and technological advantages are all-important. The trend of spiraling weapons' tactical capabilities hit a wall. The law of marginal utility makes advances uneconomical, and few improvements—too complex, unreliable, and expensive—will pass the test on the battlefield. New war will see qualitatively new weapons: inexpensive, mass-produced; not hundred-million dollar planes or million-dollar UAVs, but thousand-dollar disposable "toy" planes targeting enemy machines and installations in masses; not super-equipped soldiers and personnel carriers, but myriads of all-terrain "toy" vehicles moving on enemy positions. People die for high values, killing enemies perhaps the most urgent of them. Exchanging one's life for a few mass-produced cheap machines means losing life and will seed horror. Israel should invent a new army, not the means of financing the old one.

Riot control

Israel needs new techniques to control riots. Resin bullets are too little for some, since the rioters riot on, and too much for others, like the mass media that focus on a few gruesome injuries. Israel should consider non-contact devices, like infrasound to stimulate unconscious horror, super-loud sound, foul smelling additives in the water used to disperse crowds, skin irritating gases, and "fun gasses" which first cause hyperactivity and then lassitude. A less technical approach is to cultivate the opposition and set them to break up demonstrations by turning them into street fights.

Many governments deal harshly with demonstrations. American police killed strikers during the labor movement. In the 1990s, Russia twice met Moscow protesters with tanks; the violence in the provinces was barbaric. France quashed riots in Indochina and Algeria; Britain, in Ireland; and Spain, in Basque country. Arab countries do not let Indian guest workers protest, nor does the Shia minority press demands. The situation in Israel is no romance; stop treating demonstrators as if it were.

Avoid urban combat

The Nazis show that guerrillas can be beaten, provided you are willing to be inhumane. Or if you want to be humane, take care of your own people first and protect them from terrorists. The same applies to urban warfare, like Israel waged in Beirut. Trying to spare Arabs, the Israeli government got many Jews killed. In the world of pretentious humanity, it takes courage to kill. Israel's mass media sponsored disregard of her own troops in favor of enemy civilians hurts army morale like nothing else. War

142

assumes enemy civilian casualties. It is better to kill enemy civilians than to lose Israeli conscripts. If Israel is not ready to accept that theorem, Israel should not go to war, sue for a peace acceptable to the Arabs. Israel should not involve infantry in urban warfare but bomb and bombard after giving civilians a chance to leave.

Practical counter-terror measures

Israel can destroy popular support for terrorism among Arabs by assailing the civilian population, razing Arab settlements, and exiling the inhabitants. Eradicate financial support by attacking countries and people who support the terrorists. Practice infiltration and espionage, offer bounties for known terrorists, and go after them without counting civilian losses. Israel must hunt down anyone with even the slightest relation to terrorists. The current situation of known terrorists moving freely is ludicrous. Prohibit all weapons in the territories other than light police firearms, and impose an embargo when illicit weapons appear. Owning weapons should be a felony.

After the 1917 revolution, the Soviets rooted out monarchist and democratic opposition both in Russia and abroad by setting up phony opposition organizations, promoting them with daring operations in Russia, and snaring every one who came within reach. Israel prefers collaborators to provocateurs, with predictably lamentable results.

Clamp down in Israel: fingerprint passports, biosecurity locks in every public building, face-recognition cameras, detectors that sense tension in the voice, unusual static electricity on the fingers, and traces of explosives or toxic chemicals, Geiger counters everywhere, and a broad no-pass border zone. The whole country must become a gigantic lab, with chemical and radiological sensors everywhere. Special restrictions and strict control over the movements of Arabs in Israel are chauvinistic but necessary. Israel could start with foreign Arabs and slowly include Israeli Arabs, generally loyal though many support Palestine. Such measures would alienate Israeli Arabs and run them out of the country.

Microlevel warfare requires microlevel intelligence. Israel should establish a heuristic database tracking immigration irregularities, education, medical conditions, police history, work, finances, consumer habits, library and video rentals, tax payments, personal contacts, phone calls, ground and e-mail correspondence, internet sites visited, municipal services consumed, travel, domestic destinations, friends and business associates, medications, neighbor's reports, and other data. Like Echelon, the American computer system that scans phone calls and e-mail, the system should comb through keyword patterns in phone conversations and e-mail. It should be integrated with foreign databases wherever possible. This system will not eliminate terrorism but will detect some terrorists and cause others to make mistakes. Police use networks of informants and data collection even against low-level criminals; without aggressive data analysis, individual terrorists fly below government radar but are too dangerous to leave alone. Reporting without names and releasing them only with court warrant will prevent abuses. The data could be initially collected on non-Jews.

Nations should issue only passports with biometric data and extend the practice to domestic ID affairs, such as airport security, internal passports, and bank transactions. Fingerprints should replace passports, driver licenses, and credit cards.

Replacing cash money with electronic transactions would facilitate finding aliens who enter Israel illegally. Visitors to Israel could be given temporary bank accounts upon arrival. Electronic payments should cover all payments down to market vendors and bus ticket sales. Fingerprint scanning is inexpensive and faster than other modes of payment.

Influence of counterterrorism on freedom

A centralized database would make it very hard for known terrorists to hide. Yes, for other people, too, but why resist efficient application of a democratically adopted law? Libertarians oppose pervasive internal control with appeals to wrong convictions, but for every mistaken challenge or detention, dozens of criminals slip by. Governments do not need total surveillance to track political opponents. The resources of a modern state are up to the task: governments in power use money against their opponents anyway. Pervasive control is needed only to detect and track criminals and terrorists.

The law prohibits only invasion of privacy. Passive monitoring is not intrusive. Reasonable law-abiding citizens cannot rationally object to some machine collecting data on them. Problems arise when someone abuses the data. That is an issue of control of the collected data; collection itself is harmless. Governments misuse firearms, but no one suggests disarming the police. The British experience with controlling the uncontrollable is instructive: Parliament renews the secret service's license for extrajudicial operations annually; if any cause a public outcry, the license expires, a shrewd system which relies on the mass media to do the investigative part of judicial oversight. Legislators correctly reasoned that evidence suppressed in the courts often turns up under media scrutiny and institutionalized the phenomenon. Though the public is entitled to transparent government, people usually trust their leaders more or less blindly. When the details of monetary policy and pension fund strategies are disclosed, experts offer contradictory opinions at once, and the average citizen has no idea whether his government is right or wrong. Covert operations, active anti-terrorist agencies, and personal data collection are important in the era of asymmetric warfare, and trust deserves to be formalized as legal policy. If the media bring facts to light that kill trust, the license expires.

There are no absolute liberties. Different liberties remain in dynamic equilibrium. Thus, one's freedom of speech is constrained by

144

some other's freedom from defamation. Mass media freedom is limited in wartime for national security purposes. The right to privacy can be violated by a court with probable cause. In times of peril, when terrorists seek weapons of mass destruction, the balance should be tilted to freedom of life. There is no absolute protection for freedom of life, since the law of marginal utility comes into play and curtails other liberties. The problem is to find the balance without creating a police state with more security but fewer chances to enjoy it. That is where public control comes in. The West is far from fascist repression today. On the contrary, freedom of speech and privacy are taken to extremes that pose a potential threat to the freedom of life.

Citizens ordinarily do not have even a marginal use for extremes of freedom. They do not need freedom to incite to murder, to collect money for terrorists, or to cross borders illegally. They do not need to visit the Afghan mountains or own a machine gun. Liberty taken to the extreme becomes its opposite. Extreme liberties are useful only to terrorists and their supporters, run against vital interests of the rest of population, and should be removed.

The Israeli experience suggests that even given great license, her secret security agencies cannot contain terror. Yes and no. Yes, in that freedom of life cannot be absolute. Short of turning the country into a police station, the possibility of assault will always be there. Israel can only try to reduce the possibility at reasonable economic and moral cost to society. No, in several senses. The bureaucracy rides Mossad and Shin Beth. The situation calls for a return to an earlier *modus operandi*, relying on several smaller, less accountable, less politicized agencies able to make the necessary security decisions. Israeli security services are burdened by constraints—no pervasive data collection, overwhelming concern for civilian collateral damage, and impediments to attacking subversive elements. Still, Israel's security services foil several attempts for every one carried out and publicized.

Deal with WMD terrorism reasonably

No security measures can contain terrorism completely. That should be evident from the Israeli experience, where a tiny country with a very security conscious population cannot prevent every terrorist act. Tightened airport security in Israel only sent the terrorists to other weak spots, like nightclubs and buses. When the border with Gaza was sealed, terrorists crossed from the West Bank. Like people who evade taxes, terrorists always circumvent security. The offense stays one step ahead of the defense, which reacts. The only good security is pro-active, pre-emptive: attack the terrorists before they attack you.

Isolating the Arabs in the occupied territories and segregating Israeli Arabs would be useful but not a way to prevent terrorism. Terrorists can use mail bombs with GPS receivers detonating before security checks, transit cargo containers, and cruise ships docking at Israeli ports. The Arabs are rich enough to hire mercenary terrorists, and circumvent restrictive visa regime. They can continuously strike Israelis abroad until they stop traveling or local businesses stop accommodating them. The good news is that Jewish terrorist groups, should any appear, would deliver their blows even more ingeniously, forcing accommodation from Arab governments.

Since Israel cannot eradicate terrorism completely, she must limit it as much as possible. Problems could be turned into competitive advantages. Being the first to deal with "the war of the future," Israel can take a leading position in the counter-terrorism devices and services sector, a market that will be at least the equal of the current market for conventional weapons.

Terrorists will split their limited quantity of plutonium into several minimum-size bombs for maximum reliability and political effect. A chemical, biological, nuclear terrorist strike against any Israeli target would not be the end of the country. Pervasive security will minimize the risk, and a growing population can be dispersed out of crowded centers. Israel might pioneer the infrastructure of the future: people connected by videoconferencing and data networks instead of being locked into place. While Israel should not tolerate CBN threats, she should expect terrorists to use them. The likelihood that some Muslim government will eventually opt to swap Mecca for Tel Aviv calls for unorthodox measures. Israel has to consider genetic banks and be ready to use telegenesis and cloning. Genetic engineering to increase resistance to viruses and radiation should be welcomed, not feared. When enough loose nuclear weapons make their way to terrorists, Israel should put Jewish lives above Jewish ideals, and evacuate to Australia, Arizona, or any other location that is not politically sensitive.

Paranoia about a WMD attack is counter-productive. Security services panic and run after every potential threat, chase every piece of information or disinformation. The one who does all, does nothing. Any probability is higher than zero, but the national security agency should ignore what they perceive as false alarms, even at the risk of errors of judgment with disastrous results. The doomsday scenarios are improbable, and the security agencies should concentrate instead on credible threats.

Israeli-Arab Policy

The clash of European and Arab mentalities

The Jews brought their European mentality to the Middle East, and its clash with Arab mentality is largely responsible for the war. Muslims tolerated the Christian Kingdom of Jerusalem during the crusades, and certainly some accommodation could have been made for Israel. But the Jews disregarded Middle Eastern customs and took hold by power—guerrilla warfare, foreign support, and money. Not up to crushing Arab resistance completely, Israeli power only provoked more, especially since Israel based her claims on a religion other than Islam. The violence could have been avoided. The Jews already there had good relations with their Arab neighbors and bad relations with European Jews. With so many Jews flooding in from Europe, so much blood spilled, and so many calamities befallen, a return to the *status quo ante* became impossible.

Arabs tolerated the Jews before the 1920s when the notion of an Israeli state appeared. Muslims persecuted Jews far less than Christians up to then. The conflict is between the Middle Eastern and European cultures and not about religion or territory. The Arabs previously gave in to territorial manipulation quietly. The British drew the political map of the Arab world the way they wanted it. Though outsiders tend to see Arabs as a coherent unity, they do not see themselves that way. The usual explanation for the ease with which the British operated—that they only subdivided a single nation—is wrong. The way Arabs removed from pan-Muslim ideology and politically ambitious Arab rulers see it, land was taken from some and given to others, and the reason for their compliance lies elsewhere. The British understood their mentality, similar to the European mindset centuries ago. They rode in on military power, arrogant but respectful, treating the Arabs as friends and allies; the people on the scene learned Arabic and adopted the local dress. The Russians ruled Central Asia with a heavy hand but with little direct involvement, thus in a sense respectfully. Jews did exactly the opposite: they came weak, running from European persecution, and showed no respect for the locals. If this were not enough, the Israelis pontificated and moralized, assuring the Arabs that dispossession was a blessing. Had they planned for two millennia, they could not have made their return more difficult and obnoxious.

A peaceful solutions must accommodate the Arab mentality

A peace settlement must accommodate the Middle Eastern mentality and the way things are done in the region. Israelis should admit that they provoked the war, by trying to impose European ideas and *modus operandi* on an indigenous culture. They acted from the colonialist assumption of European superiority, especially ironic for the Jews many Europeans despised. The Arabs smelled the lie and turned their hatred of foreigners onto the Israelis, unmitigated by their respect for Europeans. The possibility of accommodation retreated into the future.

Worse, Israeli Jews, with all their political analysts, historians, and psychologists, still do not recognize their behavioral incompatibility. Why are the British and, to a lesser extent, the French welcomed in the countries they colonized until recently, where they committed atrocities far worse than Israel's persecution of Arabs? The reason is simple: people forgive power when respect accompanies it. Arabs see Israel as a powerless American proxy, humbly suing for peace, vacillating between fear and neurotic bravery—and despising, not respecting, her antagonists.

Only a culturally and economically appealing empire can keep conquered people happy. Scores of monotheist Jews settled in pagan Rome both before and after the revolt of 132 C.E. Unlike the Mexicans, who lost a third of their territory to the United States, Arabs will never accept Israeli domination so long as her ideology is anti-Arab. The official Israeli animosity to Arabs is still more puzzling when Israel has the opportunity to operate from biblical posture of seeing the Arabs as cousins of the Jews. Israeli propaganda should paint them as Israel's closest and best neighbors, facing the infidel world with Israel, even if that would look disingenuous in light of Israel's deeds. Few care about deeds; most get sidetracked on words. A lie cannot stand forever, but while it does, Israel could befriend the Arabs.

There is another option: present Jews as *dhimmi* who need their Arab brothers' support. To such an appeal, Arabs would respond with military guarantees and perhaps money. Jewish communities flourished in the Muslim world without military duty or burdensome taxes for centuries. Whether Israelis would sacrifice their self-respect to achieve that solution is a matter of choice.

Jews should respect Arabs and demand respect from them

The line between cautious respect and hatred is thin. Power and cruelty provoke both. Indeed, powerlessness engenders aggression and anti-Semitism. It is tempting and probably necessary to use terror in response to anti-Israeli organizations, which abound in Muslim countries, anything from defaming their leaders to blowing up their offices. But is Israel's harsh reaction to acts of terror and insubordination enough? No. Current policy only provokes more Arab hatred and resolve to strike back, either openly or in terrorist acts. To earn respect, Israel must show herself strong, regardless of American help.[107] She must be fair and respectful with her enemies. Most

---

[107] Israel does not need to refuse American aid but rather to demonstrate that she can make war on her own, by introducing more local-made weapons which, though perhaps less effective than the best American ones, would still be better than those the Arabs possess. The doctrine of the first use of nuclear weapons can also undermine the myth of Israeli dependence on

of all, she must stop vacillating between asking for peace and proclaiming far-reaching territorial objectives with the ephemeral bravery the tactical victory of 1967 brought.

Arabs respect force and honor. Israel must become aware of signs of Arab disrespect for Israel, including mistreatment of her citizens, absence of her flags at international conferences in Arab countries, and concessions to terrorists. Unless Israel presents herself as a superpower, Arabs will not treat her so. They do not want an affectionate cousin—unless that cousin is strong. Training, military or otherwise, counts. Military personnel, often narrow-minded, are vulnerable to technical indoctrination and loyal to the system that educated them. Training enemies is not a risk. To begin with, Arabs know the Israeli army's tactics. The Russians and the Germans studied in each other's military schools before WWII, but they used different tactics and achieved very different results.[108] If Israel offered to train them, the Arab military would become accustomed to Israel, know the people better, and see that Arabs and Israel need not be enemies.

Divide the Arabs

Instead of unwittingly uniting the Arabs into a common enemy, Israel should divide them. The first step would be to stop using the word *Arab* in the media and replace it with *Palestinian*. Israel should treat other Arabs better than she treats Palestinians. Current policy is the opposite. Israel gives Palestinians visa-free entry, labor permits, and a common market. She should cooperate with distant Muslim nations like Bangladesh and Pakistan who might be lured into collaboration if offered control of the Islamic shrines in Jerusalem. Israel could stir up conflict among Muslims by agreeing to transfer the administration of Islamic shrines to a representative body of all Islamic countries, including the non-Arab ones. That would channel the discussion away from religion and onto the political plane.

Central Asia's oil and gas reserves position it as new Saudi Arabia, a gravity center of the Islamic world. Untainted with supporting foreign terrorism, in need of help to counter the terrorists at home, less xenophobic, these countries are better partners for the West than Arabs. Rising nationalism need not deter the West: it is a viable alternative to Islamism. Israel has no quarrel with the Turkish and Persian peoples of Central Asia who are in any case less politically active than other Muslims. Israel needs to secure the cooperation of rulers, not of entire nations. The West and Israel have a chance to influence former Soviet Muslim states which are almost entirely secular after years of communist rule and now apt to

---

the U.S. But a strong economy is the most important factor in gaining international respect.

[108] The Russians soon killed almost all their officers who participated in joint studies.

embrace either Islamic or Western culture. Their governments need political and military assistance to deal with local, but foreign supported, Islamic insurgents and agitators. Israel could be either an American or a Russian proxy; the choice is hers. Russia would offer less money but more obsolete arms, which Israel could pass to her clients; America, more political support and cultural attraction. America recognizes Russian interests in the region, so Israel might want to side with Russia. Israel needs closer relations with Russia and therefore with France anyway,[109] and Central Asia presents a good opportunity for cooperation. Turkey, with which Israel extensively cooperates in military affairs, also has vested interests in those countries and would welcome further Israeli involvement, especially since joint expansion there with Israel would mean United States license for extending Turkish influence—about which Washington is hesitant.

Unlike Arab Egypt, Persian Iran cannot dominate Dar al-Islam on its own, though it strives to, and offers an opportunity for balance of power politics. America cannot keep its assistance secret, and France would be too proud of the *rapprochement* to hide it. Iran will prefer Israel for clandestine aid. Arrogant Persians look down on Arabs, and Iran is more open to the West than other large Middle East countries, including Egypt. Persians, unlike Arabs, are long post-nomadic, have some work ethic, respect education and property, and thus are poised for economic advance. They were historically friendly to Jews. Iran without fundamentalists, a development possible soon, might be Israel's best Muslim friend.

Israel should support Arab insurgents. The Middle East, many mini-states fighting one another with limited military resources, may be a safe place for Israel. She could become their arbiter and when after prolonged internal strife the region achieves unification, Israel would be an integral part of the political landscape, respected instead of suspected.

The mirror image of Middle East "Afghanization," states disintegrating into a web of warring clans, would be the proliferation of anti-Israel terrorist groups harbored by local warlords. Strong Arab governments are better equipped to suppress terrorists, but the combined pressures of democratization and fundamentalism will likely dismantle the current Arab regimes or weaken them so they will not be able to suppress terrorist support. With the Arab states failing, Israel could strike at terrorist bases lacking effective sovereign protection.

---

[109] Israel's shift to the United States during Kissinger's administration alienated France and prompted it to forge closer ties with Islamic states. Israel's move was unnecessarily direct and offensive to France which had supported Israel for many years. Current good relations with Germany could help Israeli *rapprochement* with France. Otherwise, EU would further tie up with Palestinians, replacing the Soviet sponsor and inhibiting Israeli retaliation.

Arab regimes and fundamentalist clerics use anti-Israeli rhetoric to identify their domestic opponents' progressive views with the Israeli agenda or Western culture in general. Calling domestic opponents a fifth column was a standard tactic in the U.S.S.R. Such accusations are impossible to disprove, and Israel must learn to use them. After the U.S.S.R. accused hordes of innocent people of imperialist conspiracy, their successors cozied up to the Western powers and in fact established the *rapprochement* they were earlier falsely accused of. Israel, acting through European proxies, should contact Arab dissidents: the Shiites, the few moderate Islamists, democratizers of any hue, even socialists, and offer international fraternal assistance.

Fighting Israel is the Arabs' only military goal today. Israel should offer them other targets. She could sponsor a Christian state in Lebanon. Syria, which does not want to see Lebanon become a rival Muslim state, would support the idea, and Syria's Christians would welcome a Christian state nearby. Such a state could not be absorbed into Greater (Muslim) Syria and would check Syrian expansionism. Or Israel could stir up Christian-Muslim hostilities throughout the Middle East, and then pose as arbiter. She could incite Christian radicals to attack Muslim shrines to retaliate for Islamic terrorist attacks in the West. Yet another option is to support the Shia minority and the Kurds who are genetically close to Jews.

Sabotage oil exports

Arabs are important in the modern world only because they have oil. Without it they have no economic value. The Arabs' geopolitical importance has declined ever since the Portuguese found the water route to India and without oil is minuscule in the age of airplanes and missiles. Only oil props the Arab states up.

During the Cold War, the Arabs were pampered and rewarded to get them to keep the international oil market stable in case of international conflict. Today oil firms lobby the Western governments for irrational regional involvement from corporate self-interest. Therefore, Israel should work at opening Russian and Asian oil production concessions for Western companies to take their attention off the Arab world. Bringing Western oil producers to non-O.P.E.C. oil regions will help lower prices and Arab income.

Even the Arabs' importance as oil suppliers is often exaggerated. All they have done is raise prices. Russia and other Israel-neutral countries can meet all the demand for oil. A boycott of the Arab oil cartel might lower prices from their current monopolistic levels, unrelated to the cost of extraction, and arranging an international boycott is not so difficult. Israel would find allies among various consumer and ecologist groups, anti-corporate movements, and citizens concerned with lobbying and transparency, perhaps also among special interests, like automotive firms. A consensus among oil importers would be desirable though not critical. Arab oil sales finance the war against Israel, and Israel should hamper them with military means.

While the U.S.S.R. would have opposed Israeli aggression against Arab oil facilities, Russia likely would not. Oil producers influence the Russian government both through the conventional corruption and state tax revenues. Those producers have a stake in opening the American oil market and would lobby the Russian government to support, or at least tolerate, Israeli disruption of Arab oil sales. Recent Arab attempts to enter the liquefied petroleum gas market put them on a collision course with mighty Gazprom, Russia's biggest corporation and a major gas supplier. Until the second Iraqi war, Russian hopes for Iraqi oil concessions would have blocked that policy, but now the Russian companies are all in for war against the Arab oil countries. Russian oil and gas producers can pressure their government to support Israeli attacks on Arab oil infrastructure, especially in Saudi Arabia, which openly supports Chechen insurgents. Islamic terrorism in Russia will drive the Russian government to closer relations with Israel who alone has significant experience in antiterrorism.

A few targeted terrorist actions against tankers and pipelines would stop exports. In 2002, Al Qaeda made an appeal to Muslims for intelligence about American oil company pipelines, so they are already implicated. Iraqi insurgents have attacked the oil infrastructure ever since the American invasion. Israel need not claim laurels for the attacks.

The legendary Arab wealth is a chimera: if their current income drops, Arab leaders will not spend on useless weaponry, and the largest Arab investments are vulnerable. Financial scams could be more effective than sabotaging civic structures. Wrecking Islam's economic base is the best military policy. Israel should dedicate more funds to sabotaging her enemies and spare the Israeli Defense Force.

Unhindered development of nuclear power will reduce the oil demand. Israel should mobilize scientists and media to disprove the science fiction of the dangers of nuclear power plants. Ecologists could lobby to prohibit cars with combustion engines in Western city centers, switching to electric cars. With oil pushed out, Muslims will fall into oblivion.

Policy toward Palestine and Israeli Arabs

Only cruelty can instill fear in poor people

Deterrence works only with people who value themselves. Poor people who live in camps, like the Palestinians, do not fear missile attacks, which rarely target civilian homes. The futility of bombing paupers was demonstrated in Egypt, Lebanon, and Palestine, where bombardment was hardly noticeable amid the pervasive poverty.

Increasing the brutality to scare them is one option. Another is making them richer to make brutality more threatening. Israel could threaten rich Palestinians and destroy their villas instead of villages. Wealthy Arabs would pressure people to stop supporting the terrorists. An international public relations campaign, shaming other Arabs for not helping their Palestinian brethren, could force them to pay for building an affluent society in Palestine. A civil infrastructure built by other Arabs in Palestine would be a target for Israeli retaliation. Affluent societies are not prone to terrorism. Fruitful employment reduces the propensity to war, while poverty and unstructured free time foster aggression. Welfare engenders spongers with plenty of time for radicalism, and Israel should push the relief organizations from Palestine.

Saddam killed many more Kurds than Israel has killed Palestinians and razed villages while moving inhabitants to concentrations camps. That policy did not quench the resistance. Violence is a mode, not a policy, and is only an important auxiliary to relocation.

Israel has no interest in making Arabs rich

Imagine Rome supporting Carthage with grain shipments, temple-building technology, and conferences on Greek philosophy. What has changed in human nature or war objectives? Why should Israel help Arabs attain prosperity?

Two extremes are safe for Israel. Permanent low-level intra-Arab strife is one; a stable, prosperous Middle East is the other. The question is how to cross the danger zones leading to either pole. While a prosperous environment would be better in the long run, Arabs would need decades to build a just society, and Israel would be in serious danger all the way, especially as Arab state governments get rich enough to afford aggression. Intra-Arab strife can be created much more quickly and would relieve Israel of most of the current threat. Indeed, even if Israel talked somebody into building factories in the Arab world, the terrorists would sabotage them, scare people off, and keep them poor—a perfect recruiting base.

Israel should not try to buy Arab goodwill. People do not thank those who help them, especially if they detect self-interest in their benefactors, but rather denigrate donors to esteem themselves. Benevolence increases demand, and failure to meet it generates resentment. The

Palestinians, economically the fastest-growing non-oil Arab group in the Middle East, support the *intifada*, although it impoverishes them and kills thousands.

Giving the Palestinians temporary jobs in Israel would create an immigration problem not unlike America's with Mexican illegal immigrants. A ban on Palestinian immigration might not work just now but is the best long-term solution. Isolating Palestinian Arabs does not preclude overall economic cooperation with Muslims. The hundreds of thousands of Arabs who work in Israel and sell farm produce are economically expendable and can be replaced. Israel needs only a few, financially viable Arabs. An electronic fence would show the Palestinians that Israel wants to forget about them and their "state" and its problems. They should be barred from Israel for any reason.

No country cares about its poor neighbors' job opportunities, and Israel has nothing to do with the Palestinians' problems. They are responsible for their own lives. Israelis turned deserts and swamps into a garden without help and is not obliged to help anyone. The biblical injunction is to do no harm, not to curry favor by helping people—and certainly not to build another nation's economy.

Israel doesn't need to promote wealth in Palestine

Whether Israel decides to annex the West Bank or give it away, there is no reason to help the Palestinians. Subsidies to the Palestinian Authority are nothing but blackmail, just like Soviet grain shipments to Germany before World War II. Israel has no business whatsoever pensioning Palestinians and should not require Israeli employers to give them pension benefits. Transfer whatever money the Histadrut has accumulated to a Palestinian administration to steal. Better still, use pension funds to compensate Israeli victims of terrorists.

Economic aid is wrong; people have to prosper by themselves. Many rich Arabs are potential aggressors. Assistance only sharpens inequities and makes Arab peasants jealous of Israel. Israel should give away only intangible know-how to better her enemies' lives.[110] They will always be enemies, as a poll taken after 9/11 showed: in spite of American military aid, Kuwait and Saudi Arabia showed the highest support for the terrorists. Neither nations nor individual people like to accept kindness and assistance from the rich and powerful. People naturally resent gifts from richer people unless the giver seems to care for the recipient genuinely.

---

[110] Even though teaching Arabs would foster competition with Israeli farms, especially so since Arab labor is cheaper in the P.A. than in Israel, technology transfer is probably feasible. Competitiveness depends on the ability to upgrade skills continuously. Weak local competition from Arab farms would be another inducement for developing Israeli agricultural technology.

Arabs would see Israeli help as a payoff for earlier transgressions, meant to buy their silence in future confrontations.

An impoverished Palestinian Authority is good for Israel. People despise it, and poverty fosters emigration. Any Palestinian state within borders agreeable to Israel had better be wealthy to resist terrorist or fundamentalist propaganda. A Palestinian state, however, will not be wealthy, but rather a gigantic inner city living on foreign aid and thriving on crime.

There is a difference between the wealth a nation creates with work and fortuitous wealth from oil or foreign aid. Natural wealth enriches all strata of society, helping people move from political radicalism to tolerance, since everyone must practice mutual tolerance to preserve and enjoy the fruits of their labor. Wealth suppresses radicalism. On the contrary, poor people put up with intolerance among themselves and practice it with others. Envious paupers fill their empty hours with radical politics and religion. Israel should welcome natural wealth in Arab countries, but none is in sight.

Israel might try to find supporters among Westerners and rich Arabs for some kind of Marshall Plan for poor Arab countries. Though most Arabs are unprepared for life in a modern economy, the plan would have other positive effects at no cost to Israel. It would show the West's goodwill. It would create a local bourgeoisie concerned with preserving its wealth, conservative and wary of terrorists likely to dry up the cash flow. It would create targets for Israeli retaliation. It would channel some of the radicals' and the *mullahs'* energy into lobbying for more money. It would strengthen Arab dictatorships by funding growth in the governmental sector of the economy and loosen the grip of the meddlesome Islamic charities. Still, Arabs have neither the work ethic nor the education that let Germany and Japan recover quickly after 1945. No more than a small percentage of the Arab population could be employed in agriculture, with another 20-30% in other primitive industries. Assistance must start with technical education. Very likely, educated Palestinians would emigrate in search of better jobs.

A Palestinian state offers benefits

One peaceful option is to give Palestinians their own state unconditionally, transfer the relevant territories to them and withdraw. The Jewish settlements could stay with administrative autonomy under Palestinian jurisdiction. As a sovereign state, Palestine would be hard pressed to control violence and protect the settlements. Bureaucratic states are often more tolerant than their founders, and Palestine would exercise restraint with the Jewish settlements since they have a powerful sponsor next door.

Israel could lobby the international community to declare Palestine a terrorist state. The nations that created Israel seem to think that, statehood achieved, she should be content and grateful—and submissive in the face of aggression. That attitude explains their disregard of Israel's security when they pressure her to give in to Arab demands. The same attitude will emerge toward a Palestinian state, making it easy for Israel to push it around.

Israel will be free to retaliate against a Palestinian state, not restraining herself to police actions. The Palestinian leadership will no longer be able to avoid its responsibility to maintain order in its own territory. If it does not, Israel will have sufficient cause to dismantle the failed state on her borders. The whole population will be legally responsible for terrorist actions originating in Palestine. Israel will not need to search out terrorists nests but will be free to strike any target within the state in retaliation. She will need only to show world public opinion that the Palestinians tolerate terrorists. Complicity in aggression is an obvious *casus belli*.

Even annexation might be easier dealing with a sovereign state. World opinion today sides with the suffering Palestinians in the territories, but with a sovereign Palestinian state, world opinion might take the Israeli side in a conflict between two states, one failed and riddled with terrorist nests. Israel must now ask permission of the international community and the Arab powers to annex land. With a Palestinian state, she could force the government to make concessions far more readily than she can extort them from a civilian population the West pampers. Since many Palestinian factions, including perhaps the P.L.O. mainstream, did not reject the 1974 Phased Plan but rather accepted a reduced Palestine from which to attack Israel, Palestinian asymmetric aggression is likely to become a reality. If Palestine blows her chance at statehood after the West's efforts to provide it, the world community will not object if Israel swallows it to repel aggression. The West objected to Israel annexing the lands taken from Syria and Egypt after preempting their aggression in 1967, but the case is different with Palestine: insignificant state, no Soviet sponsor.

Establishing a Palestinian state would make control and annexation easier for another reason. While Israel is the Palestinians' only enemy today, factions would grow up at once within their own state. With a little support from Israel, Palestine would plunge into turmoil, and a collaborationist government might sign a peace treaty that includes annexation. Quisling's plan failed only because Germany overextended the fronts. With peacefully indifferent Israel, in the absence of an external enemy to cement national resolve, internal strife would push Palestinians to emigrate.

Necessary cruel steps to annexation

On the other hand, if Israel decides to annex the territories immediately, then Palestinian industry and infrastructure, including medicine and education, must be annihilated in response to terrorist acts, forcing people to emigrate. Yet that solution is not economically feasible.

The cost to Israel of a drawn out conflict would offset any profit from the territories. If Israel categorically rejects the creation of a Palestinian state, Palestinians hostility might cool over time, provided subsequent Israeli governments hold firm and refuse to resume the concessions game. At any rate, Israel should not appear willing to transfer the territories, unless she does it now and without conditions.

Administrative autonomy for the Palestinians within Israel will not work, but Israel could create a federal state of warring cantons. Yugoslavia, Ireland, and Chechnya prove that such entities are unstable; yet world opinion decries state repression of minorities.

The only alternative to a Palestinian state is to expel the Palestinians. Morality aside, that solution is more reliable, more certain, cheaper, and more effective than trying to make Arabs loyal Israelis or good neighbors.

Frightening the Palestinians into submission is impossible as a long-term policy while the United Nations, the mass media, the human-rights watchdogs, and popular opinion are around. Thus, repression must be swift to settle the problem once and for all by driving the Palestinians out and dispersing them. Any other policy will cost Israel dearly in lives, materiel, money, and public support. Any firm policy is better than none. Even if Israel decides to keep the territories and the Palestinians on them, she should say so, pass laws, shoot extremists, give limited citizenship and work to the rest, and let them get along with no hope of national sovereignty, exactly as other Israeli Arabs do.

Theoretically, there is another way to make a subjugated people accept new rulers: benevolence. But walking the thin line between kindness and weakness is beyond Israeli politicians. Benevolence to previously repressed people would bring in destructive welfare and affirmative action.

Downgrade Israeli Arabs' citizen rights

The Torah's requirement to love strangers in the midst of Israel refers to proselytes, people who live in the Promised Land according to the laws of the Torah, not to superficially loyal potential enemies. The *oppression* of aliens the Torah prohibited is that of the Hebrews in Egypt: they should not be arbitrarily enslaved. They do not have the same rights as Jews, and building shrines to idols is explicitly prohibited.

Jews in Arab countries lived in isolation, in part because of Muslim reservations about religious aliens. In the 20th century, most Arab governments and populations were hostile to the Jews under their jurisdiction. Israel should return the favor to Israeli Arabs, showing them passive hostility and refusing to employ them.

The Arabs restricted Jews' religious and property rights for 1,300 years where they could. Jews had no basic rights in the Arab world: they could not testify against Muslims in court nor work in the bureaucracy theoretically (though that provision was not always upheld), and many

Islamic jurists refused to recognize the murder of a Jew as a capital offense—unlike the murder of a Muslim. As recently as the 1990s, the rights of the small remnant of a 2,500-year old Jewish community in Syria were severely restricted, and few Jews survived in other Muslim countries.

Saudi Arabia, the flagship of fundamentalism, prohibits non-Islamic worship on its territory; Israel is entitled to do the same regarding Islamic worship in her land, especially since Torah explicitly dictates such a policy toward other religions. When Sadat retracted the Egyptian government's legal protection of Christians to strengthen his shaky political position as leader of the Muslim league, Israel should have retracted her protection of Muslims. When those born in the United Arab Emirates, even in the third generation, are not accorded citizenship if they are not from the original local tribes, there could be no objection to Israel downgrading her Arabs from citizens to resident aliens. When Egypt prohibits non-Muslims from the Hussein mosque, Israel should banish non-Jews from the Temple Mount. Egypt interned about 3,000 Jews without trial after the 1956 war; Israel can apply that approach to hostile Palestinians. Reciprocal vengeance for recent offense is ethically acceptable and serves Israel's practical needs.

Israelis might decide to help the Palestinians develop and become good neighbors, but that has nothing to do with Israeli-Arab citizenship. Resettling them in the territories or in Jordan would help as much. A peaceful neighbor is secondary to preserving Israel's Jewish identity. A national religious identity is neither a new nor a uniquely Israeli concept. Saudi Arabia is exclusively Muslim, and such nations were common until populations became too intermingled to maintain ethnic exclusivity.[111] Political correctness moved white Americans to assimilate blacks only a few decades ago, and many white citizens are still not color-blind. Unlike other people, the Jewish *raison d'être* is to be different. After two millennia of waiting and working to re-establish the Jewish state, to see it populated by Muslims is bizarre. Israel incomprehensibly subsidizes Arabs, gives them free infrastructure, education, insurance, and family benefits.

If nothing is done, the Arabs' birth rate will make them a majority, or at least the largest coherent faction in the Knesset, in a few decades. The more the Arabs breed, the harder it will be to get rid of them. Even if their growth rate slows, Arabs already produced enough youth to almost square with the Jews in fifty years. Israel has no guilt before Israeli Arabs. She did not ship their ancestors from Africa or systematically kill them while colonizing. Israeli Arabs do not suffer discrimination but on the contrary have tax advantages over Jews. The Muslim economic input in Israel is almost zero, perhaps less, considering what the government pays to educate them, house them, and take care of them. Israeli Arabs enjoy high incomes

---

[111] Jews retained their identity in exile, but they only nominally lived in mixed states – rather in isolated Jewish communities. Jewish ghettos in Israel is not an option.

and social guarantees compared to their brethren elsewhere. Israeli Muslims generally do not serve in the I.D.F. and defend the state. Yet they constantly demand accommodation of Israel's enemies. Israeli Arabs are not proper citizens in any normal sense, and Israel has no obligation to them. Preferences like exemptions from taxes and conscription and the official status of the Arabic language must be rescinded; subsidies and free education must cease. If Arabs do not want to serve the military in support services or public works, they should pay higher taxes, as Jews have to Arabs for centuries.[112] Making Arabs serve in I.D.F., and engaging them in clashes with West Bank Palestinians is the best way to force the youth to emigrate or betray their brethren, causing a major intra-Arab conflict. Serving in infantry with light weapons and prohibited from taking weapons home, Arabs will not subvert the I.D.F. Israelis should not, however, deceive themselves about friendly Arabs. Bedouins now cooperate with Israel because she pays and protects them in clashes with settled Arabs. Neither can she count on Druzes, an odd crowd that worships the bizarre and murderous medieval caliph Hakim.

Israeli Arabs are not inherently bad or disloyal, but Israel cannot accept their political objectives, suppressed for the time being because economic advancement is more important for poor Arabs. Unlike American Indians who do not want sovereignty, Israeli Arabs will always have the stimulating example of their brethren living independently. Unlike American Muslims, they are contemptuous of the dominant host culture. People are irrational: Israeli Arabs will eventually develop nationalist aspirations and trade them for the economic benefits they enjoy as loyal Israelis.

A state is first a community of neighbors sharing basic values and ready to support each other, an impossible state of affairs between Israeli Jews and Israeli Arabs. Police and payoffs could quash some of the discontent and factionalism, but Israel will never be a U.S.-style melting pot. The Jews do not want to assimilate the Arabs. Many of the Jews in Israel could live better elsewhere and are there by choice for the strong sense of national identity that outweighs economics. A large Arab population threatens that identity. The legacy of Arab hostility would linger for decades after any peace settlement. Israel with Arabs is as odd as Yugoslavia, and an Arab population explosion will eventually force the question.

---

[112] While the exact amount of *jizyah*, the tax imposed oh *dhimmis*, is disputed, the authoritative book of Muwatta, written by Mohammed's contemporary Malik, in 17.24.46 requires 10% of the investment for itinerant traders. Assuming an average net profit rate of 20% in the pre-modern period , that corresponds to a verbal tradition of 50% income tax, besides land taxes and various humiliating obligations, like stationing Arab army horses in synagogues. Failure to pay taxes resulted in death.

Australia, the United States, Japan, and other civilized countries repressed their aborigines. Beyond a few sops, Americans do not care about their Indians, nor imagine restituting the country to them. Relocation of indigenous population is the only way the states are created.

The relocation should be as stress-free as practically possible. Arabs must have plenty of time to sell their real estate, with the government as the last-resort fair buyer. Israel might procure residence permits and citizenship for Palestinians in other countries, primarily in Asia and Latin America. Israel might offer some subsidies and loan guarantees. The Arabs' pension savings with Israeli agencies should be disbursed in full. Israel might even subsidize their children's education in the new countries to compensate for the free education in Israel. Palestinians who resettle on the West Bank—if Israel concedes to a Palestinian state—should get perpetual leases of large tracts of agricultural land Jews own there; that property is impractical in independent Palestine anyway. To soften the transition, Israel could refuse citizenship only to future Arab children.

Short of driving the Israeli Arabs out, Israel should withdraw their political franchise. Following the Torah's lead—of cursing idolaters to the fourth generation—Israel should enfranchise Arabs only after four generations of demonstrated loyalty and revoke the franchise the minute Arab loyalty comes into question. Since a rebellious relative could likely be found in every family, their traditional dependence on extended family arrangements would teach them to police each other and stifle disloyal activity of whatever kind. If not, whole families would be expelled. Such collective responsibility makes sense, both because poor Arabs generally adhere to family decisions and because dissidents usually incite their families and rely on them for assistance.

Israeli Arabs could be given *dhimmi* status with all the rights of resident aliens: participation in local but not national elections, a generous approach compared to the policy of most Arab states which exclude non-Arabs from citizenship or property ownership, even if they live in the country for generations. Israeli Arabs would have almost the full spectrum of rights and be able to own or lease land. Even such rights are dangerous, because Muslim countries could finance Israeli Arabs to lease the land in Jerusalem, reversing the method the Jews employed to create their state. Non-Jews may be prohibited from beneficial lease of politically sensitive land, but the Supreme Court would strike that restriction as racist. Governments use the doctrine of immanent domain to buy real estate of public interest. A Jewish state has great public interest in keeping the land Jewish. Israel might buy all the real estate belonging to Arabs at a fair price.

Since the Arabs want to stay in Israel only for the economic advantages, an economic boycott is worth considering. Most Israeli Arabs work as farmers or hired labor. If Jews refused their produce or labor, they would have to emigrate. Such a policy is no different from common "buy local" patriotic consumer programs.

The Arab birthrate means their percentage of Israeli voters will increase, a process exacerbated by the influx of other non-Jewish immigrants. Any generous policy with aliens undermines the homogenous character of the Jewish state. Some argue that even with a large proportion of non-Jews, Israel would be different from Diaspora settlements in one important respect: the Jews own the country and write the laws. Nothing could be farther from the truth. Democracy gives the country to all its citizens, not just Jews, and as there are non-Jews in the Knesset, Jews do not write the laws. They may have a majority, but that is only a quantitative difference. Jews influence legislation in many countries. In the fragmented Knesset, a small but coherent group of Arabs has disproportional influence. Jewish politicians form majorities with the ultra-orthodox parties to avoid collaborating with the Arabs, but as the demography shifts, that will not always be possible.

Israel is not a democratic state in the usual meaning of the term, like the United States, but rather a state of a single national ethos following a single religious practice—not rigorously but sufficiently enough to be persecuted for centuries. Some try mistakenly to liken this situation to Nazism, but Israel actually embodies a liberal ideal: an autonomous community. As philatelist clubs accept only philatelists, a Jewish nation may accept only Jews.[113] A history of repressions justifies the drive for homogeneity.

To qualify the difference between Judenrein Germany and Israel without Arabs from the position of imminent threat is wrong. Germans were sure the Jews posed a mortal threat to them, while Israeli Arabs may opt for the Jewish state. The desire to live in relative cultural homogeneity is what matters.

For centuries, Europeans wanted the Jews to go. "Jews, go to Palestine" was a common graffiti ten years before the State of Israel was founded. Nazis tried to exterminate the Jews by relocating them to Polish marshes, and Russians in 1953 prepared to drive the remaining Jews to Siberia. The Jews moved to Palestine, drained marshes and cultivated the

---

[113] Many states practice national exclusivism. Athenian democracy granted citizenship only to the descendants of the original inhabitants. From 1803 into the 1960s, it was illegal in France to give children Breton names. Many fringe religious groups face government opposition in most countries. Anti-Semitic propaganda is pandemic in Muslim world. Even America, the least xenophobic of all, sets ethnic immigration quotas. Core ethnic groups want to dominate.

Germany facilitated immigration of ethnic Germans, but not other peoples, from Poland, Russia, and other countries without evoking charges of racism. All states practice territorial exclusivism, and offer more rights to people born within their boundaries than to foreigners. How is religious or national exclusivism worse than the exclusivism defined by arbitrary and ever-changing borders?

local equivalent of tundra. They worked the place the world exiled them to, the land largely uninhabitable by any standards. Now the world finds it too much that the Jews will have that tiny speck of land for themselves. Back in ghettos, pogrom mobs came to take what they deemed Jewish surplus; now the world demands that the Jews share with Arabs the country they built from marshes and sand – built with no significant help of local Arabs and fierce opposition of their brethren.

Americans live in a secure state. Police efficiently protect them. Yet many Americans move to private communities, if they can afford to. Private communities set their rules, regulate visitors, and prohibit trespassers. Wealthy Americans do not want to live near the poor. Ethnic communities often settle compactly inside cities. Why are Jews refused that basic human right – to live by themselves, without strangers among them who can live comfortablyin their state fifty miles away?

Ideally, homogenous states should seek vacant inhabitable land, but there is none. Arabs inhabited Israel sparsely when in the late nineteenth century Jews started to settle there. If the Arabs cannot push the Jews back out, the only practical choice is between a pluralist society of inimical groups or living apart, which would necessarily mean some displacement. In Israel, the displacement is about fifty miles, less than some people drive to work. The advantages of a peaceful living arrangement are worth that minor inconvenience. Arabs do not want to stay in Israel from patriotic attachment but for economic reasons. Let them build a prosperous state in the West Bank or Jordan. Re-settlement need not be violent. Emigrating Israeli Arabs should be compensated for real estate and other property. Israel could offer them abandoned Jewish settlements in the West Bank and build new infrastructure, so they would not suffer like Jewish immigrants coming to Palestine. Jews could induce Arab emigration by offering large bonuses and double the fair property value to the families moving out. Soft policies, however, would provoke harsh reaction and extend suffering; relocation should be swift and closed to argument.

Israeli Arabs who want to live in a multinational democracy, in an Islamic state, or in a secular Arab country can go where they want to go. Dislodging Israeli Arabs or Palestinians from the territories has nothing in common with the Holocaust. No one wants to kill them; they are free to go.

Israeli Arabs are a fifth column who support and vote for Israel's enemies. They will either eventually have enough votes to destroy Israel's Jewish identity, or the Jews will have to run them out. Israel might become a regular democracy of diverse ethnic groups, without the distinctive Jewishness her founders sought. With the current birth rate, Arabs could become a majority and vote Israel out of existence.[114] Hostile groups might separate and tiny Israel be cantonized.

Restricting Arabs' rights is only a temporary solution, since they can launch an anti-apartheid struggle for equality to which some weak Israeli government would surely yield. After a century of enforced institutionalized oppression of blacks, white America not only legislated full citizenship for Afro-Americans but also paid reparations in welfare and affirmative action programs. Democracy and liberalism work only in countries where all society's constituents respect one another and share similar notions of culture, education, and work. But a Jewish state cannot be an ethnically blind democracy.

Israel is a country like the Vatican, not like America. It's a minuscule country, established for religious reasons in an area of religious importance. It is sufficiently small to cause no severe dispossession of the displaced indigenous population. Israeli size makes disenfranchisement of her Arabs unnecessary; they may retain full citizenship rights in a nearby state of their own.

Successful states are monocultural because only the groups that share basic values cooperate. People with different values are unknown, unpredictable, suspected, and not trusted. Cooperation requires a degree of trust. The American culture is liberalism; people of any nation could be converted to that culture. Israeli culture is Judaism; Arabs cannot be converted to it.

Every state imposes its cultural values on citizens. A Jewish state, however, includes specifically Jewish values which non-Jews, by definition, do not welcome or participate in. Could the Jews practice those values without forcing them on others? That would relegate Israel from the Jewish state to a country no different from the United States or France: there, too, Jews can practice their religion and ethics. A Jewish state cannot treat Jews and Arabs equally. Divesting the country of Arabs is the only alternative to oppressing them.

How about the atheist Jews who do not want to live according to the specific Jewish values? Should Israel divest of them, too? Many Jews, brainwashed by socialists, may return to Jewish ethics, if not immediately to religion. Atheist Jews are ready to defend Israel and proudly stand up to the national anthem, *The Hope*. Israel could not expect that from Arabs.

Multinational states also sometimes have problems similar to Israel's, but with non-citizen immigrants—not non-Jews. There is no essential difference between a state for its citizens, not aliens, and a state for a single ethnic group, not others. It is hard to see the difference between nationalist Israel and "citizenist" France: both discourage some people from

---

[114] This will happen in a *single* generation. The number of Jewish and Arab youth in Israel in 0-14 age category is about the same. In many important locations, Arabs already constitute majority.

becoming citizens. France grants citizenship to very few, and according to particular guidelines. Israel should offer citizenship, according to its own guidelines, only to Jews to prevent the Arab population from increasing. Great Britain long ago abandoned the anchor-baby provision, which recognized everyone born in its territory as a citizen. Modern Westerners accept ethnic diversity and increasingly reject nationalism because they mixed, but the rise of a nationalist right shows that ethnic diversity troubles some. France is a state of French values, and its citizens object to aliens among them. Israel is a state of Jewish values, and she does not want Arabs in her midst. Calling Israel a Jewish state is no more racist than calling the United States a country of immigrants. The United States denies citizenship to ex-Nazis and active communists who have no designs on it; Israel is justified in denying citizenship to potentially hostile Muslims. Groups could be defined along many lines: ethnic, religious, political, military, or many others. Nation-states deliberately suppress other definitions besides artificial allegiance to a particular state. Separatist movements in places from Canada to Nigeria to the Philippines show that the citizenist definition does not work. People accept citizenism only when it runs along more powerful boundaries, like economic ideology in the United States or the political ideology in the USSR. In Israel, the only practical criterion of citizenship is Jewishness.

Nationalist resurgence is most likely. Nationalism, in fact, never entirely subsided. Governments, at the most, made it politically incorrect. Relatively few American whites associate with blacks even after decades of affirmative action, as American Blacks historically prefer their own ethnic neighborhoods and clubs, even with other avenues open to them. And Americans objected in 2006 to the Dubai Arabs operating the United States ports, though they had no problem with the British operating them. If Americans do not want Arabs to control their strategic assets, Israel might not want Arabs to control the Jewish state.

Spouses can divest of another out of dislike. Police largely control spousal violence, but terrorism, the inter-group violence, is dangerous. Nations must be able to divest of aliens they dislike. As in families, dislike need not and cannot be justified; the absence of liking suffices. People move to get new jobs; surely they will move to live in comfortably homogenous communities.

Racism calls for oppression of the ostensibly inferior ethnic groups. Unwillingness to live with strangers is entirely different. The feeling is natural. People are more comfortable among people like themselves. Democracies depend on shared values, and antagonistic groups cannot coexist in a state. Idyllic theories of ethnically egalitarian societies and political correctness persuade people to drop natural contempt of aliens and live with strangers. America will not easily assimilate Hispanics and blacks, Canada Chinese, France Muslims, and Germany Turks. The European Union objected to Turkey's membership, and Europeans are better

164

predisposed to Catholic Poles than to Muslim immigrants. Almost all countries exiled Jews. Israel is entitled to expel non-Jews if she chooses, especially if they can relocate nearby and be compensated for the property they surrender.

A population exchange resolved Turkish-Greek tensions. Relocation would have prevented the Yugoslavian war. The U.N. in 1947 prescribed both Jewish and Arab states in Palestine, not one mixed state. Israel has attracted the Jews who lived in Arab countries. Now it is the Arabs' turn to move out. Relocating the Palestinians only fifty miles would prevent the inevitable conflict that will come when Israeli Jews see their dominance threatened.

Israel was wrong to accept Arabs as citizens. That error, made under extreme duress, need not be perpetuated. Israel should revoke the Arabs' citizenship and pay them off.

Most Israelis understand that something needs to be done, but they shrink from harsh decisions. Yet, Israelis insist that theirs is a Jewish state, and implicitly discriminate against Arabs. Offending a neighbor is the worst policy, and Jewish weakness is provocative. Israeli Arabs will demand equality—and will get super-equality, like Afro-Americans in the United States. Israel will embark on the way of concessions: admitting Arabs for state employment and giving Arab Knesset members ministerial portfolios; what precludes them from claiming commanding positions in the IDF? The army might revolt and drive Arabs out of Israel. Much more likely, Jewish politicians would convince themselves that an Israeli nation that includes Arabs is as good as a Jewish nation, and forsake Judaism for Israeli democratic nationalism. The resulting assimilation and denial of Jewishness could easily lead to another holocaust. Hypocritical Israeli politicians made the country a trap for the Jews, and are posed to succeed where gentiles failed: destroying Jewish identity and abrogating the Jewish law.

The usefulness of sharia

Islamic law, *sharia*, condones many actions which seem harsh to Westerners. *Jihadi* may not kill women and children—unless they attack first, as in anti-Israeli riots. Muslim conquerors may claim all the property of the vanquished and their families; Israelis reciprocally need not compensate the refugees and may exile the subversive population. Muslims are not required to check for the particular individuals who oppose them or who do not; Israel could similarly apply collective responsibility. Muslims are admonished to fight their brethren, if rebels, and so have no excuse for tolerating terrorists.

The terrorist Abu Hajer asserted that it is perfectly legal to kill civilian Muslims who happen to be present at the scene of a military action. That, of course, is what the terrorists accuse Israel of doing. Abu Hajer's justification also applies to assaults by Israel: good Muslims go to paradise, bad ones go to hell; so if they die, there is no problem.

Sharia condones discrimination against non-Muslims. The Umayyad caliphate, the Wahhabis' model, gave no political rights to non-Arabs or even to half-breed Arabs. Why should Israel to non-Jews?

Israel can use many features of Islamic fundamentalism. Its condemnation of the state as an instrument of oppression and a promoter of inequality could undermine Arab support for their governments and foment insurrection—which would keep those governments busy with their own problems.

On other hand, Israel could search the large body of *hadith* for condemnations of terrorism and killing women and children, as well as instructions to respect Jews. Quoting the *sharia* to people who hate Israel will not change them, but some might see that they do not betray Islam by refusing to support the *jihadi*.

Create the Palestinian state in Jordan

The Hashemite dynasty in Jordan is ripe for overthrow. Democratic elections will empower a Palestinian majority; two-thirds of Jordanians are Palestinian, and Jordan is by all logic a Palestinian state. Few monarchies survive, and it is wishful thinking to hope the friendly Jordanian dynasty will last. A reckless government in Iraq or Syria might try to annex Jordan. In a war, Jordan would be of little use to Israel as a buffer; even if technically neutral, it could not stop Iraqi troops from crossing its territory.

The Jordanian dynasty is the lid on the simmering kettle of Jordanian society. The Palestinian majority resents its inadequate status. The dynasty relies increasingly on brute force and seeks both American guarantees and fundamentalist Islamic approval to shore itself up. That precarious balance will not last. If a Palestinian majority seizes power, Israel should exploit the situation while she can.

Israel should re-evaluate the earlier plan of establishing a Palestinian state in Jordan, reducing the dispute from Palestinian statehood to the inclusion of the West Bank in their state. A Palestinian state in Jordan could be viable, unlike an insultingly small state in the West Bank. Israel could promise secretly to help Palestinians stage a *Putsch* in Jordan in return for annulling Palestinian claims to Judea and Samaria. A semi-democratic, popularly supported government in Jordan would be better for the West than an unstable, unpredictable monarchy. Now is a good time to promote the coup: the Jordanian population is increasingly hostile to Western influence. Polls indicate the support sinking to 4% after the second Iraqi war. The Jordanian government listens to its subjects, even to the extent of refusing to air the Shared Values commercials designed to convince Muslims that America is after terrorists, not Islam. Jordan does not curb anti-Western propaganda in its press and universities. It accommodates Israel because it fears reprisal and the United States for protection against Iraq. With Saddam gone, Jordan has little reason to side with the United States.

The West supported Kurdish independence from Iraq—at least autonomy—but is content for Turkey to retain the territory of Turkish Kurds. The same logic applies to the Palestinians: transform Jordan, or part of it, into the Palestinian state and leave the territories in the West Bank and the Gaza strip under Israeli sovereignty. Chomsky's argument—that resettling Palestinians in Jordan is akin to suggesting Jews have their own jurisdiction in New York—is off base. Jews are not a majority in New York. Even if they were, they could not make it secede. New York is much farther from Israel than Jordan is from Palestine. Relocating a few dozen miles does not affect Palestinian national aspirations. Insisting on a separate Palestinian state in the territories is like the Jews demanding a piece of New York for an independent Jewish state, in addition to the one they have in Israel. The Jordanian option is by far the most practical solution of the Palestinian problem.

The idea has legal sanction. Everyone understood that the initial arrangement under the British mandate established a Jewish Israel in all the territory of the mandate, including Jordan, but in 1922 the Council of the League of Nations excised what was to become Jordan from the Jewish homeland. Only when a British-affiliated tribal dynasty usurped power in Jordan was it necessary to carve out additional territory for the Palestinians living on land already allocated to the Jews.

Sharia also sanctions ethnically homogenous states. Quoting the Prophet's dictum, "Let there be no two religions in Arabia," Caliph Umar relocated the Jews to Palestine and made it a preserve for non-Islamic groups in the region. Since most Islamic scholars say pious Muslims cannot live among infidels, Palestinians have no stake in the territory Umar gave to Jews—and, theoretically, to Christians as well.

A Palestinian state could be created in Southern Lebanon. Lebanon, an artificial country of perpetually warring ethnic and religious groups, cannot survive. Israel already tried to pacify that failed state—to no avail, since she acted humanely. Syrians might prove better pacificators and suppress Hezbollah, if only because the outfit promotes Lebanese nationalism. America and Israel could abstain from opposing Greater Syria's ambitions militarily in return for carving a small state for Palestinians separated from Israel by a Christian enclave, perhaps also a state. Syria could annex all of Lebanon or leave a piece to local Muslims.

Cooperation with the Palestinian authorities is not impossible. They have passed the stage of radicalism. Since the P.A. does not curb the radicals, some figured that that proved Arafat was a terrorist. In fact he was simply not up to rooting the terrorists out.[115] Like Stalin after World War II, he was worn out. He would have liked to see Israel disappear and objected

---

[115] Arafat's attempt to demilitarize the factions in Gaza led to an armed standoff, and lacking support from the I.D.F., he simply retracted his demands. Israel should destroy the terrorist facilities herself without expecting the Palestinians to do it.

to Hamas or P.I.J. doing the job only because they obstructed his political goals: a larger Palestinian state. Guerrillas threaten the Palestinian government more than Israel does and create a basis for *rapprochement* against mutual threat.

Instead of pushing the Palestinian leadership to divide its power democratically and end up with a radical Islamic government, Israel should help create a strong police state, able to deal with terrorists and keep the place from becoming a terrorist haven. The radicals could be absorbed into the politics of a Palestinian state where they will be easier to control. When the Irgun was dismantled, many fighters joined the Israeli Defense Force. At least one faction, the Fatah Hawks, has already joined the Palestinian Authority police. Israel has extensive experience building the armies of Latin American dictatorships and could do the same for a Palestinian autocrat, freeing him from dependence on fringe paramilitaries. If the paramilitaries were strong and entrenched, as they were in Colombia, Israeli could at least stir up trouble and keep Palestine distracted for years, prompting emigration. Since Israeli support would discredit a Palestinian government like nothing else, it would have to rely increasingly on Israel— and make concessions to her. That Arabs would hate Israel still more for supporting an oppressive Palestinian administration means nothing. That the Palestinian elite does not want statehood, shifting it from the focus of the struggle to the periphery of troublesome non-viable states, is also unimportant. Israel needs a stable, controlled Palestine, not necessarily a state, and should support an Arab dictator there—though not elsewhere among Arab countries. Israel would control any Palestinian dictator and keep him from buying arms to use against Israel.

Judea

The case for Judea

Israeli society is deeply split. On one hand, many believe that preserving *Eretz Israel* within the boundaries of the Promised Land is the Jew's utmost obligation. That opinion is valid, since it is based on Torah, and some degree of adherence to the scroll is that which makes Jews Jews. Others, mostly secular-minded but some deeply religious as well, believe that no territory is worth the life of a single Jew, since the commandments were given for life, not for death.

Both parties have many other valid arguments. While adherents of the *Eretz* argue that only acquiring all the Promised Land fulfills the nation's destiny, their opponents just as reasonably point to the practical impossibility of attaining that goal in the foreseeable future after Sinai went back to the Egyptians. Conquering Jordan and Iraq to the Euphrates is a long way off. If the covenant promise cannot be fulfilled now, why kill a lot of people and spend a lot of money for the territories, which have no value in themselves and, except Sinai, lack significant defense value? Opponents of the *Eretz*-now goal believe that economic growth unhindered by war would be a better source of national pride, prevent emigration, and attract Diaspora Jews to Israel.

The Israeli government vacillates between those views. One cabinet builds a tremendously expensive Bar-Lev line to protect Sinai forever;[116] another gives up the land, biblically and strategically important, for paper guarantees. One cabinet encourages and finances settlements; the next dismantles them. Such wild swings of policy indicate the relative balance between two visions of Israeli goals and the impossibility of bringing them together.

That is only natural, since anybody's worldview is just a set of axioms. Some people believe that the size of the Holy Land the Jews control is more important, while others believe that preserving life and its quality take precedence. It is almost futile to argue about axioms, which are matters of conviction.

A country, however, cannot have two mutually exclusive policies. Under pro-expansion governments, even those who do not want more territory have to fight and die for it, as well as suffer economically. Under conciliatory governments, biblical partisans watch helplessly as the government gives land away. In the long run, nobody is happy with the

---

[116] A strategically ludicrous line of fortifications on the Israeli bank of the Suez Canal, praised before 1973 as the ultimate defense against the Egyptians

government. But all involved want a coherent leadership that shares their ideals, and that goal can be achieved.

In ancient times, two Jewish entities, Israel and later Galilee, formed an economically viable, cosmopolitan state. Judea, centered in the barren hills, was content with a subsistence economy, jealously guarded religious purity, and a national consciousness. In our time, history repeats itself. Zealots flock to *kibbutzim*[117] and other settlements, where the priority is not economic development but preserving certain ideological goals and values—which many Israelis do not share. Their military and fiscal obligations to the state are also different.[118] Everything is in place for a split into two states.

Judea would encompass the contested territories, with the aim of eventual expansion into Sinai and all of *Eretz Israel*. Although Judea would not be economically self-sustaining in industry, she would get the lion's share of material support that pours into Israel from Jews around the world. Judea could defend herself without great expense and depend on Israel and the West for last-resort protection against major aggression.

Being a profoundly religious state offers advantages that secular nations do not possess. Judea would be free to clear out indigenous inhabitants. Following biblical guidelines, she could use measures otherwise unacceptable in the modern world—though the nations that decry them were themselves established in fire and blood.

As Johann Tilly put it, "States create wars, wars create states." Even ostensibly humane states fight all the time: the United Kingdom and Argentina over the Falklands Islands, Spain and Morocco over an island, the United States and Cuba in Grenada, the Coalition in Afghanistan and Iraq. Third-world countries fight to establish boundaries. Only six decades have passed since the bloodbath of two world wars, not enough to change the mentality of nations. And it did not change: the Americans bombed Hiroshima and Nagasaki, and only fear of reprisal prevented them from doing the same in Korea. The French and their allies slaughtered millions in Algeria and Indochina. Russia has killed thousands in the dispute with breakaway Chechnya. The same nations that suffered the First World War's devastation marched straight into World War II. Current restraint springs from the fear of escalation, not humane scruple.

Judea can forget the notion of civil rights and obey religious law. Unlike Israel, she can afford to stop non-Jewish immigration, directly or through inter-marriage with gentiles, and limit non-Orthodox conversions

---

[117] Communal agrarian settlements, very important in the early days of immigration but ineffective, costing Israel dearly in subsidies.

[118] Religious Jews generally do not do active military duty, a policy with flimsy theological substantiation, especially shameful because they demand confrontation with the Arabs. The clergy get government funds and numerous tax breaks.

170

and other Reformist practices, which, though compatible with modern secular values, significantly water down the Jews' religious identity.

Judea could become a classic theocracy, organized along the lines of pre-kingdom Israel ruled by the judges, giving rabbis the judicial functions of the late Second Temple period onward. She could use Talmudic law, instead of contemporary legislation. An influx of fresh ideas into the body of the Talmud, updated to accommodate present reality, would benefit the tradition and spark renewed interest in it. Judea's official language would be the beautifully powerful biblical Hebrew, not the modern garbled substitute.

Israel could withdraw from the contested territories, enjoy peace with her neighbors, and concentrate on rapid economic development. That would win her some international respect. Israel could become the dominant regional economy, replacing Switzerland, the United States, and Russia as the source of financial, technological, and military commodities and services. Western powers will not compete with her for hegemony in a Middle East plunged in incessant wars after Muslims lose the common enemy.

Relieving Israel of her military expenditures will let her work to recapture Jewish prominence in banking and trade, fundamental research and technology, and the arts.Dividing Israel into two states would not cause enmity among Jews, rather, it would eliminate the enmity currently brewing in Israel where whatever policy the government chooses displeases about half the population. The division would let either state "specialize" and limit its liability. Israel would not be responsible for Judea's expansionism, while Judea might disregard the economic consequences of its decisions.

Incompatible objectives

No Arab army threatens the survival of Israel in the 1948 borders. The people who want to expand the country to its biblical borders cannot make others fight for that goal. It is wrong to get people killed or to make them suffer economically for something they do not believe in.[119] On the other hand, the faith in the Promised Land, on which Jews have survived for over two millennia, should not be destroyed by democratic political decisions. Israel should divide the house and give both incompatible viewpoints a place to live.

Division into coherent, homogenous communities would undermine any state if taken to the extreme. Yet many minorities long for self-determination, and some majorities would be only too happy to get rid of them. But look deeper. In any community, be it a family or a country, people continuously choose between living together or alone, between enjoying and benefiting from other people and finding them bothersome. The community persists only so long as the benefits outweigh the costs.

---

[119] Resolute expansionism, though, need not be costly; e.g., the Six-Day War.

When accommodation is easy, as in Catholic-Protestant Germany and French-British Canada, the state is in no danger, though religious differences can become acute. In Israel, however, accommodation is costly: kill and die for somebody else's ideals or forsake your own dearest principles. Given the strategic benefits and the political irrelevance of a division, there is no reason to live together. Jews could choose Israel or Judea, and live and work happily to realize their dreams.

Judea might engage in annexation

As in ancient times, Judea's population would be stricter about religion, willing to risk their lives and pay taxes to fund a war. Judea would seek to expand and not hesitate to answer the terrorists in kind. Judea would likely aim to conquer not only Palestine but also Jordan and parts of Lebanon. If she moved quickly and re-settled the present populations without prolonged suffering, the Western powers would accept reality after a time.

Annexation has judicial precedents. Jews accepted Israel's borders the United Nations set in 1947 as a temporary compromise. The United Nations refused to recognize the country's *de facto* enlargement, which took place in 1967. The United States ignored the United Nations resolutions, biased by special interests and accommodating insignificant members. The United States again disregarded United Nations cautions regarding Iraq in 2003 and invaded. Its dismissal of the U.N. is laudable, since it rejects the unworkable notion of one country, one vote, and reasserts the balance of power. United Nations votes do not reflect the realities of the balance of economic, demographic, or any other power, and Israel should jump on the bandwagon to discredit and disable the United Nations. Judea would have precedent for disregarding the United Nations partition and the post-1967 resolutions, which demanded a return to the original borders, and pursuing her interests with force. If international law does not benefit Israel, why should she pay it any attention?

Judea's probable religion-driven policy might be beneficial in yet another respect. People respect deep religious convictions, however alien they are, provided they conform to generally accepted moral conventions. Judea's coherent policies would command more respect than the half-hearted Israeli democracy, if only she slips not in bizarre fundamentalism.

Redressing the conflict in religious terms makes sense for Israel by making Israeli policy coherent, comprehensible, and defensible, as well as eliminating foreign pressures for a peaceful settlement. Leaders of Christian countries urge political settlement with Palestinians more forcefully than religious compromise with Muslims. Arabs are cynical about religion. Arab societies are undergoing the secularization the West has embraced since the eighteenth century, confronting modern culture and empirical science, which argue against some religious moral precepts. Religious parties rarely claim more than 20% of votes. Muslims might care less about the religious dispute than nationalist war. Arabs would find a country with rigid religiously inspired policies more comprehensible than liberal, democratic Israel's.

Is not, however, Judaism a religion of peace? It is not. Christianity is, if only theoretically, but Judaism is a religion of realism: love neighbors, do not oppress aliens, and fight enemies vehemently. Jews praise Moses for killing an Egyptian attacker, Joshua for ostensibly exterminating the Canaanites, Maccabees for fighting Jewish Hellenizers, and cheer the Purim crowd that killed *en masse* and looted the hostile civilians. Torah, indeed, prescribes helping an enemy to unburden his fallen donkey. That, however, is an altogether different enemy—a neighbor whose conflict with oneself is superficial, not rooted in incompatible interests. Judaism is uncompromising to the Jews' enemies; Israeli politicians accommodate them.

Technical details of establishing Judea

Israel might create Judea from her territory along the border with Gaza. That territory would proclaim itself a state and seek United Nations recognition[120], which would be granted since at that point Judea, infringes on no one's land. Then Judea would invite settlers and offer them citizenship. Next Judea would overpower under the pretext of stopping the ongoing violence. Israel would have no reason to remove Jewish militants from another state, and Palestine wouldn't be able to ask for foreign help, since military build-up would provoke Israeli preemption. Military stronger than the opposing Gazans, Judea would expand more easily than Israel before 1948. Israeli politicians, lackeys of the West, will try to prevent Judeans from occupying Gaza, but in the face of Arab counter-attack enough Jews will support Judea. Some religious Jews won't support Judean acquisition of Gaza, a place of limited biblical importance. They might find a common interest with the Israeli government in proclaiming Judea in East Jerusalem. Many countries recognized Israeli jurisdiction over united Jerusalem, and cannot question her right to cede a part of her territory to another state, Judea. Arabs would have a harder time demanding East Jerusalem, since that would amount to abrogating a state, not merely adjusting the Israeli border. Judea will handle the politically incorrect issue of removing Arabs from Jerusalem, and reinstate Jewish access to the places of worship.

At the very least, the Jews can found Judea in any small settlement across the border from Israel, preferably at a point where Israelis rectified the border to Palestinian demands and are not happy with the outcome. The

---

[120] There is no contradiction between finding a pretext to disobey U.N. resolutions on Israeli borders on one hand and seeking U.N. recognition of Judean borders, on the other. Jews should benefit even from an organization as useless and wrong as the U.N.

settlers may renounce their Israeli citizenship to escape Israeli jurisdiction and prevent their forced removal from Judea by loyal Israeli troops. If the removal is attempted, the settlers may threaten collective suicide or bring enough supporters to make government violence not feasible. The tactics of concentration was impossible for large settlement in Hebron or for the network of villages in Gaza, but could be implemented in a single small place. Fifty thousands armed and zealous Jews assembled in one town could effectively oppose their removal. Palestinians, much less than Israelis, would risk a confrontation certain to cause negative publicity. After Israel will de facto accept the Judean settlement, the Jews may start enlarging it at the expense of the Palestinians.

Jews readily fought the British to establish their state, but existence of Israel undermines their resolve. Only when zealous Jews grow hostile to liberal gentilized Israel, will they establish Judea. Israeli leftists might well enjoy ridding the country of the adherents to Judaism, and turn a blind eye to their exodus to form Judea. The money Diaspora Jews now send to Israel would mostly go to the more religiously zealous Judea. Judean lobbyists could make a much stronger case to wealthy Diaspora Jews than Israel's leaders can now, since most would favor the religious revival. Israeli policy is controversial. Aid being critical to Judea, few would refuse. True, some secular Jews scorn ultra-Orthodox Jews, but their skepticism would vanish once Judea imposed her agenda and forced international opinion to accept it. After the normalization of Jews, comes the normalization of Judaism. When the ultra-Orthodox have their own state, coherent, motivated, and powerful, they will command respect if they avoid grossly violating human rights. Arab money began flowing to Islamic fundamentalist groups once they became militant and effective. Many people are tired of weak democracy and mutual accommodation and long for action. Radicals rarely lack financial backing.

Jews may adopt the Muslim tactics of moderates sponsoring radicals. A Palestinian state may be a terrorist outcast, but Saudi Arabia, which pays for it, is internationally respected. Saudis achieve their goal of Israeli military attrition through Palestinian proxy, poor enough that it does not care of economic consequences of its policies and nationalist enough to be respected and protected by the world. Judea would be Israeli's proxy for expansion.

Judea will be able to maintain a small army, enough to handle Palestine, Jordan, and Lebanon. Israel would guarantee Judea's borders, even if they expanded, against aggression from Arab regular armies. In fact, Judea would generate unexpected military benefits. A theocratic state would not hesitate to use chemical, biological, and nuclear weapons instead of watching Jews die by the thousands in a protracted war. Judea will produce zealots ready to answer the Islamic asymmetrical warfare in kind.

Spiritual aspects of Judea

The creation of a theocratic Judea would save some Jews from ethnic assimilation. Judea may forbid non-Jewish immigration altogether or let in only Christians on temporary work permits who would be extensively screened to assure their loyalty. A desirable side effect of forbidding immigration would be the elimination of suicide terrorists, since no Arabs will be allowed. Fences and extensive Soviet-type border patrols would keep them from coming in illegally.

Judea's symbol should be the ancient, unique menorah, not the Star of David, which did not become a specifically Jewish symbol until the nineteenth century.

The capital of Judea, if not Jerusalem, should be called Zion, tapping into the energy of messianic expectations.

Judea's language should be biblical Hebrew, an artful language, superior to its modern surrogate, which insufficiently incorporates biblical lexicology and etymological conventions. Hebrew morphology is flexible enough to accommodate many new words while preserving the ancient roots and two-letter root cells. Reviving the simple, powerful, and beautiful biblical Hebrew would make the study of scriptures by gentiles livelier since it would reanimate meanings lost in translation. It is ironic for Israel, the last civilized country repressing reformist religion,[121] to embrace reformist language, the Hebrew newspeak. The message of Torah is inseparable from its language. Restoration of ancient grammar must be paralleled by a return to guttural pronunciation. Israeli Jews no more live in a cold European climate and could safely pronounce gutturals in the original Semitic phonetics, as Arabs still do. The current situation, when Torah and prayers are recited in a garbled tongue, should not continue.

Public opinion, given to secularization under the euphemism of religious tolerance, will not let Israel repress Reform Judaism much longer, especially since its lax observance is attractive to secular Jews and their gentile spouses, and a strictly observant Judea would give Orthodoxy a home. As the Torah requires, Judea would have only one religion, and be more or less orthodox. A theocracy cannot honestly accommodate factions without slipping into religious superficiality or cynicism: deviation and toleration prop each other.

Religious jurisdiction

Judea would restore the Hebrew system of religious jurisprudence and establish rabbinical courts in the Diaspora. Because legalism permeates modern social relations, that step would restore Jewish self-awareness, re-asserting their difference from other people, now blurred by assimilation. Decisions of rabbinical courts are binding on every Jew under the threat of

---

[121] Israel does not recognize Reformist Judaism

excommunication. Since Israeli law recognizes converts approved by Orthodox rabbis as Jews, excommunication should mean loss of status as a Jew, including descendants. Few Jews would ignore that threat. Rabbinical courts were hailed historically as reasonable and honest, and gentiles appealed to them for arbitrage in antiquity.

Imposing the authority of rabbinical courts would create a closed Jewish economy, since Jewish companies would prefer to deal with one another, just as secular businesses prefer to deal with others within a given legal system. A Jewish "business union" would gain competitiveness by acting as one in competition with other companies. Something like that economic support system was present at the micro-level in small Jewish communities before World War II, but now many prefer the minor benefits of dealing with outsiders to making sacrifices for the common good of Jews. Societies lose communal unity when economic and social pressures undo their internal interdependence. But Jews have a basis for interdependence: a common goal and purpose which, properly and continuously explained, could restore national unity.

With no ambition of becoming a major state and relying on Israel for protection, Judea could be a biblical theocracy built on religious-judiciary, not kingly-administrative, power. Since the law of Torah is exhaustive and administrative power an evil denounced in scripture,[122] Judea could become a state of liberal ideals without legislative or executive functions.

Judean theocracy would be a free society for conforming citizens. Everyone would be free to emigrate upon reaching adulthood, and before thirteen, there are few responsibilities or obligations. In Israeli *kibbutzim,* adolescents often do not share their parents' ideals and move away as adults. Some Jews leave Israel. People leave ultra-orthodox families and communities. Dissenters would be equally free to leave Judea. People who found Judean policy too rigid would move out, while more religiously motivated people would move in, and the influx of immigrants would sustain and increase the population even beyond what fecund Orthodox Jews would breed.

No concern with secular ethics

Judea would pay no attention to commonly accepted moral conventions. Following the Hebrew doctrine of just retribution, she would deal harshly with hostile aliens and bring terrorists and hostile Palestinians to justice. Following the Torah, Judea could enforce religious separation and resettlement of Arabs, something few secular states would legislate.

---

[122] By Samuel on explicit divine instruction in the strongest terms before the inauguration of the first monarch, Saul. The Bible in other parts recognizes monarchy *de facto*, demonstrating the Judaic tendency to regulate evil instead of trying unrealistically to eradicate it.

She would prohibit intermarriage and prohibit other religions from setting up places of worship: after all, there are no synagogues in Vatican.

Talmudic law would rule a country without prisons, relying on timely punishment and very rare executions. Many people oppose capital punishment, not because they think particular criminals do not deserve death but because judgments are sometimes passed in error. The Sanhedrin's due process is so rigid that error is unlikely. A Jewish court accepts no circumstantial evidence. For example, if a person sees someone entering a house, hears screams inside, sees him coming out waving a knife dripping with blood, and there was a murder at that time in the house, the witness is disqualified, since he did not see the murder. Sentencing errors exist in any legal system, and possible errors, including capital punishments, under Talmudic law compare favorably with the myriad years Westerners collectively lose in jails on wrong verdicts and for unwarrantedly defined transgressions. The major problem with Talmudic law would be not the cruelty of punishments but rather the practical impossibility of convictions because of safeguards. This might require revoking the Talmudic protections introduced as a face-saving measure when Jewish courts in the Diaspora lacked criminal jurisdiction. The issue of justice is almost irrelevant in a deeply religious society like Judea, with no outsiders to hate and persecute. The Talmudic due process leaves execution for various deviations only in theory.

Judaic prohibitions of abominable things from pornography to idolatry do not infringe on freedom of expression. They are rather like the Western zoning laws. Jews will not be prohibited from watching those things elsewhere, but the Promised Land must be preserved ritually clean. This is the idea behind the biblical "expunge the evil" – not necessarily kill the perpetrator.

Judea will be intolerant, but even restaurants enforce dress code, states punish flag defamation, and few families allow swearing at home. Secular states enforce myriad ethical norms, such as about prostitution, gambling, drugs, public nudity, and many others, often by brutal, disproportionate punishment. Judea will be sufficiently small so that the dissenters can easily move out.

The government of Judea could do things secular Israel would not if she wants to be a state like any other. For example, modern war crimes legislation allows claims against the Vatican and other European powers for persecuting Jews, even in the Middle Ages, and provides for the restitution of property, too staggering to consider.

Instead of lauding the *Nostra Aetate*, Israel should only accept the Vatican's repentance according to the Judaic law – preceded by full restitution and a fine. The Vatican has no obligation to act by the Jewish law, but Israel has such an obligation. The Vatican may excuse itself in mere words, but the Jews should not accept, much less laud, such excuse.

The Nuremberg tribunal meted out justice for crimes against humanity, applying legal innovations retroactively. While criminal charges cannot be brought against the descendants of the original perpetrators, claims for property stolen from Jews and still being enjoyed by the descendants of the thieves are quite possible. European governments did not return all real estate stolen from Jews in World War II (or earlier) to Jews. The Vatican's wealth comes in part from looted Jewish property, and its libraries stock ancient Jewish books stolen during massacres. Europeans did not even return all synagogues to the Jews; Judea has every reason to claim the buildings.

Judea would take the heat off Israel

Throughout history, anti-Semites have used the actions of a few Jews, from Zealots to tavern-keepers, to incriminate all Jews. Today all Jews are accused of maltreating Palestinians. Creating Judea would let Israelis shift the blame from the Jewish nation to a state that pays no attention to gentile opinion. Israel, which would have almost no problems with Palestinians, would become a good neighbor.

With Judea siphoning off religious radicals, Israel could move away from theocracy. Jews who do not observe the whole of the Talmudic law may feel themselves not proper Jews, though keeping it precisely is virtually impossible under normal circumstances. Ignoring the rabbinical law identified with Jewishness pushes them toward atheism and away from Israel. Israel could adopt Sadducean Judaism, which expects obedience only to the Torah's explicit commandments[123] to let people feel themselves fully Jewish.

---

[123] In addition to the Decalogue, Jewish law developed 603 further commandments of Torah interpreting the Ten, the Mishnah to interpret scripture legally, and the Gemara to explain the Mishnah. Only the radically orthodox see all commandments as divine, but they have great benefit of doubt when questioned.

Prospects for War and Guarantees of Peace: Doubtful

The Israeli Defense Force is not invincible

The alleged invincibility of the Israeli army is dubious. It won the War of 1948 against unorganized Arab gangs, not real armies. Even the Arab Legion was not professional by European standards. The Jews needed little more than common sense and minimal strategic planning to overcome the Arabs, albeit with heavy losses. But when the Jews met experienced commanders, such as the Egyptian commander Taha Bey, they lost.

In 1967, the Israelis won with sleight and luck. When luck abandoned them in 1973, they fell back on their advantage in weaponry, skills, and the will to fight. Of course, "luck favors prepared minds," but the margin was too narrow to depend on again. Arab armies today have modern weapons.

In 1982 Israel learned that even overwhelming firepower couldn't help an army lacking strategy and motivation, a disadvantage that has grown worse ever since. The army is not to blame. Soldiers can hardly adapt to wild swings in political objectives. As if to make things worse, the I.D.F. has lost the adventurous spirit it once had as it becomes more and more a politically oriented, bureaucratic machine.

In all her wars, Israel has had the advantage of no determined enemy. In 1948, Arabs wanted violence and loot rather than nationalist objectives, and later Egyptian and Syrian soldiers cared little about Sinai and Golan. Arab nationalism may change that.

American support is not guaranteed

The American military involvement in the Middle East necessitates cooperation with Arabs and dilutes partnership with Israel—a good reason she should have opposed the Iraqi invasion. It is a mistake to believe the United States would keep supporting Israel if only to prevent her from using nuclear weapons. There are other ways to do that, most easily by offering American protection to Arabs.

America's support for Israel is not built in. Alliances are based on concrete mutual interests, not metaphysics. France is more important for America in Europe than Israel in the Middle East, yet U.S.-French relations fluctuate wildly. Henry Kissinger brought the U.S. commitment to Israel to its current level to corner the Soviets; but that need has passed, and another determined man could extinguish the support. The United States has walked away from allies before: the South Vietnamese, the Kurds. America stood by while the Soviets butchered the Czechs whom American-funded radio incited to revolt. France for years subverted an American client, the Shah of Iran, unopposed. Israel hopes she is different, but she is not, not for the American Protestant establishment. America refused bombing Nazi death camps, did not help Israelis threatened with annihilation in the 1948 war, and did not stop Arabs from launching the 1967 war, expected at the time to destroy or economically suffocate Israel. Israelis must be mad to count on America.

Massive terrorist acts on American soil will erode popular support for Israel and prompt anti-Semitism because terrorists blame the Zionist lobby. America will seek escape in isolationism, especially when counter-terrorism measures prove ineffective. Prolonging the Palestinian imbroglio will further diminish American goodwill toward Israel. People sympathize with victims, no matter their moral complexion. The United States will likely rationalize a defeat in Iraq[124] as it did the Vietnamese disaster by invented humanitarian concerns: Iraqis, like Vietnamese, will become nice people not deserving military repression. Like Vietnamese, unknown to the Americans before the war and hated during it, America would welcome Iraqi immigrants, affecting the vote. Similarly, when the U.S. loses the war with Islamic terrorists and withdraws into isolationism, American attitudes toward both Muslims and Israel will change. Withdrawing of American support for Israel will upset subjective balance of power, and prompt the Muslims to reevaluate any treaties with her.

The Arabs say they have no general fight with the West but oppose specific infringements of Muslim sovereignty, specifically the matter of Israel. An implicit suggestion is that the West abandon Israel—but that would not work. Said Qutb, the spiritual godfather of today's Islamists, hated the United States long before it got behind Israel. If the U.S. cut Israel loose, the Arabs would claim victory over the infidels and press on, just as the Soviet defeat in Afghanistan led to the Chechen war. Islamists see the French decision to disallow veils in public schools and the United States dislike of polygamy as a cause for asymmetric warfare. Islamic fundamentalists hate Western values and the West's decadent culture, though it is not America culturally encroaching on Dar al-Islam but Muslims fascinated with Western culture, bringing it into their countries,

---

[124] Saddam seemed to accommodate Israel: in the Gulf War, only one Israeli died from thirty-nine Iraqi barrages. SCUD missiles hit reliably even when slightly out of range, and many misses are not easily explained other than by Saddam's instructions. He showed the Arab world his anti-Israeli stance, and kept Israel from retaliation. Next to nothing evidences Saddam's support for terrorists; he was at odds with Kurdish and fundamentalist outfits, and Iran. Now Israel faces a failed state with massive terrorist presence instead of a well-established dictatorship with no designs on her. Iraq made Arabs dependent on the U.S. for protection, and thus tolerant to Israel. Iraq drained Saudi Arabia and Iran through military buildup; the Gulf War almost bankrupted Saudis. Attacking Iraq, a long-time U.S. ally with no nuclear weapons, instead of clerical Iran, a long-time enemy active in acquiring them, was absurd. Now that replacing Saddam with another strongman is unlikely, the best Israel could do is to push for democratic elections which would bring Shia majority to power, dividing the Muslim world, and greatly destabilizing the region close to Saudi oil fields.

the fundamentalists fear. Terrorists do not deal in mutual deterrence. They would promote Islamic values against Western culture in any case. Democratic Western freedom of speech provides opportunities for peaceful agitation as well, and if the United States security agencies crack down on Islamists for inciting *jihad*, the fundamentalists will cry religious persecution and call for more terrorism.

While Israel inevitably imports Western influence into *Dar al-Islam*, other forces beyond Israel are in play—satellite TV, the internet, movies, McDonald's, godless physics, too low oil prices, unfavorable exchange rates, and so on and on. If the West, on the contrary, shut down TV satellites and blocked the internet, Muslims would cry discrimination. Muslims inevitably import Western influence, since they must spend the oil proceeds in dollars and euros—for Western consumer goods. America cannot meet Islamist demands of pressuring Russia, China, and India to stop local persecution of nominally Muslim minorities. Those three countries, historically insouciant about human losses, will not accede to terrorists, and America could do nothing to resolve the issue. If Israel vanished, the Islamists would go on to Chechnya, Bosnia, Kashmir, Indonesia. They see it their duty to protect Muslims living among the infidels and insist the West to let them live under *sharia*, not local law. Even if America found some unimaginable way to satisfy all the Muslim demands by severing cultural and political ties while preserving economic relations, that would end only the defensive *jihad.* That tremendous victory would clear the way for an offensive *jihad* to bring Western infidels under the Koran and *sharia*. Without Israel, the American problems with Islam would suddenly become many.

Why doesn't America pressure Israel to settle the Palestinian conflict? American influence on Israel is limited: she won her wars without the U.S. assistance. America does not pressure Palestinians into the settlement, either. America is not bound with Israel by a special relationship and is as indecisive as any democracy. America twisted Israel's arms and stopped her military advance in 1956, 1967, and 1973, even forcing a partial retreat never demanded from Arabs—yet shrieks when Israel overextends its influence.

American support of Israel is not exceptional. The United States gave France a billion dollars annually for the colonial conflict in Vietnam before getting directly involved there at much greater cost.[125] American stakes in the Middle East are much higher, well hedged by supporting both Israel and various Arab states, particularly, Egypt, which receives only a little less aid than Israel, though no country threatens Egypt. Comparing the aid per head is wrong, since America pays—very economically—for

---

[125] America repeats this error in the Middle East now. Dissatisfied with its proxy Israel, the U.S. military wants to take over, largely to justify bizarre defense procurement; they drag America into another irresolvable conflict.

regional influence, irrelevant to population. The cost of weapons increases faster than the amount of aid, diminishing its importance. America even pays the P.L.O., openly and vehemently anti-American, instead of suffocating it. Palestine gets $2 billion annually, 120% of its GDP. Israel's special relationship is a delusion.

American military aid to Israel is modest compared to what it gives Muslim countries—which received even more from the Soviet Union. The aid to Muslims should be counted combined, because their power is combined in conflicts with Israel. Saudi Arabia and Egypt routinely buy more American weapons than Israel, and China becomes an important and uncontrollable supplier of inexpensive arms. Kuwait buys almost as much as Israel, and tiny Qatar sometimes even more. The United Arab Emirates, a country never threatened, bought a large number of F-16 attack jets superior to those of the USAF, uniquely receiving a software code that lets them target United States or Israeli planes, and several Arab countries are expected to buy next-generation Joint Strike Force jets. The United States fought for Kuwait, something it did not do for Israel in 1973. America cooperated with the Iraqi military during the Reagan—pro-Israeli—years and gave Saddam the green light to use chemical weapons. American support for another Muslim state, Indonesia, far exceeds what it offers Israel in terms of atrocities tolerated. After liberating Kuwait, America did not tell it to sign a peace treaty with Israel or sell her oil to break a boycott. The U.S. supports Saudi Arabia and Kuwait, both bastions of radical Islam. America arranged no cease-fires when Israel needed them, but always when truces benefited Arabs,[126] and never firmly opposed Soviet arms shipments to Muslims, vastly exceeding American military aid to Israel. America never prevented an Arab military build-up or military concentration at Israel's borders, yet heavy-handedly stopped Israel from preemption in 1973.[127] Jewish influence did little for Israel before 1973 when the U.S. first critically supported Israel to prevent the region from falling prey to the Soviets.

The relationship is even less special for the American elite. The Bush family keeps close ties both with Israel and Saudi Arabia. Arab oil economies with concentrated wealth can offer much more to the governing families of America than Israel could. Their corporate friends often influence world leaders more than intelligence provided by objective experts, if such exist. Most American corporate interests are aligned with the Arabs, not with Israel, and lobby Arab interests more strongly, though less pompously, than Jews do through media and contacts open to public scrutiny.

---

[126] Arabs, unlike Israel, routinely refused unprofitable armistices.

[127] Worst of all, illusory dependence on foreign power produces real dependence on foreign public opinion, and prevents Israel from taking efficient but unpopular measures.

Jews, individualists and not team players, are inept politicians and bad schemers. They cause too much bang for the buck they receive through lobbying. A minor Jordanian princeling out-lobbied the world Jewry, and received for his unreasonable and illegitimate state much of the land the Balfour Declaration promised them. Jews lost much of the remaining land to the Palestinian peasants in 1947. Israelis did not exploit 1967 and 1973 territorial advances. Jewish lobbyists could not convince the U.S. government during the WWII to bomb death camps, and could not procure just ten thousands trucks to exchange for a million Jews herded for extermination.

Jewish mass media and corporate ownership have declined in recent years with more Japanese and Arab investment and ownership shifts to corporations lacking individual controlling shareholders. Jews also hold relatively fewer jobs in media outlets. Arabs could buy journalists and media and turn American voters against Israel. There are more anti-Semites than Jewish votes in the United States.

The Saudis lobby and suborn foreign-policy officials all over the world, promising sympathetic politicians golden parachute jobs upon retirement. Some American officials work with the Saudis after they leave office; almost none, with Israelis. The bin Laden family firm built the American army bases in Saudi Arabia and has strong relations with the Carlyle Group, whose leadership includes George Bush, John Major, James Baker, and others of similar standing. With such vested interests, it is no wonder the United States has a hard time pressuring Saudi Arabia to stop supporting terrorists and fundamentalists.

Historically, privileged Jews in European and other countries have aroused resentment, escalating persecution against them, often after a major political or economic change. American policy presently favors Israel and seeks to preserve America's as arbiter of the balance of power in a protracted conflict—but that could change any time.

Wealth buys influence. Thirty years of oil wealth have given Arabs wealth that challenges Jewish riches acquired over the centuries. Technological advances create much of the capital today. The Jews' traditional role as bankers is considerably diminished, along with a lot of their lobbying leverage. The Saudis alone of all Muslims hold about a trillion dollars in the Western assets. They buy more U.S. made weapons than Israel. Israel must be blind not to see she is losing economic advantage and stupid not to reverse the trend by occupying the oil fields.

An Arab diaspora is occurring. They have money, Western education, connections—and many of them are smart. They make up important voting groups and have considerable political influence. As in Vietnam, an American defeat in Iraq may lead to an influx of refugees. Arabs also occupy important posts in business and will eventually level the ground with Jews in the competition for influence. Only Islam unites the Arabs, especially its aggressive fundamentalist strain. That is dangerous.

A Palestinian state would get a lot of United States aid and take Americans' eyes off Israel, as happened in Egypt, now supported by many bureaucrats administering foreign aid and military assistance programs there.

Israeli lobbyists should not accept defeat but rather resist the trend as much as possible. Quite often, temporary arrangements last a long time. Jews must lobby for making the Holocaust a mandatory course in American schools.[128] Besides offering positive reasons for supporting Israel (geopolitical interests, cultural affinity, loyalty to an ally), Israeli lobbyists must show the consequences of withdrawing American support. Forcing Israel to settle with Arabs would leave the region without the major unifying force, a common enemy, and plunge it into destabilizing border wars. Without American conventional weaponry, Israel would use the nuclear deterrent, which tempts Arab states to generate nuclear programs with the likelihood that nukes will one day land in the hands of anti-American terrorists. If Israel lost American support, it would likely turn to Russia (as happened in 1948), France (as was the case until the 1960s)—and China. Whatever the choice, a country unfriendly if not hostile to the United States would influence the oil-producing region (a magic word for gasoline addicts) and force concessions from America far in excess of what it now gives to Israel.

Jews should promote American idealism to reject compromises with Muslim dictatorships—virtually every Muslim state—and emphasize the American mission of supporting liberty and democracy everywhere and the ostensible immorality of isolationism. Israel should court the American left, which denounces accommodation of regimes that abuse human rights, and the American right, which sees Islam as the new object of containment. Jews in America should pressure the United States government to establish clearer foreign policy guidelines about international police actions to stop atrocities, about national self-determination and resettlement,[129] about zero tolerance of the proliferation of weapons of mass destruction, and about allies—who should not be abandoned while loyal and democratic. Published guidelines would be morally correct and exclude cooperation with oppressive Muslim regimes. Clear objectives would help Muslims understand American actions instead of resorting to conspiracy theories and would make coalitions unnecessary, keeping whatever little special relationship Israel enjoys undiluted. Now coalitions establish the moral

---

[128] Though the courses in American schools are set by independent school boards, Israeli lobbyists conducted public relations campaigns addressing non-government entities. Not only Jews exploit the public opinion: politicians, ecologists, trade unions manipulate it as cynically.

[129] America supported independent Christian East Timor but not Islamic Kashmir ostensibly because Kashmiri Muslims can move to nearby Pakistan, while Timorese have no Christian state nearby to go to.

184

legitimacy of American actions, quantity compensating for the lack of goals.

Israel and the United States share great historical affinity. Many settlers fled hostile Europe to the land of promise. They fought Britain for independence. They tried to avoid violence by buying land from the natives who eventually resisted the aliens, even though they benefited from the technology transfer and the land was big enough for all. People in both countries see themselves as a beacon on a hill with messianic ambitions. Both were players in the Cold War. Both are resented for being prosperous and powerful, yet restrained. They have a common enemy, radical fundamentalist Islam.

Israel should resist American isolationism. Supporting a country with shared values differs from promoting one's values by force. To democratize Afghanistan is senseless. Supporting an endangered ally, the only democracy in the Middle East, makes sense. Most people would not doubt the validity of United States intervention to save Christians from Muslim atrocities. Similarly, United States intervention to save the liberal state is justified. Two world wars have shown the impossibility of total isolation. Some allies are too close to cut loose, and some enemies too evil to tolerate. Pro-active measures, like supporting Israel militarily, are better than last-ditch reactions.

Closing the United States bases in Saudi Arabia would not show respect for national sovereignty but rather submission to Islamic fundamentalists who are offended if a non-Muslim steps onto the land of Hijaz.[130] The macho mentality suggests a reciprocal refusal of Jerusalem to Muslims.

No Middle Eastern state other than Israel is loyal to America. American aid to Saudi Arabia has bought neither lower oil prices nor Saudi cooperation against terrorism nor Saudi opposition to the spread of anti-American Islamic fundamentalism. Economic and political concessions to Muslims, from acquiescence to oil rackets to support of atrocious regimes, cost Americans far more than support for Israel.

The Middle East supplies only about 10% of the oil America consumes, and holding Saudi Arabia accountable causes no disruption of the supply at the nearest gasoline station. There are other sources; the Russians would replace the Arabs gladly. Indeed, buying oil from Russia is better than giving the loans it defaults upon.

Instability in the Middle East, intensified by the U.S. invasion in Iraq, increases oil prices and corporate profits. Many American corporate interests would not welcome regional stability under Israeli control. Israel

---

[130] Saudi opposition could be circumvented by all American soldiers there proclaiming *Allah Akbar*, declaring themselves nominally Muslims. Americans mean something different by "God is great."

should appeal directly to the American public and multitude of companies who suffer from high oil prices, and might support Israeli expansion.

Israel should support American isolationism when, as the current trend suggests, the U.S. assistance to Arabs would grossly overweight the help to Israel. The American aid sustains systemic deviations in Israeli economy, and allows the U.S. to restrain Israeli government from militarily efficient policies. Israel can live and fight without the U.S.; Arabs cannot. Israel, refusing the U.S. aid and asking for parallel cessation of the aid to Arabs, would preserve goodwill of the American people instead of invoking contempt of the donors.

Honesty, perhaps cynical, is the best policy in surprisingly many cases: public cannot be fooled forever. Israel should explain that she is driven to cooperation with atrocious regimes because the American corrupt military-industrial complex excludes her from United States government procurement and from major export markets, and overcharges taxpayers for military hardware. Israel, whose internal market is very small, must export to sustain her vital military industries.

U.S. economic assistance does Israel no good but rather promotes ineffective policies, from excessive military spending to permanent budget deficits. Israel should seek access to American military procurement through an American/Israeli defense free-trade agreement—which would also stanch the Israeli brain-drain.

A Likud government should change the way Israel packages her policies. There is little difference between Likud and Labor policies, but they present them differently. While Likud's simple, clear-cut approach often provokes an outcry among Western liberals, Labor masks its to avoid offending public sensitivities. Likud builds more settlements in a time of crisis; Labor beefs up what is already there. Israel must take into account both Arabs and the West. Everyone knows the pill is bitter; sugarcoating demonstrates respectful concern for consumers.

America rewards its allies little but bribes its foes. Israel might stop demonstrating unconditional loyalty and flirt with France, which might elicit better terms from the United States, more aid and more political leeway. Israel could disobey America by attacking her Arab neighbors or annexing the territories and reclaim the center of attention, which she lost to Iraq.

Israel could befriend the American Catholic minority by giving it control over some contested Christian sites. Rapprochement with American Catholics will improve Israel's position in the Catholic countries of Europe and Latin America. The ties would not outrage the U.S. Protestant establishment, which is only nominally religious, and Israel could offer Protestants biblical sites held by Muslims.

Israel should defend the perceived property rights of the Orthodox Church against other factions in return for its support of Israeli interests with the Russian government. The Armenian Church is perhaps Israel's

186

only other important ecclesiastical ally and influences Armenian-American voters. Israel should disregard property claims from politically unimportant Christian sects.

Many Americans are conservative Christian moralists; few people can expound morality other than in religious terms. American politicians of a particular stripe endlessly invoke Christian principles to support legislative positions. The secularization of the state, so urgent in Locke's time, is no longer a problem. Rather, the loss of religion undermines moral axioms. Jews should lobby for more space for religion in public discourse. Children indoctrinated with Judeo-Christianity would be less tolerant to Islam.

The small-scale Arab-Israeli war allows the United States to manipulate the balance of power and arbitrate differences, a policy the United States decried a century ago in Europe but adopted in the Middle East. The Palestinian conflict presents no serious threat to Israel, and America props it up instead of ignoring it, but the war with Egypt destabilized the situation beyond America's capacity to control events. The terrorist war of attrition in the Middle East benefits American strategic interest.

Imagine living on a mountain and depending on a village below for important supplies—like oil. Good if the villagers are accommodating, but likely they would overcharge, offer your competitors better terms, and generally not treat you as the hub of the universe. A natural solution is inciting the villagers to fight each other—not too much, so that they do not disrupt your traffic, but enough so they depend on your aid and protection in the worst-case scenario. This is the American Middle East policy in a nutshell: reasonable, cynical, and self-interested. Now that Caspian oil is available, cash-strapped Russia is willing to supply the West with all the oil it needs. In that scenario, the Arab village is less important.

Rising anti–American sentiment in Europe after the demise of the Soviet Union poses a dilemma for Israel: American support for Israel pushes the European Union toward the Arabs as the best way to oppose the United States in the Middle East. Even the best friend is not absolute, and Israel should regenerate her European support base with active participation in European elections and political processes in general, as much as in America. Israel behaved so in France and other countries before late 1970s when she found increased American aid more profitable.[131] American leaders might welcome Israeli influence in Europe. Playing America against Europe for support requires a leader of Sadat's caliber, whom Israel lacks.

---

[131] The estrangement was not entirely Israel's fault but stemmed from France's return to its traditional support of Muslims. Francois Mitterand, a friend of the Soviets and of Vichy police commissioner Rene Bousquot who oversaw deportation of Jews, was unreliable partner.

Israel should pursue *rapprochement* with China. Near the ex-Soviet oil producing republics, China does not need the Arabs. China has problems with ethnic minorities and with nuclear proliferation in North Korea, India, and Pakistan. China needs Israeli technology and Israeli weapons. The trick is to overcome China's historical isolationism. Increasing Chinese involvement in formerly Soviet Asia suggests that could be done.

Modern anti-Semitism

Anti-Semitism did not disappear with the establishment of a Jewish state, when Jews became people like others. Modern anti-Semitism does not look like the traditional version. Its line of thinking is, "The Israelis have got more than they deserve. They should stop arguing with the Arabs and be glad we gave them any state at all." Israeli security issues are only relatively important to her allies: terrorists do not blow up Christian children in Israeli school buses. The allies are willing to help, but if treaty-based security does not work out, they lose nothing. Nothing happens to them if Israel is destroyed. Centuries ago, Israel asked for the protection of a superpower, Assyria, which soon annexed it. The same happened with Rome. Israel should not ignore history's lessons and be aware of how America manipulates her. Israel must be strong since militant anti-Semitism is alive. Centuries after the medieval mass murders of Jews, civilized people were sure the atrocities would not recur. Then in the mid-seventeenth century, a throng led by Bohdan Hmelnitsky (the hero of modern Ukraine) decimated the Jewish population of Ukraine, claiming to have killed a million Jews. Decades after Russian pogroms, written off as an aberration perpetrated by barbarous Mongolized mobs, no one imagined the highly educated Germans would bring about the Holocaust. It happened, however, only sixty years ago, not long enough to hope for a change of mentality. The anti-Semites are never quiet for long.[132] A new clash is neither impossible nor unlikely but all but inevitable. Jews must make it a fight, not an atrocity.

Adherence to Judaism makes the Jews defiantly different from others, and will perpetually cause hatred. Anti-Semitism does not evaporate from societies and then re-appear. It is always brewing, ready to burn. Jewish organizations are wrong in trying to suppress anti-Semitism to invisibility. They fool Jews, not Gentiles. Jews forget that they must be strong to survive, and resettle in Diaspora and assimilate – until the next wave of atrocities. Even to the extent of cooperating with Neo-Nazi organizations, the Jews must keep anti-Semitism on the surface: a controllable, but clear danger.

---

[132] The inactivity is relative. Racial killing of a Jew and pogroms in Brooklyn occurred only a decade ago. In mid-twentieth century, Americans were as anti-Semitic as Europeans. For all the sense of guilt, 22% of the Germans polled believe there are too many Jews around. (*The New York Times*, 09.15.94, p.A21)

188

The Need to Reconsider Values

Looming disillusionment

Does Israeli youth not see they are being herded to a war, not to defend themselves but to realize the doubtful projects of self-righteous politicians, a war which a well thought-out foreign policy would stop? The politicians bicker endlessly about the size of Israel, from the 1947 minimum to a cautious bit more in 1948 to the biblical boundaries in 1967, giving up part of Sinai in 1973, the territories in 1979, Golan in 1995, part of Jerusalem—almost—in 2000, and back to the 1948 borders. What's left is more or less what Sadat offered in return for a comprehensive peace back in 1972. Only the foolish could tolerate such shenanigans, especially when succeeding doctrinal swings get people killed. The army is good when ideology drives it, but skepticism cripples it, as was seen in Lebanon.

A soldier can be asked to sacrifice his life for higher values, but what are Israeli values? For decades Arabs have plotted to annihilate Israel, which justified asking Israelis to risk their lives to oppose that threat. But what higher idea is at play when Arabs want only a tiny speck of land, when they are negotiating partners instead of sworn enemies? Many Israelis don't believe in the diabolic trickery of the Phased Plan; Palestinian intentions at settlement could be genuine. Israelis are no longer desperate and therefore not resolute. Freedom of speech allows the defamation of nationalist and religious ideals and the possibility that they are not worth dying for. Who would die for a flag he can burn, whose very existence flouts religious law? The best thing the Arabs could have done—and did— to demoralize the Jewish army was to deny any design on Israeli lives or land Jews owned in 1948. If the Arab terrorists had the sense not to attack civilians, the Israeli Defense Force would lose what moral integrity it has.

Some Israelis are no longer proud of being Jews. The Soviet people stopped being proud of their country when they compared it to the West. It is hard to be proud of an economically weak country with absurdly outdated socialist regulations, rampant corruption, and political instability. Israel has the highest ratio of public expenditure to GNP in the civilized world. Israeli tourists are known the world over for their poverty. The country lacks large locally owned banks, stock markets, and other entities where Jews traditionally thrive. More important, scientific, literary, and artistic achievements are minuscule.

Reliance on someone else for welfare and military protection harms morale. Israel is both socialist and subservient to an empire. The necessary but immoral persecution of the native population erodes Jewish morality, which prescribes compassion for the underdog. A country cannot make war for long without damaging its morale. The war created the police state and taught youngsters to admire brute force more than education and virtue. Killers, even people ready to kill, are not good peacetime citizens. Teaching killing in wartime lays the foundation for civil troubles in peacetime. Israeli politicians are so accustomed to daily killing that one doubts whether they value even the Jews.

Israeli conscripts have to kill for reasons they may not support. They are forced to commit what they view as murder, against their conscience. To compensate, many Jews choose to hate Arabs, the only way to preserve self-esteem. Germans similarly moved in only few years from dislike to irrational hatred of Jews, which allowed the Germans to acquiesce in repressions. Nations given to hatred lose rationality. Japanese Zen masters taught that it takes clear head to fight well.

Living under the siege not only damages morality, but also curbs intellectual productivity. The war reverberates through Israeli society in myriad losses.

The loss of Zionist values exacerbates matters. In the early twentieth century, socialism filled the void left in the hearts of Jews who abandoned Judaism; even such an ideology is lacking now. The racism and the militarism of Israeli youth is a product of easy victories and youthful radicalism and has nothing to do with Zionism, which is often dragooned to cover ignoble ideas. Living side by side with a hated, weaker enemy has produced a master's syndrome in many who treat Arabs like slaves or animals, not respected enemies—not a majority, but the number grows. Fear and guilt—the other side of the master's syndrome—erode the will to sustain confrontation. Jews who shed their religious identity, rootless and lost, find Arab claims to the land persuasive—because religiously and ideologically zealous Arabs *are* persuaded. Since integrating Arabs into Jewish society would dilute the state's Jewish identity, separation is inevitable, relocating Israeli Arabs in a state of their own. Daily contact does neither hostile people any good.

Define ethnic boundaries

Many young Israelis emigrate, since they have never lived among gentiles, an experience that deterred older Jews who fled Eastern Europe. In the modern cosmopolitan world, young Israelis adapt much more easily than their ancestors. Assimilation is increasing, as it often does in prosperity, especially as anti-Semitism subsides before cosmopolitanism, eroding Jewish borders and self-awareness. Jewish organizations should not fight mild anti-Semitism and opposition to Israeli mildly imperialist ambitions.

Israel is not a closed society organized to prevent assimilation. The country initially agreed to unite different ethnic groups under the umbrella of Judaism. Yet assimilation is in some ways like the Holocaust. An assimilated Jew is no longer a Jew.

Strictly religious groups are doomed in the atheist world. Christians two centuries ago and Muslims until recently did not marry unconverted members of other faiths. Now they do. Atheist Jews likewise feel free to marry gentiles. Only a web of mutually supportive distinctions can prevent assimilation: a religion divine at least in its core, unique ethics, proud chosenness, ethnicity, cultural difference, and economic, military, and political advantages. The example of Maccabees shows that the Hellenized Jews turn to their religion when their state is successful.

The way to decide who is a Jew is to distinguish between ethnic Jews and religious Jews, which will mean acknowledging atheist Jews and proselytes. True, the Hebrews mixed with other nations during the Exodus when other aliens in Egypt joined them. The Assyrians resettled aliens in Judea; Idumeans and many other ethnic groups were in at the formation of the modern Jewish nation. Yet Hebrew genetic features are traceable. The current standards are hypocritical. Why let maternal descent determine Jewishness? Among Jews, paternal lineage defines nationality. The Torah pays no attention to a mother's nationality.[133] The rabbinical teaching that one can be certain of a child's mother but not its father not only insults the morals of Jewish mothers but is also illogical because it ignores the unknown variable. DNA testing obviates the rabbinical argument, which is also impractical: Jewish males often converted their gentile wives, and children were raised as Jews, though children of mixed marriages with Jewish mothers rarely turned to Judaism. If, however, gentiles converted to Judaism are Jews, why care at all about parentage? Genetics does matter, though it is not predominant after the influx of Egyptians, Assyrians, Edomites, Khazars, and others. Studies of mtDNA in various Jewish communities show that the women are largely of local origin, related to neighboring groups but not to Middle Eastern genetic patterns, as are the paternal Y-chromosomes. That confirms the empirical observation that Jewish men frequently marry converted gentile females. The guidelines must be honest and sensible, perhaps combining genetic relevance with acceptance of the Torah's basic tenets.

Throughout the history, people of other nations joined the Jewish nation. The influx was sufficiently gradual that the Jews retained their culture. And so it should continue. Jews need not become a misanthropic closed society – isolated by practicing rigorous ethical standards, yes, but not closed. Individual Jews may fall in love with Gentiles, and seek to bring them to Judaism.

---

[133] To prove that the Torah prohibits male Jews to marry gentile women, the Talmud (Kiddushin 3:12) twists Deut 7:3-4, especially since Deuteronomy limits the prohibition to the Canaanites (Kiddushin 68b unconvincingly extends the injunction to other nations). The Talmudic argument is intended to deal with situations of dubious paternity. Lev24:10, adduced to show that son of Israelite mother, even if his father is Egyptian, is liable according to the Jewish law, tells just the opposite, that such a person is prone to blasphemy. Besides, many non-Jews joined the Exodus and effectively converted, and the example does not prove matrilineal descent without conversion.

Genetic issues should be studied, not dismissed as curiosities. Who are the Cohanim with their peculiar haplotype? What is the historical affinity between Jews, Kurds, and Palestinians that explains their genetic similarities? Thirteen Jewish haplotypes surprisingly correspond to the thirteen biblical founding males and tribes, though probably without a common Abrahamic sire.

Why consider proselytes Jews? Ethnic Jews do not always observe the Law, but converted gentiles must. Today ethnic traits decide who is a Jew, with a concession for proselytes. The rabbis are glad the government pretends to determine Jewishness by religious standards, though the policy makes no sense, since atheist Jews are also Jews for purposes of immigration—on the unlikely presumption that apostate Jews still have a spark of Judaism and can always return to the Law.

The question affects black Jews. Ethiopian Jews, though they have much the strongest credentials to be the "lost tribe" of Namibia, genetically one not only with Jews in general but with the Cohanim in particular, are disregarded. The issue is especially relevant because insufficient learning ethics, idleness of welfare programs, and replacement of the religion with consumerist values transform many Sephardic Jews into Israeli Afro-Americans.

The next question is, to whom should the state of Israel belong? To all the Jews in the world who don't pay Israeli taxes or vote, to her citizens (including gentiles), or to some other group like Israeli Jews?

The answers to those questions bear on many issues. Jewish society has a proper interest in proliferation for metaphysical and economic reasons and could offer subsidies to families, though offering them mostly to large families promotes religious orthodoxy and has little economic effect, since many of the orthodox do not work productively but hold religious sinecures. A just system would subsidize families with three children but no more and certainly not Arab families—Israel needs larger Jewish population, not just any population.[134] Israel might offer bonuses for every Jewish child born and deduct a billion dollars a year from the inflated military budget. Not weapons but Jewish minds are Israel's hope. A better option would be to promote child-bearing by working families by 20% tax break for each child under eighteen with further tax breaks for grandchildren to stimulate early child-bearing. Still better, reduce the welfare provisions to the sustenance minimum the Torah prescribes, so that people will have more children to make a safety net for themselves.

To identify Jews (potential citizens of Israel) with adherents of Judaism leads to absurdity when converts are discouraged, often by a humiliating conversion experience. Otherwise Israel would face massive immigration of superficial converts, technically Jews, from poor countries.

---

[134] In yet another twist of pluralistic socialism, Jews financially support unproductive Arabs through subsidies.

At the beginning of this era, the cynical pagan population found Judaism attractive as the religious embodiment of many philosophical notions, and there were many proselytes, as could be now. Israel must become a state for Jews, not for all believers. Whether Jews want to encourage conversion or not is another question, but converts should not be given permanent residence to remove the economic advantages of conversion. Instead of the current policy of not giving the converts Israeli visas, the government could give them the option of living in the territories. State propaganda should emphasize conversion,[135] drawing more people to the religion Jews believe to be true and increasing Israel's base of foreign political influence. The ancient Jews were not told to convert conquered people by force since in the messianic age all nations would turn to God. They would still be different from the Israelites, suggesting the importance of ethnic traits. At the very least, proselytes should not have the same rights as Jews until four generations have passed. Proselytes have always been at a disadvantage in Judaism, *e.g.*, in marital matters. Temporary economic and political disadvantages for converts would filter out frivolous converts if the Jews decide to proselytize actively.

Defining Jewishness was not important previously because persecution united all Jews. A person oppressed as a Jew was a Jew. Since anti-Semites did not bother with minute differences, Jewishness was very broad. Even earlier, a Jew was anyone who sacrificed to the God of the Hebrews. Since no other worship was licit in Judea, the local population automatically became Jewish. Normalization mitigated the anti-Semitism, which generated persecution, and religious tolerance blunted many Jews' dedication to Torah. Unless Jews define Jewishness practically, assimilation will accelerate.

Muslims recruit Western sympathizers. Mosques and Arab cultural centers are open throughout the world. Arab cultural expansion hopes to turn public opinion against the Jews, who should respond that Judaism is culturally much more nearly Western. Israel should emphasize her kinship with Christianity and particularly promote the sects that view the Gospels as human works, Jesus as prophet, and accept the Mosaic Law.

Reliance on religion should be restrained

Scholarly biblical criticism threatens Zionism's ideological pillars. Much of the Bible is not revelation, not history, but saga, yet the Israelis flirt with theocracy, compounding the confusion instead of resolving it. The people who should lead the national revival, the rabbis, oppose the discussion. Jewish fundamentalism is as assertive in Israel as Islamic

---

[135] Right now, only few books on Judaism are available for non-Hebrew speakers. The Talmud is not translated into most languages, and even the English translation is not widely available. In contrast, thousands of Christian theological texts, many of high quality, can be downloaded free from the internet.

fundamentalism in Muslim countries—coherent, confident, and funded, gaining support from the uncritical.

Cosmopolitan Western culture fills the resulting void. Israel has no nationalist ideology to promote state values, and the moral and material aspects of living in a state at war for half a century are unattractive. Nationalism in bi-national Israel will speak of "us, Jews and Arabs" and destroy Jewish identity.[136]

Better to admit honestly that the historical parts of the Torah are not factual,[137] get past the myths, and offer sustainable ideals—from Maimonides' rationalization to Halevi's poetry, from biblical minimalism to the Tanakh. There must be lively and honest discussion. Such discussion did not break Judaism in Talmudic times, and will only help it now; participatory democracy similarly strengthens societies. Attempts to gloss over the weaknesses of Tanakh and the Talmud do not work in the light of modern criticism. Thoughtful criticism is better than unthinking acceptance. Criticism channels doubts which can lead to rejection of Judaism if they are repressed or not informed. Modern rabbis are like Shammai, who pushed the inquiring gentile away, while Hillel explained the essence of Judaism in a single sentence. Since most Jews never read the Tanakh, let alone the Talmud or the commentaries, rabbis should generate popular literature on Judaism—anthologies, commentaries, and anecdotes, like the short commentaries of the Lubavitcher Rabbi. The effort must be large scale. Christian foundations distribute their publications free, and both Christians and Muslims offer free religious instruction. Jews should do likewise. Synagogues in Israel and abroad should invite local Jews to participate in the events and provide background material on the ceremonies, even through bulk mail.

Changing the army

The present policy is indecisive. Another more practical strategy is air superiority with unhindered use of armor-piercing cluster and vacuum bombs,[138] chemical weapons, and tactical nuclear micro-charges to prevent extended military conflict and obviate Israel's need for a large infantry.

---

[136] Many people have no problem with this. But would they accept mixed Jewish – Negro nation, if a Jewish state had been set in Uganda? Creating a nation based on territorial arrangement is wrong; by this token, Jews in the Diaspora should marry locals and assimilate.

[137] Talmud teaches that historical descriptions are given in the Bible only for their interpretation, Wajikra rabbah, 1.

[138] Restricted by various arrangements supposedly because of their extreme power, but actually a concession to states not possessing such powerful weapons and to advocates of humane war, preferably with boxing gloves. "Softening" warfare is a reaction to unwillingness of modern soldiers to fight for political objectives. The proper response is not fighting unnecessary wars; making them somewhat less painful only provokes more confrontations.

Intelligence and commando units can identify targets. Tank units and small contingents of mechanized infantry can perform clean-up operations. Israel should rely on WMD for deterrence, antiaircraft artillery for tactical defense, and a reasonable number of aircraft for strategic defense. Although Israel's nearly six hundred combat aircraft are several times less than the cumulative assets of her enemies, their planes are mostly outdated, and even earlier Israel usually destroyed at a more than a 10:1 shoot-to-loss ratio. Israelis bragged they would achieve similar results in air battles with Syrians, even if they exchanged their planes. The point is well-taken; invest in training, and let Arabs spend their budgets on ultra-modern weapons, sure to become obsolete before seeing conflict.

Naval data are misleading: although Israel's military maritime capabilities are minuscule compared to those of the U.S. or Russia, she does not have to protect her seas. She maintains 50+ ships only to boost the egos of the military bureaucracy.

There is no need to spend a fortune getting ready for all-out war. Armaments obsolesce. There is no reason to buy and stockpile readily available supplies for an unforeseeable future. Israel can buy arms when the situation deteriorates or, better, make treaties with major military powers to buy arms at any time. Israel cannot keep pace with the cumulative military spending of her enemies, almost ten times her own.

Keeping masses of ground troops is an outdated and expensive approach to warfare. Israel's standing army of 175,000 costs the GDP in losses from lack of productive employment of about $3.5 billion, in addition to about $10 billion in direct costs of the I.D.F. which could be decreased at least by a third by cutting the size of the standing army. Bureaucratic accommodation of military establishments and the military-industrial complex preserves a large army; beside, soldiers are cheap and no commander ended up in jail for wasting them—though many should have. The enemy should be bombed into submission, either to terms or to an imposed administration, and kept in line with the threat of violence. The Arab armies cannot compete with the Israeli Defense Force in high-technology warfare.

The bourgeoning Israeli military-industrial complex poses all the dangers of corruption and eventually unavoidable inefficiency known in the United States, the militarism of the Soviet Union, and also a unique danger of collaboration with enemies. American military companies also cooperate with enemies, but a small volume of trade compared to the U.S. internal procurement poses no danger to the giant American army. The extent of Israeli military companies' cooperation with hostile regimes cannot be publicly discussed, but it already hinges on clear and present danger to Israel.

The Israeli army is more than sufficient to deter Muslim armies. Arabs are generally wealthier than in 1948 and not prone to aggression. Israel need not enlarge her armed forces and bring on an arms race with the

Arabs. War costs rise exponentially to maintain the army, build infrastructure in the territories, suffer from little foreign investment, and cover the loss in GDP when productive workers are mobilized. The money spent for the military is needed for education, research, and culture. Young Israelis should be proud of those, not of military apparel.

The army must become professional. Peacetime conscription is economically unsound. Young people should not spend their most creative years in the army. Israel must reduce the term of service to a few months of basic training at most. That would allow for rapid mobilization in case of necessity. Conscription should target older people. Most firepower is now concentrated in mechanized units, and so physical strength is not paramount anymore. Mature moral strength is more valuable on the battlefield. Fatalities among young soldiers are usually higher than among mature adults. Conscripting active voters from thirty to fifty years of age for both peacetime duty and first-response warriors might change many Israeli opinions. Currently, young people are herded to the battlefield before they are old enough to stand for election and change the policy; most of them have not yet had a chance to vote against the politicians sending them to the slaughter. Lowering the voting age to *bar/bat mitzvah* is sensible in an honestly religious Jewish society but not a substitute for raising the draft age.

Drafting women for combat or as front-line support personnel is questionable. Girls should learn to be mothers, not killers. Military life changes people's outlook on basic values. Being ready to kill an enemy child, even accidentally or in self-defense, is antithetical to the tenderness a woman feels for her own child. Equality before the law does not change the fact that men and women are different; if crime is predominantly a male occupation, war is even more so. Women are little represented in the essential air or tank forces. Israel does not anticipate another all-out war like 1948, where every Israeli counted since weapons were so scarce. Israel needs more mothers, not more soldiers.

After 1948, Israel won through mobility because her armies were better, not larger. A huge conventional army is obsolete and useless in guerrilla warfare. Size compensates for the inefficiency developed both from self-restraint and people's unwillingness to fight for changing political doctrines, unlike 1948 and 1973 when the danger was clear and present. The I.D.F. crosses a dangerous barrier toward the American-style bureaucratized saber-rattling monster, with expensive useless or insufficiently tested weapons, corps hanging onto similar weapons and losing specialization, commanders guided by self-aggrandizement instead of efficiency and demanding more weapons without cooperative regard to procurement needs of other corps and the capacity of the Israeli economy. The I.D.F. became too big to retain its early venturesome spirit. Elected commanders instead of conformist political appointees and drastically reduced financing or increased participation in regional conflicts might slow the army's deterioration.

It makes sense to change Israel's peacetime armed forces. Equipment maintenance can be outsourced to private companies, reducing costs and creating an internationally competitive sector of the economy. Army personnel can be reduced to a nucleus adequate to command, control, and intelligence needs, swiftly expandable by conscription if necessary. That would, however, mean a pre-emptive-strike policy, since otherwise Israel's enemies could easily disrupt her economy by faking mobilization to keep Israel always mobilized.

Political reform

Israelis refuse socialist or totalitarian rulers, but a plethora or small parties fills the political vacuum they leave and create political instability and endless internal political skirmishes. Most state functions should return to the people and the market to create a liberal economy.

Both Israeli left and right first argue for expansion, and then give away the territories. Leaders are chosen with little regard for their abilities, especially since the population votes for a party whose leader, often chosen by *apparatchik* intrigues, becomes the head of government. A parliamentary republic makes ministers and executive officers of politicians, not professionals, and aggravates the problem with short-term appointments, relieving the appointees of both the chance to finish their programs and responsibility for failure. Parties introduce ministers regardless of how they will cooperate with the prime minister, often determined to oppose him or her. This is acceptable for a parliament, but pluralism does not suit an executive body. Once a policy is determined, it should be carried out coherently until completed or proven wrong. More often a new government uproots what the previous one did. Since no party wants to laud the other's achievements, campaign rhetoric binds challengers to change course, whether the course was bad or not. Parties prefer any action to none; hectic activity pleases voters but is generally counterproductive. The result is huge expenses without achievement.

A collegial prime ministry, with three or four recent prime ministers working together, could provide political continuity, making decisions by consensus or some weighted voting system. That system is not immune to exploitation, but the present system is worse.

Most politicians are alike. Rotation only aggravates their incompetence and lack of consensus among Jews. A presidential republic where the president serves ten years would be best for Israel. Even a moderately capable president could produce sustained, consistent, acceptable results, far better than the periodic policy reversals Israel now lives with. Some countries suspend elections during wartime, and Israel is at war. Presidential government is also closer to traditional kingship, preferable for a state built on ancient values. A visible, authoritarian ruler would attract some of the hatred the Arabs direct to Jews at large, the way Arafat was blamed for the whole Palestinian problem.

Though Israel's rulers often have military experience, a prime minister does not have to have the supreme military authority. The Israeli Chief of Staff is more competent to make decisions. Shared responsibility would ease internationally unpopular decisions and deflect blame from the political establishment. Democratic politicians, eager for shows, are more militaristic than the military, and shared responsibility will add conservatism to policy. When, on the contrary, politicians vacillate to please the Western sponsors, the military will push the necessary decisions through. Ideally, on the model of Prussian theorists, the cabinet should make war policies and not interfere with the military until victory or defeat is clear. Specifically, the C.G.S. should authorize preemptive strikes, which are a tactical matter for a country without depth of defense. Absent political meddling, the Israeli army might have whipped a peace treaty out of Arabs long ago.

Military authority over the country's war effort will prompt political appointments of the weakest possible Chief of Staff, to control him informally. To prevent this, troops should be allowed to elect commanders all the way to the top, with government and the staff having veto right. Citizens might elect demagogues for commanders, but soldiers, for whom these are life-and-death decisions, will not err grossly. The bottom-up control of appointments will inhibit pork barrel military purchases: soldiers want practical, not lobbied, weapons.

Steps to be taken in the Diaspora communities

Israel may have been mistaken to resettle flourishing Jewish communities in Arab countries in Israel. They could have been powerful agents of influence. Israel must establish close ties with foreign Jews and encourage them to work for Israel's benefit. Few likely feel much affinity with Israel in everyday life.

Justice is indispensable for communal identity. People who appeal to external courts accept alien protection and laws, abrogating their own. Diaspora Jews historically relied on simple and honest rabbinical arbitrage. Israel should sponsor courts of arbitrage, based on religious or Israeli civil law, obligatory for Jews under the threat of excommunication. Many Diaspora Jews rarely see a rabbi in their lifetime, and still fewer visit synagogues or community centers. The Israeli government should send good lecturers to address Jews in every place, to reinvigorate their sense of identity and bring them together on the basis of reasonable religious duties, pride in their history and nation, and a sense of election and mission.

The Israeli government should create a worldwide network of Jewish interests, with people in national governments, major corporations, and run-of-the-mill enterprises. The old Jewish network dissipated after

World War II, many became secular and assimilated, and increased wealth fostered independence from the community for social support.

The Israeli government should court the loyalty of the Diaspora Jews, not by denying media reports of Israeli cruelty but by offering inexpensive travel to Israel, a kind of international Sharon tours.[139] Every Jew should get a birthday card from the prime minister and a holiday greeting from the chief rabbi. Bulk mail is better than no contact at all. Diaspora Jews should be asked to buy major mass media outlets or buy show rights on the Arab-Israeli war to limit media coverage. That would mitigate international pressures on Israel and free her hand to some extent. Israel might foster her movie industry, a major propaganda device. Though most Americans watch few foreign films, some intellectuals and opinion-makers do, as does the more cosmopolitan European audience.

Israel should come to the defense of any Jews anywhere who are persecuted illegally, never mind the cost or consequences. The expense would not likely be large, since Jews are usually law-abiding, and would buy increased loyalty to Israel. On the contrary, Israel did nothing to stop persecution of Jews in Dominica and Argentina and, before the media outcry, in Ethiopia. Said Nosair, the Arab who murdered Rabbi Kahane, initially got away with a short prison term: the Israelis could have reached him in jail.[140] Indeed, Arabs killed Jewish Defense League' activist Earl Krugel in the American prison. The bureaucratic establishment, the Supreme Court, and the Mossad failed to enforce justice on Ivan the Terrible and Dr. Mengele.[141] That should never happen. Israel tolerates many terrorists working for the Palestinian Authority. Why leave them alive? Jewish Diaspora communities are easy targets for terrorists. Increasing their security to Israeli level would pay in attachments and support for Israel.

---

[139] Free bus tours to the territories introduced by Ariel Sharon for Israelis during elections to demonstrate to them how vulnerable the country is to bombardment from the hills and to induce voters to support the policy of holding the territories.

[140] The Israeli establishment, threatened by Kahane the gadfly, was only too happy to have him killed. Jabotinsky, ostracized by the Jewish establishment during his lifetime, was attached to the pantheon *post mortem*. The years before us will see a similar conversion of Rabbi Kahane's image emasculated of his ideas.

Israel and the U.S. put Rabbi Meir Kahane's political organization on the terrorist list with murderous Muslim guerrilla groups. Odd terrorist he was, organizing self-defense of Brooklyn Jews against Black pogroms, urging Israelis to evict Arabs to disarm the demographic time bomb, and calling on the Orthodox rabbis to upheld the Torah where it lacks political correctness.

[141] The Israeli Supreme Court acquitted one of the most notorious Nazi death camp operators. The Mossad refused to kidnap Mengele for prosecution in Israel, or hunt him out and kill him on the spot. The shame is not only the establishment's: no Jew came up to deal with Ivan the Terrible after Israeli court acquitted him.

200

Israel should prosecute anti-Semitism elsewhere. Anti-Semitism flourishes because it is allowed to, but there are legal remedies that are likely to succeed. After the terrorist attacks in the West, many agreed to limit freedom of speech, interpreting incitement broadly. Anti-Semitism is on the rise in Israel, not only among Arabs but also among non-Jewish Eastern European immigrants. That should be stopped at once with immediate deportation, regardless of family ties, for the first offense. Not only are anti-Semites a fifth column that undermines Israeli resolve, but also Jews do not want them around. There is more than sufficient reason for expulsion.

It is not enough to call the charges of hypocrisy leveled at Jewish organizations anti-Semitism. The Anti-Defamation League and the rest are too big and visible to use means reserved for secret services or covert operations. Israel should operate clandestine smear campaigns to avoid smirching the image of the major Jewish entities. Jews should also oppose people with tarnished reputations in leadership positions, since the mass media regularly expose their illegal or morally questionable sources of enrichment, about which the A.D.L. can do nothing. That situation is even more painful in Eastern Europe and Latin America where the impoverished population despises the oligarchs who lead local Jewish communities.[142] That led to pogroms in the past and is certainly no help now. Prominent Jews are at times accused of criminal activity, even of selling arms to the Arabs. Jewish organizations accept money from people who are neither religious nor pious, parading them at receptions and other events. That should change. Moral merits, not contributions, should take the front seat. Jews should pressure agencies to meet rigid standards of integrity, and breaking the commandments should exclude people from the Jewish social and political hierarchy; current tolerance borders on forgiveness. Large private donations do not equal the financial capacity of the State of Israel, and some are dubious, like when wealthy foreign Jews buy lands in the territories at rock bottom prices. Israel should publicize the economic benefits of holding the territories to attract Jewish investors from abroad. Diverse ownership creates better support. Even selling the land to Christian charities with restriction on transfer to Arabs is better than to Jewish oligarchs. Encouraging many small donations from Jewish Diaspora communities instead of big ones from a few plutocrats would also increase participation and knit the worldwide Jewish community together. Even if Israel wants funding and other assistance from donors whose assets are of questionable origin, they need to make less noise about it.

The same logic applies within Israel. While ordinary people undergo humiliating interrogation in Israeli embassies to get tourist visas, important for the Israeli economy, numerous known criminals find safe

---

[142] Gentiles see leaders of Jewish organizations as representatives of Jewish people, but Jews at large do not elect and often do not even know them.

haven there and travel the world with Israeli passports. Though Israel is not a center of offshore financial activity, she is criticized for protecting a few shady businessmen and companies. Though Israel does not profit significantly from arms sales and military services, the country is involved in many notoriously dirty endeavors with some of the world's worst dictators. Gentiles must see Jews as people of high moral quality, especially during the Palestinian conflict. In a typical show of stupidity, Israel deals immorally in publicized cases at little profit instead of disregarding morals only for large profit when publicity is minor.

When faking compassion, do it credibly. The "Save Darfur" campaign fooled few people. It was too transparent an attempt by Israeli lobbyists to publicize Arab atrocities. Jewish organizations, often ruled by rich sponsors with little understanding of the mob mindset, cannot refine the public relations. Heavy-handedness is more practical: prove empty pronouncements with actions. If Israel wanted to save Darfur, she should openly arm the Fur tribe and force the transports of food through the Baggara cordons. That would have created the world's goodwill to Israel; mere words would not.

Jews should criticize Muslims on myriad of minor issues instead of a few vulnerable problems. Trumpet the private concerns of many Egyptologists about the ambitions of one Zahi Hawass who imagines himself the keeper of Pharaonic Egypt. Scream of the destruction of the Red Sea coral reefs by coastal over-development. No one is going to check or analyze Jewish involvement in so many insignificant issues, and a barrage of critique on many fronts will impair Muslim reputation much more than concentrated attack on a single issue quickly discounted in the Western public' minds as irresolvable.

Interfaith dialogue is a sham. Religions allow no compromises. "We accept Jesus as a historical figure and maybe a prophet, and you scale down on the notion of Trinity" is not an option. Nothing precludes Jews from befriending Christians or Muslims. Nothing in Judaism allows Jews to consider other religions.

New goals

Israel normalized the Jews by making them a "normal" nation with a state. The Jews should normalize Israel, making her into a "normal" state unburdened by perpetual war and socialism.[143]

Any reform must begin with the economy, breaking from the socialist past and moving toward a free market, so suitable for enterprising Jews. A dynamic economy will make Israelis proud and others respectful.

---

[143] Many Jews lean to socialism which promised in the Diaspora to elevate them to equality with other nations. Jews want a big government which protects them from mobs, and which they can use to rise above the mobs. Second-generation Israelis, largely free from the fear of gentiles, can abandon socialism.

202

Decent neighbor will replace American client. The first priority should not be to extend Israel's borders but to create attractive conditions in the country: peace, low taxes, and minimal government intervention. Israel must create a welcoming climate for research and development, investment, banking, and other high value-added services. She should emulate Japan, Hong Kong, Switzerland, and the United States all at once. But to do that, Israel should become the voice of the Middle East in the Western world, not the voice of Western democracy in the Middle East.

The Israeli government should worry less about grabbing desert and other useless land and more about creating the vibrant economy that will let her become a scientific, financial, and trade center. The problem is not terrorism but the paucity of Nobel laureates, multinational corporations, banks, and stock and commodity exchanges. Israel has only about as many scientists per million people as the United States, and in terms of publications and patents, Israeli scientists are about half as effective as their American colleagues. The conditions in Israel are so bad that many researchers emigrate, as do highly educated youth who see little reason to work in Israel for a fraction of the salary they can get in the United States. *That* is the real problem, not the Palestinian issue.

Socialism quickly metastasizes through societies. Appealing to the deepest desires of protection and equality, it changes national mentality. No society abandoned socialism easily, and most – violently. The possibility of peaceful transformation of Israel into free market society is uncertain – there are too many ex-Soviet people and other semi-communists to allow for velvet revolution. The generation of slavery died in Sinai, but Israel missed a chance to let the Soviet Jews develop Negev.

Israel should explicitly encourage immigration of highly skilled gentiles from the Third World, from workers to scientists unable to get American residence visas. Particularly, Muslims could be lured, both promoting ties with Israel and brain-draining their countries. With comprehensive free education, Israel is in dire need of the best teachers. America should drain the world of scientists with expertise relevant to nuclear weapons, unconditionally offering them visas and well-paying jobs.

Although per capita productivity is higher in Israel than in any other Middle East country, the difference is minuscule, only about three times higher than in primitive Lebanon. Israel's public sector is much poorer than the public sector in many Arab states because of war expenditures, social programs, and the absence of oil revenues. Teaching the army to rely on small chemical, biological, and nuclear forces rather than infantry should alleviate the problem.

Social programs are alien to Torah where charity is the obligation and responsibility of the individual person; a good deed not to be replaced with government welfare. The government robs people of the opportunity to perform an important religious and ethical obligation. Jews should take care of the poor and educate their children, as they did for millennia before socialism transformed charity from beneficence for widows and orphans to entitlement for everyone. State money should go only to programs not supported by charity, such as increasing the birth rate.

The Torah envisages a liberal society, which should not give way to the preference for strong government. Israel must deny the socialist values of her founders. Torah prescribes a tithe only on basic food, later expanded to all produce, suggesting that charity is to save those who cannot work from starvation, not to equalize incomes. There must be no mandatory redistribution beyond the tithe—and, in line with the commandments, no tax on corporate income, which would boost the Israeli economy and attract foreign investment.

People love a prosperous country. Israel must define her economic goals and only then decide which political and social objectives her economic can support. The present suffocating tax system must be dismantled. As a first step, the consolidated tax rate ceiling must be fixed at 30% and gradually descend to 15%. Then the state should make decisions about military conflicts, social programs, education, or infrastructure based on the taxes collected. People who want war can pay an additional self-imposed tax, if they like, although there are not enough of them now to finance a war. Most of the people who want war cannot pay for it but vote to tax others to defray the cost. Unless Israel stops putting the cart before the horse, setting the goals and then looking for means, her economy is doomed.

The current situation, where each political party tries to get the lion's share of the budget to bribe its constituency, is a prescription for peculation and failure. Most budget spending should be fixed by consensus as a percentage of revenues to avoid lobbying. Education should be the first priority. Well-educated people do not need many social programs and can arrange market capital for infrastructure projects. Now, while the government pays for essentially socialist goals, education and academic research are under-funded, and the war makes everything worse.

Security comes from an open, interrelated economy, not from the army. Israel should imitate the Egyptians, who opened free-investment zones in areas susceptible to Israeli attacks, which in due course became living shields, since Israel dare not bomb foreign-owned factories in Egypt. Israel is not as attractive as Egypt with its huge population, but she is not bad. Real security lies in involving influential people, companies, and countries. They will pressure both the Arabs and their own governments to protect their investments in Israel.

Dar al Islam is not the enemy of the west

To expand Tolstoy's dictum about families, all happy societies are alike, all troubled societies are different. Affluent people want safety for themselves and their property and freedom. Societies that want goods might profess communism or Islam but in the end come to respect property, *ergo*

204

individualism, private initiative, practicality instead of idle contemplation, and the freedom to accumulate wealth. To realize freedom, they want responsive governments and opt for democracy.

Sage autocracies of the Singaporean type are great when sages head them and more efficient than democracies. But autocracies are vulnerable to bad rulers who quickly destroy much of what good rulers build and, most important, destroy the unquestioning discipline of people who trust their rulers' sagacity. Autocracies that do not transform themselves into democracies slide into demagogical tyranny. Only in small homogeneous societies can people agree on what constitutes sagacity; in large countries, different people understand wisdom differently. As differentiation increases with economic development, contradictory interests emerge, and consensual autocracy no longer works. Responsive and responsible democracy adapts to society's ever-changing needs better than autocracy.

Contempt of authority is not only a bulwark against tyranny but also a benchmark for dissent, as well as an indicator of development in science and business management. Obedient people are not creative.

Reforming societies by force, whether revolutionary, autocratic, or despotic, never works. Lasting benefits cannot be bestowed; they must be earned through slow and painful development. No sage can overcome the inertia of the masses. Peter's modernizing reforms were mere ripples on the marsh of Russian society; American immigrants accepted the founding fathers' liberal propositions democratically.

Freedom tilts the balance away from family and societal responsibility, from discipline and hierarchical order, to individualism. Confucian and protestant societies both move from communalism, family, discipline in politics and at work, and thrift toward individualism. Individualism is not a peculiarly Western value, and communalism is not peculiarly Asian. The scales of individualism and communalism are laden with property. As societies move to affluence, people rely less on the communal safety net and survive without the group, which tilts them toward individualism. The scales move slowly, and only a generation of prosperity began to dissolve Japan's communalism. People, who act predominantly in their own self-interest to acquire wealth, are not communalists. Communalism operates only in simple societies; elsewhere, the interests of various groups are hard to assess, impossible to quantify, and impractical to pursue all together or correlate arbitrarily. Calls for placing society above self often disguise obedience to a state.

Communalism in totalitarian states is not a philosophy but rather a rational response to an individual's *inability* to confront others, especially the many associated with government. Oppressive powers squeeze societies into masses. Individualism, on the other pole, is propped by *unwillingness* to confront others for fear of even minimal repercussions. Few people pursue communalism or individualism on their philosophical merits.

No stable society is perfectly libertarian: too much diversity irritates and freedoms clash. Materialist Western democracies are hostile to communism, Nazism, and religious fundamentalism, which threaten property rights and popular consensus. The hostility becomes prohibition only when a threat gels; normally even detested views remain legal because the public wants free speech and the right to one's opinion and dissent. Affluent societies possess a large margin of stability and expect efficient, expensive law enforcement to intervene before dissent becomes actionable and dangerous. Societies marginalize hostile opinions and contain them.

Many societies have attempted to pursue non-materialist values and failed in international competition. People are made to live in material world, and no ideology could long compete with the simple attraction of goods. Ideologies and religions that introduce different values run against nature and cover that fact in complexities and euphemisms, all the while accumulating contradictions and ambiguities trying to adjust themselves to real human wants. All the way, teachings become less attractive both to idealists who object to concessions and to pragmatists who oppose unnatural dicta. Teachings become irrelevant to the majority that cannot practice them because people live by action, not contemplation. "Truth is that which works," and people discount unworkable doctrines.

While developed societies share the desire for freedom from personal and material repression, undeveloped societies have little in common, and superficial differences in religion or ethnicity become significant in developing group attachments and identifying enemies.

Civilizations are not about religion. Most people are practical atheists or know and follow—now as before—their religions superficially. Sectarians often hate members of other sects more than followers of other religions, yet sectarians generally belong to the same civilization.

Separation of church and state does not significantly shape civilizations. Theocratic Jews respect freedom and property. Secular Western Christians do likewise, while secular Hindu society does not.

Civilizations are not strictly related to ethnicity. Blacks are slowly assimilated into American Western civilization. Rather civilizations are about the core values: freedom, life, property, and a balance between the private and the public. In that sense, twenty-first century consumerist Japan is westernized, while post-communist Russia, with deep communal and authoritarian sentiment, is not.

Cultural or ideological attachment is the poor man's way to self-esteem, to feeling meaningful by attaching himself to the grandeur of a group; poor nations, likewise, appeal to civilizational identities. People in economically developed societies can achieve on their own.

Religious societies are economically inefficient when people look to other world for fulfillment. Transforming religion into ethics, as in Judaism, Confucianism, and Protestantism boosts their development.

Affluent societies profess the religion of goods. Adherents of every other mass religion or ideology further their aims by converting others. Consumerism goes forward individually as people increase their consumption and perfect their souls simultaneously. Consumerism works only in economically developed societies where consumer aims are realistically attainable.

Consumerist societies do not agree to totalitarianism or wage wars unless they feel threatened. Wars may be waged for vague threats if they pose little danger, as did the U.S.-Vietnam war. They wage wars to obtain coveted goods, as did Spain in the New World, if war is feasible. Advanced countries produce most valuable goods and are not easy to fight. Goods are usually obtainable by trade easier than by war.

Consumerist societies are usually pacifist. They are less likely to wage war than profusely religious or ideological states, which necessarily put intellectual values ahead of life and property—else people would not subordinate themselves, their property, and their potential income to those values. Nation-states drive people away from consumerism, infuse them with ideology, and increase their propensity to war.

Growing wealth increases interaction between people and between peoples, and different values clash. Wealth promotes cultural experimentation, increasing the intra-societal divergence of values. Growing similarity offsets trends toward confrontation: fear of losing property breeds tolerance; for many people, liberalism and the avoidance of confrontation are consumerism's other face. German and Japanese chauvinist consumers buy only cars they manufacture. Such habits, though antagonistic, comfortably coexist in the larger framework of a common desire to enjoy property safely. Inexpensive communication, likewise, first challenges values, then dissolves them.

Countries develop only with open markets, and a global economy presupposes similar values. Nationalist businessmen do not survive competition with free marketers unburdened by the need to deal only with their kin. Some businessmen invest in corrupt China or the lawless emirates expecting a high return, but most are risk-averse and prefer countries with transparent laws and decent courts. Some are eager for oil concessions in Iran, but most avoid irrational regimes. Few invest in militarily adventurous, unstable, or endangered countries. Foreign trade has been high-risk and high-return throughout the history, and countries with bad business climate survive, even though they under-perform business-friendly countries that attract entrepreneurs with only moderate profits. Less profit to foreigners translates into more income left at home and accelerates domestic development.

Morals, though not natural, are acquired and universal. No one wants to fall victim to murder, looting, or fraud. Everyone extends those immunities to others as long as societies are reasonably ordered, and such behavior minimizes the chances of being victimized. The atrocities in

Kuwait and Bosnia were similarly wrong, but the West did not show a double standard by reacting differently. The standard was one: necessity, not morality. The obligation of not harming does not make help obligatory.

All people want the same rights. Even African paupers want truthful reporting and need a free press. Autocracy serves artificial states that combine hostile groups better than democracy, but that is the fault of the colonial powers, not of democracy. After borders are readjusted to create relatively homogenous societies, people prefer democracy to totalitarianism. Economic development and the increasing complexity of societies demand more safeguards and thus more extensive human rights.

Human rights and the rule of law in the broad sense are as old as the extant literature: from the codex of Ur-Namma to the Torah to the Greek and Roman civilizations and forward, those values are not uniquely Western. In the narrow sense, homosexuality was prohibited or restricted in the developed countries until recently, and liberalism is not inherent in or peculiar to Western culture. Unlimited tolerance of odd practices is a product of affluence: people enjoy expensive police protection, avoid confrontations, want fewer restrictions for themselves, and thus allow more freedoms to others.

Religions converge. Protestantism, no more like Catholicism than Orthodoxy, merged with Catholicism into Western Christian culture. Various cults are amalgamated into Hinduism, and "Judeo-Christian" has broad application. People, willing to accept ethical restrictions to avoid offending and provoking neighbors, moderate the expression of their beliefs—and eventually, the beliefs. Civil regulation and ethics, practical steps to paradise, cannot differ significantly among religions whose adherents live together. Religions adapt to modern realities, such as equal rights for women and coexistence with infidels, and reinterpretation spills onto other theological issues, revamping religions along similar lines. Scientific skepticism ridicules theological postulates, and compulsory secular education expunges religion from children's worldview. "You cannot serve God and Mammon," and people, unable to pursue two major objectives at a time, go for affluence when it is realistically attainable; pious Muslims live in Paris rather than in dar al Islam and orthodox Jews in New York rather than Jerusalem. Renaissances are rare and short-lived in religions, just as in cultures. Fundamentalists are few, and most people despise them. Religions rely on absolute authority and oppose innovation. Absent continuous updating, any system eventually dissolves into homogeneity.

Religions promote salvation, an absolute good, and rely on absolute credibility. Possibly, Absolutist monotheism could supplant polytheist cults. Accept a monotheist deity in the pantheon, and monotheism becomes the Trojan horse that forces the other deities out. Polytheism lacks the barrier of intolerance. Societies that practice polytheism and ancestor worship are vulnerable to Christianizing, which succeeded spectacularly in Korea.

People are uncomfortable with absolute values and prefer complex balancing systems. Polytheist elements eventually re-enter monotheist religion; Jews kiss the Torah scrolls, and Christians venerate the Virgin Mary.

Paganism resurfaced in the Christianity that overpowered it. Could not indigenous beliefs resurface from under Western influence? Christianity, a theory, was adapted to daily life by borrowing time-tested pagan practices. Western culture—from ethics to economy to art—was tested through centuries and found a better performer than any other. It is not, actually, Western culture but a universally optimal culture the West was the first to discover. Elites flirt with sword fighting and haiku, but populations prefer boxing and sumo, paperback thrillers and cartoons. The economy of abundance created a mass demand for culture, and that culture, serving the lowest common denominator, is alike across the globe.

After some initial irritation, people get used to others' values: Catholics and protestants are no longer hostile. Values become less urgent, and a renaissance is unlikely; few Muslims answer the fundamentalists' calls and those not for long. New, often common, enemies emerge to push former opponents toward cooperation.

Cultures likely converge, for the same reason single standards emerge. People and influences travel farther and faster, creating a more homogeneous global society. Indigenous cultures are increasingly relegated to a tint on mass culture, as major corporations build additional features on top of standards. Global culture is not static: wider audiences mean more influences. Neither is culture coherent: rather it consists of different strata catering to different layers of society. Why, then, it is not stratified by ethnic and perhaps religious preferences? Because they are weak and dissolve steadily. New trends continuously emerge in culture, stratify to meet the demands of various audiences, and blur. Ethnic identities are static; once blurred, other ethnic identities do not replace them. The Japanese attempted to reinvent their identity in the late twentieth century, and came up with their technological ultra-development. Such cases of changing identity are rare and do not last: continuously changed identities cease to identify. Japanese-Americans assimilate well.

Cultural convergence is not entirely a modern phenomenon. The Romans assimilated Greek art and science, medieval Arabs studied Greek manuscripts, and Renaissance Europeans took Roman law for their model. Culturally blank-slate societies are bound to adopt foreign practices; if Muslims wanted to develop the art of painting, they could only copy others.

Most cultural differences are only myths: bloodthirsty Muslims, patient Asians thinking in terms of millennia, Confucians seeking consensus (in autocracies), and cultured European masses. Analysts looking from afar see cultural rebound where in fact only their foreigners' awareness of that culture increases. The locals see their traditions eroding. Increased contact dissipates preconceptions.

Besides importing Western culture directly with American films, societies import it with goods symbolic of the West. Likewise, interest in Japanese culture coincided with the *Made in Japan* expansion. As long as the West retains the technological lead, it will develop most of the symbolic products and keep its culture attractive.

Muslims who watch American movies have never heard of the Magna Charta, but the name also rings hollow to many Westerners. Mass culture is not about philosophy. Hollywood blondes in Cadillacs arouse similar feelings throughout the world. Values—individualism, freedom, respect for law and property—are not imported but develop painfully and slowly alongside and mutually supportive of economic progress.

There is nothing wrong with mass culture or modern morals. Peasants and similar majorities had very simple tastes in art; refined art belonged to the elites. The divorce rate might be historically high now, but extramarital relations, essentially the same thing, were always popular. Aesthetes view mass culture with contempt, and puritans view mass morals likewise, though neither is below the historical norm. Corporate employers gripe about declining work ethics; Greek slave owners had similar complaints. Things change shape, internet newsgroups replace neighborhoods, but human nature persists.

Power does not usually expand culture. Forced conversion of the whole population and full annihilation of earlier traditions is the norm. Culture spreads through attraction. People acting in self-interest choose pleasant and indulgent cultures that further their interests, especially when elites no longer control acceptable private behavior, learning, and information to shape cultures for the communal needs of states. Victors often adopt the culture of the vanquished. The West might not remain dominant, but its culture might nonetheless survive.

Heated calls for the preservation of indigenous cultures against the onslaught of the West show that they are endangered—and doomed. Most never actually existed as a mass phenomenon. Only elites practiced them and took the indifference of populations concerned only with survival as consent. The Japanese public has no use for the complicated art forms, and the Chinese do not want Confucian obedience, which was forced on them. The Chinese adhered to the analects as little as Europeans to the idealistic dicta of the gospels.

Both no development and rapid development promote interest, desperate and proud respectively, in the indigenous culture. In the first case, old cultures become merely symbolic, a kind of *Oktoberfest* held by immigrants. In the second, it soon proves futile, unable to deliver economic progress. The Iranians got fed up with the *mullahs* in just three decades, and were more secular after they overthrew the *ayatollahs* than before. Religious observance induced by failure is superficial, just enough to experience attachment without real concern. Conservatism poses as religious resurgence: merchants protect their economic interests against foreigners, paupers claim communal welfare, and middle-aged males demand patriarchal prerogatives. Conservatism is a desperate and eventually inefficient attempt to stop the wave of modernization, and religious resurgence is similarly unsustainable.

Very poor people are traditionalist rather than religious; rural Muslims require their women to wear scarves, but few pray five times daily. A bit of modern prosperity sent them searching for values, which they see in religion. Increased social mobility and social changes made them cling to tradition identified with religion—only to see that religion does not help. Economic and social transformation need not end before people return to moderate religiosity, but people take time to get used to the changes—a matter of decades.

Culture is a means of enjoyment, and enjoyment depends largely on economic situation. Culture, thus, is related to economy. Traditional cultures are not congruent with a global technological economy.

Central planning prescribes economic behavior, and cannot work in complex societies. Tradition prescribes a still wider range of behavior and is all the more unworkable. Societies shed, reinterpret, hypocritically revere, or (most commonly) ignore tradition. Practical culture is an *ad hoc* phenomenon, ever changing and adapting to economic realities. Even such basic ethical rules, like prohibitions of murder and theft, are commonly ignored in times of distress. Prosperity changes culture no less than does hardship.

A resurgence of suppressed interests is often taken for the rebound of indigenous culture. Indian politics is being "Hinduized," not because the locals became concerned with religious intricacies but because the government, unable to satisfy the people with economic development, seeks support in old hatreds. Hindis and Muslims are not more intolerant to each other now than before. Rather, the conflict previously suppressed by totalitarian rule and backbreaking work for sustenance, erupted when the political and economic situation were right and was popularized by the media out of all proportion. Undeveloped countries still have not passed the stage of a booming economy bringing people of different faiths and ethnicities in close contact, forcing them to cooperate to satisfy their self-interest, thus blending identities. When income calls, hatreds are put aside.

Underdeveloped nations that encounter the onslaught of Western culture through media, goods and emigrants' tales are uncomfortable with it. Unable to suppress that culture, they adapt to it and bandwagon the West. They further have to adopt Western habits because many of them plead with the West for aid. Japan succeeded in modernizing while remaining distinctive because of its unique combination of cultural homogeneity, xenophobia, communalism, work ethics, passion for design, and education. The country developed with relatively little foreign assistance. By creating a sophisticated internal market, Japan prevented imports of less advanced goods and curtailed foreign influence. Even so, the habits and passion of

Japanese and American teenagers do not differ significantly. The Japanese traditionally tilt toward visual arts, now represented by comics and appliance design, but otherwise both groups are fond of movies, videogames, modern music, discos, alcohol, sex, and future income. Traditions are by definition outdated; modernizing nations shed them and, unable to develop new traditions quickly, fill the void with mass culture.

While people may refuse foreign goods, as do the Japanese, in an open, (especially) globalized society, they cannot refuse a dominant foreign language, whether it be Akkadian or English. Elites (scribes or businessmen) are fluent in the lingua franca, causing people to expand their knowledge of the language from sporadic to basic to full. The language becomes a prestigious good, a necessary means of advancement. The language of the nation with the most foreign contacts has the best chance of becoming the lingua franca. The contacts could be any: diplomatic for Akkadian, trade for Greek, military for Latin, scholarly for German. American English combines those areas of prominence and stands a good chance of surviving for a long time in simplified forms as the common language of global society. Its pidgin variants will converge as speakers across the globe communicate daily. Mandarin is too complicated for universal acceptance as a second language. Hindi exists in so many dialects that Indians prefer English for communication with speakers of other dialects. Arabic is widespread, but the economic and military value of its speakers is negligible. Except for the unlikely case of military power, the lingua franca is always the core language of an open society, even in the case of Rome. Cultural attraction is indispensable for preserving conquests and pacifying the conquered. Society must be open not just politically but also economically.

People judge teachings by their fruits: the promise of an afterlife for religions and worldly well-being for ideologies. The world might hate and envy economic leaders, yet adopt their competitive behavioral patterns; hatred often masks admiration. Envy might result in sporadic clashes and sabotage, which appear in any culture. Muslims produced Al Zawahiri, and Christians, McVeigh. Wars generally erupt to solve problems, not to vent feelings. Attacking Japan would not help American steelmakers who also face competition from South Korea, Russia, and other places too numerous to subdue.

Consumerist societies, especially those that rose to affluence through work, are averse to fighting, just as there is less crime in rich societies. They are not pacifist and employ force where retaliation is unlikely. Economically advanced countries can retaliate or arouse enough concern among others to count as retaliation, and affluent countries do not usually fight among themselves. Total wars destroy economies and cannot solve trade disputes.

Countries might be prone to fighting for cultural reasons, but culture hardly prevails over economic interests. Countries of similar culture fight over real interests, and countries of mutually exclusive religions cooperate on common interests.

Poor countries need ideology to make the citizenry consent to be ruled, but affluent countries also fall for ideology or idealism, especially when doing so poses no threat to their economic status. Abundance pushes people to seek higher values which, once found, help others to recognize those ideals, eventually with the sword. Mid-size developed economies, conscious of their vulnerability to military means and economic sanctions, are pacifist to the extent of seeking international consensus.

Declining giants are dangerous. They use force to preserve the international respect they got used to at their peak and are unable to preserve by economic activity. Another newly risen empire, acting as the world's policeman, could shorten those pangs.

Rising tigers are dangerous, unless they are very open economically and trade with the targeted countries a lot. New economies, often undemocratic and with few welfare demands, accumulate unusually large amounts in government coffers, allowing for military build-ups. As such economies peak, popular and government ambitions irreversibly outstrip capabilities and are channeled into politics and eventually into warfare. Depredation on weak neighbors is not as easy as before. Efficient transportation has allowed weak countries to acquire out-of-region sponsors capable of projecting their military power. WMD arsenals and world opinion also deter aggression. Global society offers better opportunities for increasing influence through trade and assistance rather than through war. Proclaiming warfare no longer economically rational before WWI was no mistake; it just took people some time to realize it. The economic irrationality of wars does not preclude them. The reasons given for wars often only rationalize a struggle for power, hatreds, ambitions, and plain masculine aggression. When no other pretext is found, civilizational issues go in.

Rationalist societies are potentially aggressive, since suffering has no place in rational calculations. The moral rationalism of the Enlightenment was a backlash against religious obscurantism; social rationalism reacted to the inability to comprehend the complex mechanics of social interactions. Rationalism emerges in global politics as large but irrelevant nations justify their claims to dominance.

Countries that get rich incidentally are arrogant and aggressively seek their place in world affairs to compensate for their inferior development. When incidental wealth is concentrated with government or oligarchs, poor and envious people do not fear mild international confrontations, even welcome the conflicts to sublimate and vent their discontent. Rome advanced through painstaking military labor and was remarkably tolerant; Saudi Arabia promotes *jihad*.

A sluggish economy leads to moral decline, while prosperity through work reinforces ethical values. People in poor or declining economies cannot realize their ambitions through market activities and resort to politics, radicalism, and war. Poverty or raging ambition override moral restrictions; affluent people can afford more of them, if only to feel safer.

The family is the strongest group. The broader a group, the weaker it is. Civilizations, the broadest groups, are weakest. Muslim countries join together only in declarations. People avoid helping a community and do not fight for civilizations.

The stronger a group is, stronger are the attachments and hatreds inside it. No Muslims hate infidels as much as some spouses hate each other. People sublimate myriad forms of discontent into hatred and make the people nearest by its objects. Most similar people invent distinctions among themselves to justify their hatreds. Ukrainian cynics summed up the reasons for dissolution from Russia as "They ate our bacon." Group boundaries appear when needed.

Civilizational identity, though weak, is real, and cannot be changed at whim. Turkey is still Islamic after three generations of Western secularist governments. A change of identity, a temptingly simple solution, is often counterproductive: if Turkey succeeded at Westernizing, Europeans would be called to protect a weak "cultural relative," while Muslim Turkey—moderate because economically open to Europe—is a viable buffer against the many failed states of Central Asia and the Middle East.

Humanity depends on inter-group competition for evolution. Inter-civilizational interactions are few, and civilizations do not compete significantly. They cannot, therefore, provide for evolutionary competition. Most competition—and conflict—takes place inside civilizations, which accordingly consist of antagonistic sub-groups. A world consisting of inwardly homogenous civilizations would cease to compete and develop.

Civilizational identity arises when no other identification is available, usually in times of social transition. The American melting pot showed that people of conflicting religions, cultures, and history eagerly shed their past to participate in a prosperous future.

People rarely identify themselves with nations, let alone with civilizations. Europeans warred among themselves for all their history, but the popes had a hard time assembling crusades to fight aliens. Except for rare, short wars induced by propaganda, people fight about urgent interests, and conflicting interests occur mostly among people of the same civilization who interact—and fight. Often. Inter-civilizational conflicts are almost exclusively about borders and of little practical concern to those living farther away—but they tickle people's xenophobia and make headlines. Inter-civilizational skirmishes in Bosnia roused the Europeans; millions dead in intra-Muslim conflicts left them unconcerned. Fighting over real interests is fierce and short; xenophobic wars are mild, indecisive, and thus prolonged, creating an impression of permanence.

214

Civilizational wars are rarely orderly because governments and businesses have little interests in alien lands, unless they include valuable resources, in which case the wars are unrelated to civilizations. Rather, border—including internal borders—conflicts are mob violence erupting when impunity is likely. The violence could occur along lines of property, class, religion, ethnicity, or just about any other visible trait. Impunity is critical: people do not risk their lives because of xenophobia. Clashes cease when the silent majority, quickly satiated with slaughter, implicitly revokes its support of the perpetrators. Radicals rarely influence politics; in matters of importance and consequences, the silent majority opts for moderation.

Trust is a matter of predictability, and so prevails where values are similar or easily comprehensible. Trade is simple enough that formal agreements describe its terms, and trust is unnecessary beyond the mere assurance of not cheating. Complex economic cooperation requires a different level of trust, and most businessmen prefer working with people of the same culture. That does not, however, make them willing to fight people of other cultures.

Complex adaptive systems rely on many conflicts for continuous readjustment. Family quarrels, market bargaining, and wars make societies efficient. The more interaction there is, the more readjustment is required. Since most interactions take place inside groups, most conflicts do as well. Fault line wars are the least bloody, because the enemies are clear. People are unwilling to fight over vague things; often only border populations are involved. The more blurred the lines fault lines are, the bloodier the conflicts are. Civil wars likely cause the most casualties because everyone is an enemy, and real interests are at stake.

A billion Muslims have produced only few thousand guerrillas to fight the West. Others cheer the terrorists but are too little involved against Western civilization to join them. Many guerrillas have immediate reasons to fight rather than a vague hatred of another civilization: ambitions, past abuse, or adventurism; the chance to kill with impunity and win laurels is tantalizing to many. Terrorists belong to a minor sub-group inside dar al Islam. Terrorists are Muslim, and Nazis were Christian; neither represents their civilizations.

People generally cooperate inside groups and compete with other groups. Groups are defined by behavioral traits. Different values thus mean competition and hostility. People are averse to alien habits. They rationalize hatreds and clad their interests in ideology. They draw lines to push the others behind, transforming them into aliens, a perceived threat, and legitimate prey. Moralizing made wars of plunder unacceptable and created the need to disguise conflicts in "ethnic" terms, thereby replacing plunder with murder. Ancient for-profit wars caused few casualties; ideological wars are bloodbaths.

Clashes between civilizations are limited to ideologically inspired or political goals. Real conflicts are few, often none. Touted confrontations

215

over economic issues are often irrelevant to nations and even benefit them, though they harm influential groups. Cultural frictions dissolve amid economic cooperation and rise to prominence when cooperation is insignificant; a trade portfolio, especially speculative foreign investment and oil sales, does not amount to cooperation.

Elites that fail as leaders imitate the masses; poll-based policy-making and indigenization of elites are common examples. Elites are often out of sync with their nations, Westernizing when people are not ready or pushing the old values when people want to Westernize. Failing rulers become ballast to their countries, pulling them back to the traditional past. Government support gives religion authority and draws more people to it.

States rely for their existence on nations, fictional groups, and so promote nationalism and religion, fictional group identities centered on ideas, not people. States need to prove themselves indispensable to their citizens and so are active. Ambitions prop up international involvement. States, therefore, promote the fiction of national and civilizational identities to rally people for what are really the goals of power politics. Politicians fish for religious quotes and customs to justify any policy. Much hateful rhetoric, "them versus us," remains only rhetoric, aimed at uniting the nation. Its potential for confrontation is slight.

At the other pole, political correctness produces a similarly violent backlash from people resisting multiculturalism, policies that benefit minorities, and alien immigration. Modern communications, inexpensive transportation, and political ease of movement allow immigrants to retain strong links with their homelands. Immigration is no longer a decision to change cultural identity, and unassimilated immigrants—especially the poor who depend on communal ties—form antisocial groups. Political correctness is likewise counterproductive in international relations, transforming a respected gendarme into a feared and hated nanny; people who accept intervention that stops atrocities oppose the use of force for non-essential purposes, like democratizing, economic liberalization, and preserving borders. Short interventions thus become civil wars, often with inter-civilizational dimensions. Minimizing meddling in other people's business would go a long way to eliminate the clashes of civilizations.

Saudi Arabia cannot establish an empire militarily and poses as the core of an informal Muslim empire, sponsoring schools and guerrillas and claiming to protect its kin worldwide. Poor countries and endangered Muslim communities accept the pretense of kin allegiance so long as it benefits them practically. People appeal to kinship when profitable: West Germans did not jump the wall to join their brethren, but East Germans did. Paupers agree to a common religion, ancient values, and authoritarianism if they can thereby increase the redistribution of wealth. The balance between individualism and communalism shifts toward the latter in poverty or under a threat; affluent societies rarely resort to kinship.

Kinship is often the last resort: rejected by Europe, Bulgaria turned to Russia. Appeals to kinship or other affiliation produce only limited, often token assistance: great powers invested little resources in proxy conflicts during the Cold War. Same-kin powers often find they can gain more political dividends by mediating conflicts rather than inflaming them; the Serbian government soon started trying to contain the Bosnian Serbs' aggression. If there is no kinship but real interests call for alliance, other common traits are found to satisfy the need: unable to appeal to common ethnicity or religion, Israel calls for affiliation with the West because both are democracies. Protectorates appealed to the arbitration of Rome, with which they lacked any cultural similarity. In the balance of power game, both Europeans and Arabs at times appealed to Britain.

Civilizational identities are forsaken when necessary. Kuwait appealed to America for help against Iraq, and France sabotages the US-led Western alliance in pursuit of political dividends, preferring to be in the vanguard of Muslim interests in the West than the rearguard of American interests anywhere. The Russian government supports anti-Muslim sentiment domestically to repress the Chechens but allies with Arabs against America—their allies in the war on Muslim terrorism. Governments are equally mendacious about xenophobia and kinship.

The boundaries of any civilization are pragmatically fluid and substantiate any line of conflict. The anti-communist "free world" included Japan and even Saudi Arabia. The Nazis drew civilizational line between Arians and everyone else. Nationalism surpasses religious identity in the secular world. Explaining the world as clashes of civilizations—religious confrontation, racial competition, *etc.*—is a desperate attempt to rationalize a system too complex to comprehend fully or explain simply.

People identify with different groups: family, football team fans, town, nation, religion, and civilization. Groups form around interests, not culture: diplomats and businessmen are at times more comfortable with foreign colleagues than with their compatriot voters and workers. People continuously juggle and arbitrate conflicting allegiances. The importance of any threatened group increases: soldiers forsake their families for a nation at war. Threats are relative: when prosperity decreases a town's or a family's lowers immediate problems, even cultural influence against one's civilization matters. The Cold War defined major interests in terms of allegiance to socialism or freedom; with détente, the only interests left were old religious and civilizational allegiances. Soon, however, new alliances will form around interests more meaningful than religion: trade, flow of investment, international charity.

Very poor people cannot afford concerns about civilizations, and the affluent do not fight over intangibles. Cultural hatreds are common at a specific economic level: well above sustenance yet lower than others, a point at which people can afford to pursue their ambitions by taking time from work but cannot realize them. That status can be attained either by externally acquired prosperity—welfare, international aid, or sudden improvements in agricultural productivity or medical care—or by stifling opportunities—by economic sanctions (post-WWI Germany), overregulation (USSR), or lack of education (dar al Islam).

A little sudden prosperity endangers morals: some people's ambitions surge beyond their means, while with others, consumption habits lag behind, leaving free time for radical activities and contemplation. Such people are few but enough to trouble societies.

Xenophobia is often the last resort of self-esteem. Snobbery and superiority make people despise, not hate others. Hatred is a product of envy. Instead of admitting that their own shortcomings prevent them from reaching the (usually material) level of others, people imagine they do not want that path or that level and reject the values they long for. If the object of envy is weak or acts weakly, hatred sees no barrier and intensifies. The Soviet people greatly envied American development but did not hate America—because it was strong; Muslims envy and hate America because they do not fear it.

The relevance of the demographic bulge among youth varies depending on education and economic opportunities: American baby boomers were assimilated after a short adjustment, though in Islamic countries they remain insufficiently employed and violent. Youth, however, rarely vote and exert limited influence on politics; riots culminate in revolutions only sporadically. Education may be culturally inherent, as in Japan, or a means to realistically attainable material gain, as in America. Superficial learning promotes hatred: people are conscious of scholarly defined, thus ostensibly substantial, cultural differences; unable to analyze them; ambitious because education is unusual in their milieu; unable to realize their ambitions because their education and skills are non-competitive; and lack tolerance which develops slowly through long affluence. Idealism, rationalism, ignorance of opposing views and the inability to comprehend the difficulties of social engineering substantiate revolutionary aggression.

The drive to well-being is very powerful, and people rarely choose cultural conflicts when economic opportunities are available. People working for sustenance have no time for xenophobia, unless it offers them loot (a shortcut to sustenance) or when they cannot sustain themselves regardless of toil (hunger revolts). Xenophobia is the domain of the lower-middle class, unrealized professionals and students without prospects of employment.

Xenophobia realizes ambitions either actively, through participation in politics and violence, or passively, by pinpointing culprits ostensibly responsible for the lack of opportunities. Ambitions are realized, albeit irrationally and without economic gain, in the first case, and reduced without a dent in self-esteem in the second. Like a lightning takes the random path of least resistance when a conduit is unavailable, ambitions are variously realized when economic opportunities are unavailable. Conflicts occur along cultural lines because they are clear, and rallying other losers is simple; cultural differences in themselves, however, do not cause conflicts. Cultural fault lines usually relate to religion (now, though not in tolerant polytheist antiquity) or ethnicity because those notions are superficially understandable and big enough that violence on their behalf soothes frustrated ambitions. Other cultural fault lines include class, property distinctions, or even soccer clubs. Differences are everywhere; they become fault lines only when real interests pressure them. Group allegiances become prominent in crises but generally do not cause them.

Capable opportunists sometimes head xenophobic movements, but the rank-and-file are losers who lack the resolution to compete economically. Their hatreds are similarly irresolute. Minimal opposition suffices to quash them: magistrates watched the pogroms with complacency, and anti-American protesters in dar al Islam do not fear reprisal. When, however, real interests are at stake, people are ready to suffer, like in rebellions against tyrants. Xenophobia does not make wars.

Border populations fight along civilizational fault lines when their neighbors belong to another civilization and along ethnic or religious fault lines when their neighbors belong to different ethic or religious groups. Advances in communication and transportation blurred micro-level territorial groups, and then blurred the mid-level groups, states. That process is underway in Europe, but other continents will follow. Hearing of blocs like "the free world" or "the West," other countries answer in kind, inventing extra-large groups with extra-weak bonds, such as the world of Islam. Opposition shapes affiliation.

Muslim Malaysia vents its ambitions through economic activity, fueled by its Chinese population; Muslim Iran suppresses its enterprising class and realizes ambitions by spreading fundamentalism and terrorism. Traditional Islam, unlike Confucianism, does not emphasize a work ethic, worldly gain, or education; the bureaucratized Arab and Turk empires inhibited private initiative. Those differences produced significantly different Arab-Muslim and Confucian economies and, therefore, politics. National competitiveness develops in clusters of related industries like crystals grow spontaneously in saturated liquids; growth builds on itself. Muslim culture, not seething with business activity, is not competitive. Lacking rigorous technical education, Muslim countries, unlike Russia, do not produce even isolated geniuses.

Western civilization is small in terms of population. The world is Chinese, Indian, Muslim, and Black. The West can dominate in influence, more important than raw population figures. Such dominance calls for limiting others' access to Western assets of knowledge and money, for restricting the transfer of capital (investments and imports), technology, and, most of all, education to the Third World. No company shares its hard-earned technology and no family allows strangers to live in its house, yet the countries paying lip service to idealists offer just that to aliens. Leftists demand sharing of the West's most precious assets with the Third World for the same reason they demand redistribution inside their societies: the underproductive leftists share other people's money to no harm to themselves and to the great feeling of their own goodness – at other people's expense. The West willing to dominate must exploit others rather than help them, plunder their natural resources at the monopolist buyer' prices, and stop immigration and manufactured imports. No need to harm the others through conquests or enslavement; just do not help them to your own detriment. The West intermingled with others will harm everyone; egalitarianism similarly destroyed communist economies. People of different education, innovativeness, and work ethics are not equals. Popular governments responsive to ethnically diverse electorates will never pursue economic exclusivism; they will help the competitors, and die out. Innovative corporations and minorities may form their own state-like entities and refuse to share technological knowledge with strangers.

Societies are complex adaptive systems, and no single factor responsible for development can be singled out. Rather, development depends on an almost intangible mix of factors. A mild climate benefits intellectual activity and creates agricultural surplus. Population must be dense enough to communicate, defend itself, and promote trade, yet sparse enough or isolated by terrain to make totalitarian control not feasible. Religion is not a primary factor in development; rather, economies and faiths shape each other. Random factors are at play: occasional wise rulers who establish just laws, the absence of vulnerable neighbors and slaves so people are not prone to loot and oppress, and trade opportunities that open nations to other cultures and promote education. Development cannot be modeled: an emphasis on education in the absence of employment radicalizes society, and emphasis on employment regardless of education creates low-wage-addicted economies. Free societies balance the factors empirically during a gradual advance. Development is self-reinforcing and initially accelerates when more people adopt the beneficial behavioral patterns of winners and slows when an affluent population behaves comfortably rather than efficiently.

Not all cultures are equally militaristic. Monotheist religions and ideologies opposed to common sense suppress dissent and are violent. Mature monotheist religions become, in a sense, polytheist, tolerating other confessions for political reasons. Burdensome religions, such as Islam, which permeate daily life with restrictions and obligations, keep their adherents on a short leash and make them intolerant. The same burden, however, quickly moderates those religions through interpretation or hypocrisy. After a short period of *jihad*, Islam was relatively peaceful for centuries, but the present fleeting resurgence demands a major place for Islam in the world and is aggressive. Christianity was more expansive than

Islam, bringing its teaching to Africa and America by force, and in a sense is aggressive even now.

Religious resurgence is often fundamentalist. New bigots know the religion superficially but need to identify its enemies clearly to channel the discontent. They attain energy through velocity rather than mass and compensate shallowness of knowledge with force of convictions. Their religiosity is in fact nationalism where a nation is defined in religious terms.

Edward Said's The End of the Peace Process
(New York: Pantheon Books, 2000)
A Review

Professor Said was University Professor of English and Comparative Literature at Columbia University. Born an Arab in 1935 in Jerusalem, then under the British mandate, he studied at Cairo, Princeton, and Harvard. He published more than twenty books and died in September 2003.

Building the state in the real world

Since the Arabs could not destroy the Jewish settlements with criminal gangs or regular armies, they—especially the Palestinians—have started posing as persecuted victims, crying for justice. That is dishonest, since the Arabs knew for almost a century before 1967 that the Jews were fighting for their ideals on their own. When the balance turned against the Arabs, they appealed to morality, though they cooperated with the Nazis and opposed settling Jewish refugees in Palestine. Now the Palestinians are eager for equal rights; but why should Israel agree to that, if Arab opposition to equal rights for Jews created the conflict in the first place? Some attempted to build a case for a situation in which Jews are expected to adhere to moral standards their enemies flout.

The fate of the Palestinians is not Holocaust

Said's book opens with what should be a shocking statement from *Kirkus Reviews*, calling the fate of Palestinians "one of the greatest tragedies of our time." Yet the Palestinians are not being exterminated. Their movable property has not been looted nor their women raped—by Israelis. They do not work in concentration camps but live more comfortably than Jewish immigrants did fifty years ago. They are not starving but have gotten unprecedented welfare benefits for four generations. Many emigrated to other countries long ago; those left do nothing positive. How can one compare life in a subsidized community with real tragedies like the Holocaust of Jews and gypsies in World War II, the slaughter of the two world wars, the millions dead in Algeria and Rwanda, and other catastrophes, all of which arose from the desire to kill for the sake of killing? The Jews do not want to kill Arabs. Israel took heavy losses in street fighting in Lebanon and Palestine instead of razing them from the air, as any other army would have done. Indeed, Israel's restraint with civilians led to her defeat in Lebanon—the proof of the impossibility of reestablishing order in a heavily militarized country without brutality.

Speaking of the Holocaust, Said says, "Many of us [Arabs] may wish to regard it as none of our business." But no less a Muslim authority than the Mufti of Jerusalem sat the war out in Berlin, collaborating with the Nazis with the full support of other Arabs and no dissident of distinction.

Jewish leaders conspired to drive the Arabs out, and Professor Said is quick to condemn it. But every action should be considered in its context. No one wants to live next to someone who tried to evict and kill him, even after an accepted arbitrator issued its verdict, as the United Nations did in 1947.[144] If such a neighbor could be driven out by legitimate pressure, well and good, and Israel's pressure has been mild by comparison with the violence attendant on the establishment of modern states. The Palestinian resistance to the flood of Jewish refugees could be justified, but that is not the point. The important thing is that they proved their hostility to Jews, and so the Jews have reasonably tried to run them out.

Jews and Palestinians are not equal

Palestinian apologists say that all people are equal and deserve equal treatment. That is wrong on both points. Egalitarianism is a totalitarian policy, and to demand political equality is as wrong as to demand economic equality. Equal opportunities produce unequal outcomes. Jews and Palestinians had equal opportunities in 1948. The Jews used theirs better and have prevailed.

People are not born equal. Different people have different mental abilities, and some have peculiar national traits. Women, for example, do better than men in some occupations and worse in others. It is good that there is no norm, and that all types of people are different, with people suited variously to various activities. Current scientific knowledge does not draw firm conclusions on the nature of human differences, genetic or cultural. Differences are, of course, no excuse for discrimination, but analysis should not be labeled racist or sexist.

Said does not believe in equality and finds Ben Gurion's remark likening the Arabs to American Indians offensive. If Said believed they were equal, he would not be offended. He also dislikes the suggestion that Pakistan and Bangladesh control the Muslim landmarks in Jerusalem. If he thinks his country is better than some other Muslim nations, he should not be surprised someone else does the same. He does not care about other non-

---

[144] After de facto settlement of Jews in Palestine, and de jure recognition, Palestinians cannot argue that Jews forced their way into the neighborhood. Black activists forced their way into white American neighborhoods like the Jews entered Palestine. A combination of force and legal devices substitutes for welcome reception.

Jewish people in Israel, only about the Palestinians. He has no reason to criticize people who do not care about Palestinians.

People of different nations often think differently since they have different cultures. Said calls Richard Butler's claim that Arabs have a different notions of truth from the rest of the world racist. Likely, however, most Westerners who work with Arabs would subscribe to that judgment. Not burdened by Western-style moralizing and skeptical of infidels, Arabs are very flexible about the truth and their promises. Islam expressly sanctions deceiving non-Muslims.[145] Mohammed invited the Jewish leader of Khaibar to come unarmed for negotiations, and then killed him. The phenomenon is not rare: before the invention of the notion of racism, Europeans said the American Indians were dishonest. The Indians probably thought they were just being practical. Only developed societies can afford the restraint of promises.

Equality presupposes similar or at least compatible cultural platforms, what the author calls a "reconciliation of experiences." But Western and Islamic values are irreconcilable, and equality is out of the question. Differences should be understood and tolerated but cannot be ignored.

The Palestinians claim special rights

To claim equality is often just a way to ask for special rights. Said objects to Israeli isolationism, arguing for integration with Palestine, yet later admits that most Arabs want to boycott Israel, the next best option to destroying it. Israel is not isolationist; Arabs ostracize her. Economic integration is meaningless, since Palestine has neither capital nor technology. Professor Said wants open borders, letting Palestinians flood Israel, looking for a better life and work, but that would give Palestinians preferential treatment. Israel has no reason to give Palestinians special treatment—yet she actually does. Palestinians with clean records can work at almost any job in Israel, though Arab Lebanon excludes them from dozens of occupations.

Said criticizes Israeli control of "exits and entrances" to Palestine, while what Israel in fact controls are border checkpoints. Should Israel concede control of her borders to Palestine or just leave them open? Since Palestine is not a recognized state, there is no formal border. Professor Said wants it both ways: a state but borders that work only one way. Said notes that tension and killings arise when two nations are "rubbed against each other," just co-existing. The logical solution to that is separation, not open borders.

Said's indignation that the Law of Return applies only to Jews also asks for special treatment. This law gives Diaspora Jews the right to

---

[145]The Ten Commandments similarly prohibit bearing false witness only against one's neighbor, a member of one's group.

immigrate to Israel, a state created specifically for Jews. Why should that privilege be extended to Arabs? Put it another way: would any Arab state, Palestine included, accept the descendants of Jews who moved away centuries or dozens of years ago? Clearly not. Whether they should is irrelevant.

Said in fact proposes "supra-equality," namely that not only should Palestinians be treated as equals but that others should defend their rights. He is indignant that Egypt claimed nothing for the Palestinians in the Camp David agreement. That is not true, in the first place, since the agreement posits Palestinian self-determination, which became another plank in the Palestinian platform. Further, why should Egypt or anyone champion the Palestinians? Egyptians and Palestinians are not compatriots; they have different cultures and speak different dialects; religious affinity did not inspire Palestinians to fight for Pakistan against India. Why expect support from Egypt? Egypt's treaty with Israel does not imperil the rights of other Arabs. Said denigrates all things Egyptian, even claims that "U.S.-compliant" President Mubarak is unpopular, while in fact Egyptians are fond of him.

Trying to balance equality and special rights, the professor says the Wye River Memorandum commits the Palestinian Authority to Israeli security, not the other way around. He must believe Israel is responsible for Palestinian security. Israel has no interest in Palestine's external affairs and has never infringed on P.A. security unless in reprisal. Palestinians have all the security they need: a huge police apparatus, though no army whose only prey would be Israel. The P.A. promises only not to host anti-Israeli terrorists—not a mind-boggling concession.

Professor Said also criticizes Israel for releasing about a hundred Palestinian criminals; but Palestinians should deal with their own thieves. It turns out that not all Palestinians in Israeli jails are political prisoners.

No reason for preferential treatment of Arabs

Said criticizes the American president for "showing no understanding of [the] Arab-Islamic world." What Arabs want is simple: no Israel. Why should the United States or any other country care about Arab mentality? There is the plain legal matter of recognizing Israel, a duly established state,[146] and ceasing hostilities. No one asks Arabs to love Jews. Arabs are not in kindergarten so that the powers must tailor their policy to Arab wants. Welcome to the cold world.

---

[146] Japan recognizes Russia but does not accept annexation of the Kuriles. Arabs never recognized Israel in the 1948 borders, established by U.N. resolution on the partition of Palestine, the very resolution they incessantly appeal to, demanding Israeli withdrawal from the territories.

Inequality is inherent in every conflict

There is no equality between victors and vanquished, especially if the latter were the aggressors. Whatever were the Jews' original intentions, they launched military aggression, which incidentally expelled the Arabs only after the Arabs invaded Israel in the War of Independence. Since Said speaks of "historical Palestine," he should accept other historical parallels as well. Should Netherlands claim equality with the United States? Should native Americans ask for the "end of occupation, removal of settlements, real self-determination and equality"? Moreover, those actions are mutually exclusive: what kind of equality would a Palestinian state give Jews, who may not settle there and were unwelcome in pre-1948 Palestine? Yet Said repeatedly claims that since Jews and Arabs have equal rights in Israel, they must have the same rights "in the occupied territories." How can people in occupied territories be equal to the occupiers?

Agreements reveal "the huge difference in power between the two sides," but so the real world works. Laos imposed no terms on Vietnam, which used it for anti-American operations, Italy pressured the Vatican to concede most of land holdings, and Mexico is grateful for whatever piece of free trade the United States offers it. Said claims that peace is possible only between equals. Were that true, America would be at war with everyone.

Equality requires applying much harsher standards to Jews than to Palestinians

Said does not appeal to equality unless it benefits the Palestinians. He applies a much harsher standard to Jews than to Arabs. He calls an attack by a Jewish faction on guerrillas or armed bandits hiding in Arab Dir Yassin "an atrocity by the Haganah," but does not mention about routine looting of Israeli convoys to besieged Jerusalem and the murder of civilian personnel and the wounded by the villagers who also harbored the guerrillas. Nor does he decry the Arab massacre of a convoy of doctors and nurses to Mt. Scopus Hospital during the same siege. Arabs had no qualms killing civilians in overrun *kibbutzim* and killed 850 Jewish civilians in four months after the U.N. resolution on partition. The press holds the Palestinians to less rigorous standards. Being barbarian has its advantages: the Palestinians may be inhumane, but the Israeli army must observe rigorous ethical rules.[147]

Other examples of Said's bias are too numerous to mention, but see this. How, he asks, can the Lebanese forgive Israel for a twenty-two-year occupation? Just as the Israelis can forgive the Lebanese for shelling Israel

---

[147] Even the Israeli judicial system imposes a double standard on itself. The Attorney General refused to file charges against the Arabs who lynched Baruch Goldstein after disarming him, but Israeli court sentenced a Jew for shooting Palestinian terrorist after disarming him.

from the north for years. And how can the Lebanese forgive the Palestinians for religious massacres? Are they grateful to Israel for stopping them?

Said tosses labels of inequality and chauvinism about at random. It is not chauvinism if Jews want to live separately; people prefer houses to a caravansary. The Jews have no problems with people of many other nations living in Israel, even Arabs. Their opposition to Palestine does not stem from Jewish nationalism but from the Palestinians' well-documented hostility to Israel.

Misrepresenting and fact-twisting

Said says it is unfair that Jews are "allowed" sovereignty while Palestinians are not. Both had it in the 1947 U.N. resolution that divided the mandate territory into two states.[148] Some chances lost cannot be regained. Upon what are the "rights" of nations based? Can nations roll back history and correct their mistakes? France would have had more forces at Waterloo, Russia would have retained her pre-World War I borders, Israel might not have rebelled in 132 C.E., and no Palestinian entity would have existed in the first place.

Some modern states reemerged after occupation. Some were reestablished by international pressure, like Poland after World War II. No one can stop the Palestinians trying to form a state; but there is no inherent right of sovereignty, and Said has nobody to blame but the Palestinians for blowing it in 1948.

Said claims that Arabs and Israelis have no military option but to coexist peacefully. The Arabs have lost every war with Israel and only acquiescence to ostensible Western values prevents Israel from running the Palestinians out of the territories—much as Jordan drove them out, killing several thousand in the process. That hardly aroused the Arab world, which treated the slaughter as a brotherly misunderstanding. In fact, the Arabs worry about conflicts only when non-Muslims—Israelis, Serbs, Russians—confront Muslims. Intra-Arab massacres do not trouble them.

Said claims that since Palestine was already inhabited in 1948, the creation of Israel displaced the Palestinians, when in fact the territory was only sparsely inhabited with ample space for many more people. The present Palestinian population is several times the combined Jewish and Arab population in the 1940s. The Palestinians asked the British administration to stop the influx of Jewish refugees fleeing European persecution. Though neither the Jews nor the Arabs got a hearing from the British, the Palestinians got the British to use their usual strategy of

---

[148] The Arabs never demanded a Palestinian state. The British promised the Jews both banks of the Jordan, and that promise was reiterated in WWII. The Palestinians received the newly created state of Jordan plus part of the territory previously allocated to Jews.

supporting the weaker side in the balance of power, and Britain sided first with the Jews, then with the Arabs, intermittently. When the British sided with the Arabs—often enough, since the Jews were stronger—the mandate officials restricted Jewish immigration.

Said claims that Palestinian courts operate without witnesses or defense representation or press coverage because of pressures from Israel and the United States. How so? Both Israel and the United States have due process for every citizen. Palestinian state-security courts, on the other hand, are modeled on the judicial establishment of the former Soviet Union.

The book changes the meaning of words to prove any given point. Said claims that the Israeli invasion of Lebanon was not about her northern border but was launched to defeat the Palestine Liberation Organization. But the border problem was due specifically to the P.L.O. shelling Israeli towns from the safety of Lebanon. So, no, the Lebanese war was not defensive in the narrow sense of repelling invasion, but, yes, it was defensive since it answered aggression.

The author uses that approach time and again. He says Israel is the only Middle East power with an offensive air force and nuclear ability. How about Egypt? Egypt is in Africa, and not a Middle East power, even though it is a major force there. Syria and Saudi Arabia each have large attack air fleets. Said mentions Israel's offensive air capabilities to label her the aggressor. Yet Israel's offensive air forces are used for defense, since Israel lacks depth of defense and cannot conduct war on her territory. Israeli aircraft must be able to operate in enemy territory and are therefore long-range, high-speed, maneuverable bombers, normally considered offensive. Israel needs few interceptors, because her pilots usually best their opponents ten to one.

Said says Israel is the only Middle Eastern country "totally supported by [the] world's only superpower." No regional country gets more important American support than Arab Kuwait and Saudi Arabia, which the United States protects and has fought for. The United States intervened through Israel on behalf of Jordan when Syria threatened it. There is considerable military flow between the United States and Egypt. The United States–Israeli relationship is not so special as is commonly thought. Until only few years ago, Arab countries received immense support from another world superpower. The U.S.S.R. built civil infrastructure and supplied weapons to Egypt, Syria, Iraq, and the P.L.O. Arabs are no orphans facing Uncle Sam's Jewish nephew.

Said tries to show there is no difference between bulldozing and bombing. The inhabitants of Jewish towns on the Lebanese border know all about shelling, which is very different from bulldozing. When Said says, "recently evicted Palestinian family," he means the household of a terrorist. "Palestinians under curfew" are the inhabitants of a settlement where riots or terrorist activity broke out. "Young men and women who languish in Israeli jails" are members or active supporters of illegal militant

228

organizations. "Killed in massacres" is meaningless, since the only people Israel kills in Palestine are rioters, terrorists, or civilians nearby them. Said protests that Palestinians are "deprived of the right to resist occupational policies." There is no such right. Furthermore, a strange occupation that is: Israel subsidizes the Palestinian Authority with medical and other services, jobs, and all but free speech, all the while tolerating violent demonstrations and outbreaks.

Said compares Palestine to Bosnia, though he admits that, while there were massacres in Bosnia, there have been none in Palestine. He says something *like* a massacre is taking place daily in Palestine. In fact, a house is demolished occasionally or a few people are exiled, but Israel shows little cruelty in response to terrorist acts. According to Said, Israel destroys about five hundred buildings annually, takes one square mile of land, exiles about a thousand people, less than a tenth of a percent of the population. Said admits that even the Palestinians do not take it as persecution.

Said presents contradictory figures elsewhere. In the peak year 1997, Israel demolished only two hundred houses which hosted known terrorists. In fact, Israel has carried out only about eighteen hundred demolitions in twenty years. The large queue of demolition orders not carried out yet shows the legalism of the procedure. Israelis are not the bulldozer maniacs Said portrays.

He calls Israeli concern with security "remorseless obsession, . . . exaggerated." By common standards of military conflict, Israel's security measures are tolerant and clearly inadequate, as the continuous Muslim guerrilla warfare shows.

Said's blames the British penal code of 1936 for "punishing Palestinian resistance." What was that "resistance"? Gangs of Palestinian criminals roamed the country, murdering Jews and burning their settlements and fields in what became the largest massacre of Jews in Palestine since 135 C.E., more than in the first crusade. Said evidently condones that "resistance."

Some issues Said attributes to Israeli ill will stem from objective difficulties. He says Israel does not give Arab peasants enough water. In fact they have a lot more water under Israeli rule than they had in 1948. Further, nobody in the area has enough water. The exploding Arab population and increased cultivation put pressure on the water supply. While the Jews use conservation technology, the Arabs use much less advanced, less efficient irrigation schemes. There is simply not enough water to go around. Instead of blaming Israel, the Arabs should study agriculture.

Lie

In Said's view, Britain fostered Zionism. Tell that to the Jews the British killed in Palestine or to the tens of thousands of refugees held in the camps, prohibited from entering Palestine to avoid upsetting the Arabs.

Britain played the balance of power policy, helping the weaker side, sometimes the Jews, more frequently the Arabs, historical allies against France and Turkey.

The book puzzlingly claims that the Arab armies did not mean to destroy Israel in 1948—yet that was their stated objective. The fact that the Jordanian army stopped the aggression on the West Bank in the face of fierce Jewish resistance and agreed to a secret separate settlement does not change the original objective. The Jews stopped the Arab armies, not some limited Arab agenda. What could a "limited war" have been, anyway? The Jews claimed only the territory the United Nations assigned them, no more, and the Arabs meant to destroy even that.

Said writes that after 1948 "every major leader sued for peace but was rejected by Ben Gurion." Yet fifty-five years later, most Arabs categorically reject peace with Israel. Arab leaders turned against Sadat when he signed a peace treaty with Israel. Said notes the futile attempts of several realistic Arab leaders, notably of Egypt and Jordan, to convince their people to normalize relations with Israel, yet sympathizes with Arab rejection of normalization.

Note Said's assertion that Israel has upped its demands on the Palestinians. What of continuous Israeli concessions to Palestinians since the negotiations with Egypt in 1970s? From a categorical rejection of any Palestinian self-determination whatsoever, Israel conceded their autonomy, then a state of ever-increasing size. Israel tolerated endless Palestinian terrorism. While some years back, Palestinian terrorism would have led to invasion and exile, now it brings on further concessions and negotiations.

Said says that nowhere else in the world must people struggle for a license to build a house on their own property, an assertion that contradicts his claim that Arabs cannot own land. In fact, any civilized country requires building permits. That is not perhaps the kind of freedom Palestinians enjoyed in their primitive villages before 1948, but that is how a state works. Jews and Arabs get the same building permits, and Israeli government ignores massive illegal construction in Arab villages.

Refugees: Double standards for Jewish and Palestinian refugees

The demand for Palestinian statehood and the right of return for "refugees" implies a double standard. The Palestinians can choose between an ethnically homogenous state without Jewish settlements or living in economically attractive Israel. No one, however, demands that Jews be authorized to resettle peacefully in, say, Iraq and get restitution for property their ancestors abandoned. Many reject the concept of Israel as a purely Jewish state, but the Palestinians do not want Jews in their midst. The same perverse logic is applied to the settlements: Jewish towns may not exist in the territories, even in the religiously sensitive areas for Jews, but the Arabs administer Muslim shrines in Jerusalem, including the Temple Mount, central to Judaism.

Said objects to the small Jewish settlement in Hebron whose 450 people "must be made to leave." But Hebron is significant for religious Jews and has been for three thousand years, not just for the last thirty years that Palestinians have found Jerusalem important.

Said says Israel must apologize for the grief Palestinians suffer, though he does not expect Arabs to regret what they did to Jews for years before the Israeli state was formed in 1948. He laments the Palestinians who died but excuses the Jews killed by Palestinians before 1948, during the War of Independence, in the war of attrition, in border shelling, and in terrorist attacks. If, on the balance, anyone deserves reparations for lives and property, it is Israel.

Said wants Israel not only to give away the territories but also to do so "in humility and reconciliation." Imagine Mexico asking this much of the United States. He can concede to "recognizing Israel in our [Arab] midst," provided Israel resolves certain issues to his "minimum satisfaction." That is nonsensical bravado coming from a defeated enemy. The defeated Palestinians hope to appeal to Jewish morality after failing with other means.

Most Palestinians do not want to return to Israel

The claim for right of return for third-generation descendants and other relatives of the original refugees serves only for agitation. They are already resettled elsewhere, and almost none want to return. The stream of illegal immigrants to the United States from Mexico, Asia, and Eastern Europe shows that people find ways to invade a host country—marriage, border jumping, work permits, anchor-babies, and so on. No such thing happens with former Israeli Palestinians. Israel has no problem with their return to the territories. Indeed they could have returned to the Palestine Authority long ago to satisfy their nationalist ambitions; Jews immigrated to Palestine in worse situations. Yet Arabs do not.

Said says there are four million homeless refugees—more than the population of Palestine in 1948. Between two and six hundred thousand people emigrated, and many quickly resettled in other countries. The greatly improved conditions in the U.N.-sponsored Palestinian settlements produced a population explosion. Should Israel build homes for them? They are not homeless and live better than their grandparents before the exile and many people in other Arab countries. Neither are they homeless spiritually, living a few miles from their grandparents' places. How can Israel possibly absorb enough people to double its current population?

Said says all (!) young Palestinians want to marry Americans and emigrate, which confirms the conclusion that the people in the camps are not patriots but only too uneducated and untrained to get out. He admits that Israel went the extra mile trying to resolve the refugee problem, offering

231

money and visa arrangements to resettle them in Arab countries and Latin America.

Refugees' descendants are not refugees

Some call Palestinians "refugees," but a refugee is someone forced to flee, not his third-generation descendant, no more than inner-city blacks are slaves. Said's logic taken to its extreme would give the right of return to the descendants of the Jews who fled in 70 and 135 C.E. Jews should be allowed to return to Spain, Germany, England, almost everywhere else, including Mecca with restitution of their property there. More than half a century has passed since 1948. Palestinians born elsewhere are not refugees from Palestine. Unlike the right to property, citizenship is personal and not inheritable.[149]

No legal basis for the right of return

Said asserts that international law somehow provides for the return of Palestinian refugees. Nothing in international legislation could be construed to allow third-generation descendants of refugees to return to the state in question and of which they have never been citizens in the first place. By that logic, Jews might claim their medieval property and citizenship in almost any country in the Old World. Many refugees accepted citizenship and swore allegiance to other states, often hostile to Israel. They are either disloyal to their current hosts or want to deceive Israel. No state could be expected to grant citizenship to seditious aliens.

The right of compensation

When the Ukrainians in 1991 tried to collect two barrels of gold some ruler supposedly left in the English Exchequer more than two hundred years earlier, they were laughed at. No country can afford to pay compound interest;[150] without it, the 1948 property is not worth the paperwork, to say nothing of the problem of establishing the existence and value of the property and the hereditary rights.

The amount of the claims Said vaguely estimates at billions of dollars. Although that does not seem like a high price to pay for Israel, the figure is sheer fantasy, since the whole property of several hundred thousand poor Palestinian exiles could not have amounted to more than a

---

[149] Perhaps citizenship could be inherited if it were bought and sold, but states express nationality in metaphysical terms, making it a personal right, not an attachment. Some states grant citizenship to foreign-born children of their citizens, but even so the Palestinian refugees never took Israeli citizenship.

[150] 60 guilders paid to American Indians for Manhattan, with compound interest over the centuries, amount now to more than all real estate on the island.

232

few dozen million.[151] Fleeing Jews left no less in the Arab states. They resettled in vacated Arab houses; Arabs could have done likewise. Said adds land to the claims and misrepresents the facts. Before 1948 Jews had bought about 6% of the territory of Israel, but that percentage included much of the arable land, the rest being desert, marshes, non-arable hills, or unowned vacant land. Quoted in the prices of that time, the land would now be worthless. If the value has increased, that is due to improvements in agriculture and irrigation introduced by Jews. More land was bought after 1948. United Nations decisions gave Israel other untitled land. If Said recognizes the U.N. authority, he cannot claim land the U.N. gave Israel.

Said writes that Israel took over *all* Palestine except the West Bank and Gaza after 1948. Actually, about *half* of Palestine – the area allocated by the United Nations.

Said starts with a request for equality and cessation of brutality and finally comes to the issue of compensation—not only refugees, most deceased by now, but also their numerous descendants. Never has a victor, after repelling an invader (Arabs invaded legally established Israel in 1947) paid compensation to the conquered or their supporters. Said offers the example of Iraq, which paid reparations to Kuwait; but Iraq was the aggressor and lost the war. Said wants overseas Palestinians compensated as well. Applying that logic to other cases, Jews should demand compensation from Italy, Spain, and many other European countries, as well as from the Arabs who persecuted Jews and expelled them on several occasions. There is no legal framework for such reparations; Germany offered them only after unspeakable crimes, not comparable to the relocation of Palestinians. Perhaps Jews accepted the money because Germany offered it in good faith, not in exchange. Israel never solicited reparations—but Said does.

Defeated aggressors cannot make demands

Arabs forget that they lost the war they started in 1948 trying to keep Jews out, and asking for equal treatment is absurd. Losers do not make demands, but Said asks for more than equality. In his opinion, "many [Palestinian] claims are unsettled." He dismisses Jewish claims to the property they left in Arab countries, to say nothing of the human lives and immense sums of money Israel invested to repel Arab aggression and set up a strategic deterrence. That the refugees were civilians is irrelevant, since

---

[151] A few hundred dollars is a major amount today for similarly semi-nomadic African families, so perhaps Palestinians property amounted to hundred dollars per head. Another measure, $800 per-capita GDP in Palestine now, suggests the property value of the same order. The land value should not be added, because Israel preserved titled rights. Even if accounting for the land, 1948 prices are negligible, later surge is due to development by Jews. Refugees took possessions and cattle.

many Arab villagers housed guerrillas, supported them, fought and looted Israeli settlements with them. When Palestinian gangs destroyed Jewish settlements in the 1930s, Jews did not flee nor are they asking for restitution now—though they should, if only to inhibit Palestinian claims. The Palestinians fled in 1948 after far less danger.

To make his claim for restitution plausible, Said not only ignores the fact that there was little to restore of the pre-1947 Palestinian economy, hardly better than the Iron Age, or Palestinian property, but also he misrepresents the facts. He writes that the creation of Israel usurped the whole of Palestine and destroyed their society. In fact, the Palestinians tried to annihilate the legally established Israeli state. Not until nineteen years later, after years of sustained conflict during which Palestine became a base for terrorists, did Israel take some of it back. Hardly any nation has treated the indigenous population with more restraint than Israel.

Israel does not dispute the restitution of property to which Arabs had clear title. In many expensive areas of Israel today, vacant lots belonging to Arabs who left decades ago are common. They have appreciated greatly in value because of Jewish neighborhood development and are still waiting to be claimed by the rightful heirs. Any other country would have confiscated them long ago, at least for the back taxes. Jews are legalistic, and when an Arab has the slightest claim, Jewish lawyers jump on the case. Arab property in Israel is not abused. The Arab refugees left little when they left; there is nothing to restore, certainly not as much as Jews abandoned in Arab countries.[152]

Settlements

Said maintains that the Jewish settlements are the main obstacle to peace, presumably for the Palestinians. But the townships did not exist before the late 1970s and became important when the Palestinians had nothing else left to demand concessions about. Now they demand the expulsion of Jews from the yet-to-be-created Palestinian state. Even Said sees that the settlements are not the real problem, since they appeared only after Israel took over the West Bank. What indeed was the obstacle to peace before 1967, when the Arabs held the land? The Arabs refused peace both before and after the settlements appeared. The correlation, if any, is the opposite: facing the settlements, Palestinians considered peace.

Said interprets neutral facts as Israeli mischief. What harm is there in the road network Israel built among the settlements? Roads are important to a developed economy. Said says the roads make it "impossible for Palestinians to rule their own territory." Why? There is no reason. They do

---

[152] Though Israelis reportedly steered hostilities to force immigration, persecution ranged from real in Iraq to looming in Egypt. Fear motivated Jewish refugees from Arab countries and Arab refugees from Palestine; both reacted to propaganda rather than to atrocities.

not. Said says the Israeli habit of building roads is a "mania." Because Israel operates the roads she built, the Palestinians call them "internal borders." In fact, the roads in no way infringe on Palestinian sovereignty.

The author frets about "massive building projects that transformed Palestinian geography." Jews are 8% of the Palestinian population. Israel does not blame the Palestinians who are 15% of its population for "changing the geography" of the blooming desert which the Jews created.

The Palestinian Authority refuses Jews the right of return

Said says Jews claim "fourteen Jewish buildings dating back to the Old Testament times but no longer in evidence" in Hebron. The "buildings" include what Orthodox Jews and Arabs alike believe to be the tomb of the patriarchs—and Jews are willing to live among a hostile population to be near it. But while Arabs demand free access and jurisdiction over the Aqsa and the right to settle in Jerusalem, they want to run the Jews out of Hebron.

Jews have some autonomy in the settlements but not much beyond what ancient Muslims allowed to *dhimmi*: self-government inside the settlements, arbitration of internal matters,[153] and light arms for protecting themselves, all household matters which do not infringe Palestinian jurisdiction. The settlers have no authority outside the townships. The Arabs routinely insist on evicting the Jews, not just putting the settlements under Palestinian jurisdiction or even letting Jews live in Arab settlements.

Palestinians have comparable—and uncontested—autonomy in Israel. The central government hardly involves itself in their villages, traditionally ruled by the local aristocracy or councils. Israeli Arabs are free to decide among themselves, to practice their religion, and to visit Muslim shrines in Israel. Most Israelis tolerate them; they have no formal restrictions in business or employment. They may not bear arms, but they do not need weapons since they are not threatened.

Beyond a few accidents, Jewish settlers have never instigated any violence against Palestinians. How could a few Jews locked among millions of Arabs cause trouble? Yet Said claims that "horrendous settlers are about to let loose on the largely unprotected citizens." The Palestinian security forces and the armed terrorists alone outnumber the adult settlers, and the heavily armed Palestinians are no more "unprotected" than a third-world army.

Racism and incitement

Said accuses Israel of anti-Arab racism, a curious charge from someone who writes about "our [Arab] racial prejudices." While few Jews are fond of Arabs, the hatred coming from the opposite direction—

---

[153] Muslim courts historically have jurisdiction over criminal cases even when all parties are *dhimmis*, but this is insignificant in zero-crime religious communities.

demonstrators' slogans, newspapers, walls, school textbooks full of anti-Israeli rhetoric—is blistering. Said admits that Arabs protested normalization when some anti-Zionist Jews came to an Arab conference, refusing to let even their Israeli sympathizers join them. Opinion-makers from Egypt, at peace with Israel for a quarter century, rarely visit Israel—but not because they are unwelcome. Contrast that with the freedom Said experienced in Israel, where he freely rented meeting halls and gathered audiences hostile to Israel. Few states are so tolerant.

Similarly, though Said repeatedly condemns Israeli exclusiveness, he is unconcerned about the far greater xenophobia of Arab states, like Kuwait or the United Arab Emirates, which deny citizenship even to people born there in the third or fourth generation. For that matter, any country that imposes limits on immigration or treats citizens and resident aliens differently is exclusive.

Elsewhere Said admits that the Arab states are no better than Israel, much worse if we credit his description of the "glorification of raw power, blind subservience to authority, and a frightening hatred of others." He admits a "creeping wave of anti-Semitism" in Arab thought and "political failures and human rights abuses," policies "disfigured by discredited ideas." How is Israel to respond in that environment? Should she sympathize with such people, treat them as equals, or disarm?

Professor Said suggests that somehow either Israel's exclusiveness made the Lebanese stir up religious war or that the Israeli military presence sparked the turbulence in Lebanon, although in fact the army invaded Lebanon to stop the civil war threatening Israel's borders. The civil strife in Lebanon started with the arrival of the P.L.O. Expelled from Jordan, the P.L.O. upset the fragile balance of power in Lebanon. Syrian intervention assured a prolonged conflict. Israel took the opportunity to drive the P.L.O. away from her borders and create a security zone in Lebanon, as full of weapons and terrorists as it was. Israeli support of the S.L.A. was only reasonable. The Palestinians alone are responsible for the violence in Lebanon.

In Said's opinion, the expulsion of the Palestinians in 1948 was ethnic cleansing, which in a way likens Israel to the Nazis. Jews, however, narrowly escaped the Holocaust and were fighting for survival against Arabs who promised to throw them into the sea, not just to overthrow Israeli jurisdiction.

Jews wanted a state of their own, preferably without the Arabs who bitterly opposed Jewish settlements in Palestine since the early twentieth century, long before the Jews were any problem to them. The urge to drive the Arabs out[154] was not so much government policy but a spontaneous

---

[154] With minor violence compared to more than a thousand Jews massacred in Arab riots in the 1940s only. Many Jews who survived the pogroms were beaten, etc.

reaction by the Israeli army to get rid of hostile elements. Israel, home to about a million happy gentiles, is not racist.

Similar actions may be quite different, depending on their causes. The Russians had a better moral case for killing Germans in World War II than the other way around. The Nazis did not drive the Jews into Switzerland or Palestine; they murdered them. The Arabs instigated pogroms in 1940s from pure hatred. Many countries, including Syria and Iraq, prohibited Jewish emigration to Israel, since they intended to annihilate the Jews, not expel them. The Israelis, however, drove the Arabs out for the clearly defined purpose of creating an ideologically motivated, ethnically homogenous state without hostile elements.

The Israeli government implicitly encouraged expulsion of the Arabs, but even if it had protected them, they would have run anyway. They knew about mobs: Arab governments could not stop Arab mobs, and they feared the same from the Jews. The Ben-Gurion government could not stop fringe military factions from expelling the Arabs even if he wanted to.

Though attention usually centers on the civilian deaths on both sides, other casualties may shed more light on the parties' goals. Though the Russians, for example, were more justified killing German soldiers than the other way around, both parties were wrong to rape—unless vengeance is just. The Arabs committed immeasurably more such non-lethal crimes against Jews in Arab countries and in overrun Israeli townships than Jews did against Arabs. A handful of Jewish atrocities opposed scores of Arab crimes.

A historical anecdote shows how victors may be held to stricter moral standards than the vanquished. During the American occupation of Japan, MacArthur executed two American soldiers who raped Japanese women. Japanese soldiers, who used army brothels staffed by Filipino and Korean sex slaves, went free. World opinion expects more from Jews than from Arabs, and the Jews respond to criticism. Arabs disregard it and go right ahead killing civilians.

Said calls the settlers names like "mad" and "religious fanatics." Indeed, they are zealous. Who else would leave comfortable urban civilization to build towns in a historically important wilderness? Yet they are generally more restrained than their Arab neighbors. Jews will protect their townships, but few advocate killing Arab civilians to force a political settlement, even though Palestinians use just that tactic against Israelis.

Said likes the term "historical Palestine," but that notion validates the issue of historical Israel. Jews obviously have more right to the land than the Arabs, most of whom were roaming Bedouins only a few generations ago. Jews have always lived in Jerusalem, often a majority of the city's population. It is misleading to say that Arabs have lived in the

---

Israelis perpetrated few such abuses upon Arabs. 900,000 Jewish refugees after the riots exceed the number of Arab refugees both absolutely and relatively.

land for nineteen centuries. Those were different Arabs, nomadic tribes. No single homogenous group has lived there continuously longer than the Jews, and no Arab tribe attached any significance to the land before twentieth-century nationalism appeared.

The notion of "historical Palestine" backfires in yet another way. There was no Palestinian state ever, nor had anyone thought of one before the United Nations resolution of 1947. If history is the guide, the Palestinians have no right to a state but may live in Israeli territory. There was no such thing as Palestinian ethnicity a few dozen years ago; modern nationalists invented it. Even their name does not belong to them but to the biblical Philistines. The idea of statehood did not appear in negotiations until the late 1970s.

Said clings to the belief that Israel's main concern is not security but the destruction of the Palestinians. He says the 1967 war was fought to keep the Palestinians down. That is ridiculous, since the Palestinian problem did not exist then. No Arab leader brought up the idea of a Palestinian state for another ten years.

Palestinian nationalism

At some point in Said's book, it becomes clear that his idea of Palestinian nationalism does not square with the mood of Palestinians. He prefers nationalism to fundamentalism, though many Palestinian radicals are fundamentalists. He is no liberal and concludes that a doctrine of citizenship should replace nationalism, which in turn lets him claim Israeli citizenship for Palestinians—where many of them prefer to live. Actually, that happens all over the world. Mexicans sacrifice nationalism for a better life and immigrate to the United States. But where is reciprocity? Few Arab states naturalize even Muslim immigrants, let alone Jews. Beside, while many Arabs want to move to Israel, hardly any Jews want to move the other way, which eliminates any possibility of a reciprocal citizenship policy.

Accusations against the United States

Said believes Americans have a "morbid fear and hatred of Arabs." Such language would be understandable from an Iranian fundamentalist, but Said is a professor at a major United States university. He deals with Americans daily and cannot help knowing they do not feel that way. Millions of Arabs are integrated into American society and willingly embrace their new nationality. Said contrasts United States hatred for Arabs with the tolerance of Arabs in India, though thousands of Muslims die routinely in ethnic skirmishes in India, not in the United States. Said further claims that Jewish xenophobia and intolerance infected the Arabs. But the Arabs invented the concept of *jihad*, intolerant of infidels, and tolerated Jews and Christians only as *dhimmi*. Palestinians barely tolerated the European Jews who lived in Palestine even before the 1917 Balfour Declaration.

238

United States policy is in fact pro-Arab. No democracy would support the destruction of Israel, and the United States does not support Arab goals in that regard. The United States supported Israel against Arab aggression in 1973 but pressured Israel to stop further expansion as soon as the danger passed. The United States advocated the Sinai give-away to Egypt for an unreliable treaty and pushed Israel to give away the Golan Heights for nothing. While successive American government could have quashed Palestinian hopes for statehood by withholding aid to Palestine and its Arab supporters or by threatening to unleash Israeli force, they fanned those hopes. American subsidies to Arab states, both direct transfers and military protection, far exceed aid to Israel, and per citizen benefits are higher in Kuwait than in Israel. America's moral and political affiliation with Israel arises because Jews are fully integrated in American society and Israel is the only democracy in the Middle East. Americans support Israel spiritually but cooperate with Arabs materially most of the time.

Said calls American outrage over terrorism hypocrisy, because the United States winks at Turkish persecution of the Kurds. Yet while the Arabs sponsor and export terrorism to much of the world, a threat to American strategies to preserve stability,[155] the Kurdish issue is a Turkish internal affair. Nothing has happened in Turkey like the Iraqi atrocities against the Kurds. When the struggle in Chechnya began to affect mostly civilians in Chechnya, the United States was quick to criticize her Russian partner. Said calls the Gulf War of 1991 "the utmost cruelty," which is ludicrous, since the United States showed extraordinary concern for Iraqi civilians. Said's label fits the P.L.O. and its shelling of Israeli border towns and blowing up buses with school children better.

The requirement to sympathize with the Palestinians

Said says Israelis must be compassionate with Palestinians. Are we normally compassionate with sworn enemies? Do Palestinians deserve Israeli sympathy? No Palestinian rises to defend the rights of the Tutsi, the Kurds, the Russian Jews, nor did any Palestinian of note protest the Arab invasions of Israel in 1948 and afterward. Why should Israel sympathize with the Arabs?

Said says the Palestinians are weak and need support, yet the power of the whole Muslim world is assembled on their behalf, even if nominally. Israel won in 1948 all by herself. The Palestinians are not weaker; they are less determined, simply because most of them do not care about homeland and statehood issues. Even Said admits he has not visited Palestine since his

---

[155] As the world's arbiter of the balance of power, the U.S. prefers a little instability where everyone has more or less the same power, all dependent on the U.S. but not requiring its military involvement. Asymmetric warfare undermines arbiter's credibility.

childhood. The Arabs started talking morals only when they could not get their way with violence.

While Israelis are ready to fight and die for their land, the Palestinians plead their "position as dispossessed people." Being dispossessed of territory is hardly relevant. No Arab arose to defend ancient Israel from the Seleucids or the Romans or to defend the dispossessed Jews who flooded Palestine after World War II. No Arab helped the United States against the British or Mexico against the United States. Israel is perhaps the most legal state ever created, combining historical premises, land purchases, and an act of the international community carried out with historically minimal force.

Misjudgments of military matters

Professor Said worries that the Middle East consumes over 40% of the world's weapons sales, though the actual volume of arms trade is relatively small. Most American and Russian production is for internal use, so relatively few weapons make up that 40%,[156] mostly low-end weapons. No country in the region has truly outstanding military resources. Even Israel ran out of replacement parts in the two-week 1973 war.

Said does not understand Israel's defeat in Lebanon. Israel had no clear political objectives, so it is impossible to say whether the Israeli Defense Force fulfilled its mission there or not. From a military perspective, the operation was fruitful—the P.L.O. expelled, a neighbor pacified, a border secured. Israel's troubles in the Lebanese war stemmed from her restraint from inflicting civilian casualties and zero tolerance for casualties among her own forces. It is not possible to fight an effective war under such assumptions. Said accentuates Lebanese jubilation over the Israeli withdrawal, though they were just as happy to see the P.L.O. leave.

Said says that Arab education and agriculture have declined in the face of military expenditures, which is ridiculous to anyone acquainted with the state of education and agriculture in the Arab world fifty years ago. Indeed, Israel made major innovations in desert cultivation and shared with her neighbors.

The democracy of Zionism

Said says Zionism is not democracy since it restricts the rights of non-Jews. Classical democracy was never for everyone. The Greeks refused rights to aliens, even after generations. Only males of a certain age and means could be elected. Every country today gives its citizens more rights than resident aliens. Usually, nationality is identical with citizenship. The nationality of every United States citizen is *American*. Israel defines nation by religion and includes all nominal adherents to Judaism—as was more or

---

[156] Israel's military budget is only $5.5 to $10 billion by various estimates, while Saudi Arabia alone spends $72 billion annually.

less the case everywhere in Europe until the modern notion of the nationalist state arose. It is still standard in the Muslim world, where theoretically there is no distinction between Muslims of various ethnic origins. Moreover, Israel made her understanding of nation clear well in advance of the United Nations partition resolution. Thus, the Israeli concept of national democracy is reasonable both in historic perspective and in theory. It is hypocritical to accuse others of violating democracy while few Muslim leaders have ever been elected democratically. Nevertheless, Israel accords her gentile citizens *more* rights than Jews, freeing them from army duty and taxes. Discrimination comes from private Jews who don't want to sell religiously sensitive lands to Arabs. If Israel treats her Arabs badly, why do refugees want to return?

Historical errors

Said claims that the Palestinian case is more complicated than any other in the history of independence struggles, because Palestinians live under several jurisdictions. The situation is in fact quite common. Both Kurds and Armenians live in several countries and want their own, as did Jews before 1948, a situation at least as complicated as the Palestinian imbroglio.

Said says Palestinians have endured extraordinary agonies and dispossession, but worse cases abound. The Shiites in Saddam's Iraq were far more restricted than Palestinians in the territories. Shiites are also oppressed in Saudi Arabia. Many African tribes are more persecuted. Many Chinese, Egyptians, Iraqis, Omanis are poorer than Palestinians. Compared to their fathers, today's Palestinians are doing very well on welfare programs.

Time has shown Said's reasoning on the importance of Israel's giving up the territories is wrong. He argued that Israel needed to give Syria the Golan Heights and other territory to Lebanon and Palestine to win peace. Since then, Israel foolishly returned the Golan but has no peace with Syria, nor did withdrawal from Lebanon bring peace. Muslim countries nowhere near Israel, like Bangladesh, lacking any disputes with her, are still hostile.

Terrorism

Said tacitly endorses terrorism, not entirely without reason, since guerrilla warfare is the only way to fight a more powerful enemy. Yet he ignores the consequences. If the Palestinian terrorists who attack Israeli civilians are right, then why should the Israeli Defense Force not reply in kind? Why protect Palestinian civilians who are not hostages and actively support the terrorists?

Said opposed changing the P.L.O. charter, which sets the goal of destroying Israel on the ground that unspecified Israeli laws discriminate against Arabs. Yet no Israeli law prescribes killing Palestinians.

Said says the Palestinians and the terrorists have the right to use any means to reach their goals. Why he denies Israel the same right is not clear. He admires the tactics of Mandela's African National Congress and recommends it to the Palestinians, while admitting that Mandela's outfit committed every imaginable crime, including murder and corruption.

Though he admires the South African scenario, Said ignores the real situation there: the most prosperous and stable African country is steadily slipping into civil war, corruption, nepotism, economic decay, and desolation. The same will happen in Palestine if it separates from Israel, as happened after Israel closed her borders to Palestinians in response to the *intifada*. Few people value independence that highly.

Said calls suicide attacks "desperate acts of the weak." Desperate people act on their own. The Palestinians cold-bloodedly send children on suicide bombings, children drawn in from the terrorist web, indoctrinated, and sent to death to buy mass media coverage with their lives. They use young people because they are easier to convince than adults—or are we supposed to believe that children are desperate to die? Juliet, perhaps, but not Joan of Arc. Children know nothing of ideology, except what adults feed them.

Cruelty and torture

Said says Israel alone sanctions torture, though many states, certainly all Arab states, use it. The U.S.S.R., always an Arab sponsor, practically institutionalized it, and the former Soviet republics use it. Israel pragmatically admits the need to use physical pressure on certain suspects—and regulates it. Indeed, often the only way to save lives is by making terrorists talk. A brutal war is going on, and Israel cannot oppose terrorism with due process. In fact, until recently, torturing suspects was licit even in civilized countries, and any police officer will tell you that abandoning it lets many criminals slip away—a luxury unaffordable when dealing with terrorists.[157]

Professor Said is eager to point out Israeli brutality. Imprisoning terrorist and their supporters should hardly raise an eyebrow, lest in war time, but even that is nothing compared to what Said admits the Palestinian government does to its own people, arresting them *en masse*, torturing and murdering the opposition. Israeli rule would be an improvement, though Said criticizes Israeli prisons where terrorists are held, not the Palestinian jails, full of people whose only crime is opposition to the ruling authority.

---

[157] America handed captured Saddam to Iraqi prosecutors, instead of pressing him to reveal hideouts of his associates and relatives, locations of Iraqi WMD laboratories, and details on Iraqi intelligence dealings with terrorists. The refusal to extract this information from Saddam by whatever means is detestable on the backdrop of American casualties for the same goals. The government found it easier to sacrifice its soldiers than to torture a fellow ruler.

Liberties

Said's own examples contradict his accusations of the suppression of liberties in Israel. He, a Palestinian of known anti-Israeli views, had no trouble bringing a crew to Jerusalem to film an anti-Israeli movie. Israel shuts down anti-Israeli Palestinian magazines if they violate the law against incitement. Israel upholds her Palestinian citizen's civil rights even during a war. Said repeatedly says he met no hostility from Israeli Jews, people his Palestinians compatriots have been murdering for a century, but he supports Arab violence.

He laments three Palestinians killed on the barricades in Hebron and many more injured in the fighting. There were four hundred religious Jews settled in Hebron near places of biblical importance. They were not nice to Arabs, but many neighbors treat each other worse. A huge Palestinian mob assembled at the barricades to their quarters to throw them out. The Israeli guards fired warning shots, but the situation became a full-blown encounter in which *only* three Arab attackers died.

He frets that her "paranoid" desire for security drove Israel to erect a checkpoint at Bethlehem, where one Palestinian had already been killed. But how many Jews did Palestinian terrorists from Bethlehem kill before Israel put up the checkpoint? The Palestinian who was killed there was not likely a peaceful civilian.

Refusing to accept reality

Professor Said criticizes what others would consider an unusual outbreak of reason in the Palestinian leadership, namely that it tried to forget "about its people's tragic history." Said applies the term *tragedy* loosely, since it normally denotes something more substantial than the U.N.-sanctioned relocation of semi-nomadic villagers and a primitive urban population a few dozen miles away in exchange for generous welfare programs which greatly exceeded the Palestinians' previous wealth.

What is the alternative to forgetting the past? Is it a futile fight against a superior enemy and more suffering? The Palestinians need to think less about quixotic principles and more about adapting to reality. The public outcry feeds Palestinian discontent instead of forcing them to face reality, adapt to it, and carry on with their lives, whether under Israeli-sponsored autonomy or in some other state. Jews who suffered from Romans two thousands years ago, have no humanists and relief organizations on their side, and adapted or migrated, and moved on. Seventy years ago during the massive Arab pogroms around 1936, Jews had no one to appeal to but had to fight or surrender, had to adapt. Those are the Arabs' real options. Said does not want them to adapt, rather suggests a fight. He would not say so, since the Palestinians are not up to open warfare with Israel, preferring rather to demand peace and justice as they wage undercover war.

Remembering past persecutions is not bad. Hardly any people have suffered so much or have remembered that suffering better than the Jews, but they do not bomb Spain or Germany. The problem emerges when things past determine the future, when history becomes electoral platform. Too many ideological provocateurs incite the Palestinian people to right past wrongs instead of accepting reality.

Land ownership

Said writes that only Jews benefit from the institutions of the Israeli state and at the expense of Arabs. Yet Israeli Palestinians have the same medical, pension, and education benefits as Jews, far beyond what any Arab country offers. Whatever advantages Israeli Jews enjoy may be paid for by Jewish private funds. Nothing happens at the expense of Arabs, who pay lower taxes than Jews and are exempt from military conscription. Arabs are only 15% in Israel, generally underproductive, and cannot subsidize Jews.

Said specifies only land ownership, which is not a state institution in any regular sense of the word. Land in Israel is technically controlled by a non-government fund entitled to set its own rules[158] and free to refuse to lease land to non-Jews. Further, the owners hold many Arab farms in perpetual possession, while Jews generally lease. Since Arabs are not taxed and often own vacant land, the Arab disadvantage seems slight. Many countries ban foreign nationals from buying land; religion is a more valid basis for restrictions than fluctuating citizenship. Americans don't sell the White House to Japanese investors, and for Jews there is something bigger in the ownership of the Promised Land.

The Jewish National Fund, the private land trustee, was not set up to deprive Arabs. During its hundred-year history, the J.N.F. developed more than 250,000 acres of previously useless land, planted 220 million trees, and built many reservoirs. Jews from all over the world donate to the J.N.F., letting it buy unclaimed real estate and develop it. Why should it benefit Arabs? The J.N.F. is not conquering land or getting it free from the Israeli government but buys it. Before 1948, though Jews did not control the territory, they bought massively and without incident. The J.N.F. did not force Arabs to sell the land, though some have alleged extortion. Israel is

---

[158] Nothing in liberal doctrine justifies forbidding private entities to discriminate on ethnic grounds. If a dog's owner might sell it into good hands, not just anyone, why refuse a house owner a similar right of choosing a buyer on whatever grounds? If a charity might benefit orphans, but not widows, why disallow charity for Black orphans only? People donate money to churches, benefiting only Christians, but cannot donate to charities benefiting only Christians. If people could bequest to anyone, why not to any group? Charities circumvent this hypocrisy—prohibiting people from favoring those whom they want to favor at no expense to others— through custom-tailored review policies. Jewish Trust Fund is not land monopolist, and should be able to set its preferences as any private entity.

almost[159] unique in that she bought more arable land than she conquered or obtained through international legal arrangements.

Israel does not routinely apply the doctrine of eminent domain. Private land ownership trumps public designs. Arabs own many vacant lots in major cities, and the government does not foreclose, even though they destroy neighborhood property values. Arabs must not want land in Israel, since they refuse to develop lots even in Jerusalem. No one who knows the Israeli legal system can believe unlawful restrictions impede construction on Arab land. The courts that acquitted a Nazi criminal for lack of firm evidence and which locked the Jerusalem city administration into a years-long battle over the Armenian quarter of the Old City would defend any lawful Arab claims. There is not a single instance of an Arab being dispossessed of a piece of land to which he had legal title. Even unchartered land under cultivation is assigned to Arab villages in perpetual lease.

One cannot argue that the Palestinians, like the American Indians, have no concept of private ownership of land. *Sharia* permits private land ownership, and state ownership was introduced to replace bureaucrats' wages with lease assignments, essentially tax farming. Letting the land fall out of cultivation was not due to sharing it; Arabs often give up farming for herding.

Muslim countries have denied land ownership to Jews since the time of the Prophet, so it is not self-evident why Jews should not reciprocate.

Jerusalem

There is a lot of fuss about Jerusalem. Although Said blames the Israelis for not turning the city over to the Palestinians, he admits Israel's readiness to concede control over Muslim sacred places. What more do the Arabs need?

Said says Jerusalem is off limits to Palestinians. That is simply untrue. Indeed, he admits that 40% of Arab applicants get passes, more than the United States or European Community countries issue to visitors from poor countries. The ratio is quite high, considering that Israel is at war with the Arabs. One wonders how many Palestinians visited Jerusalem's Muslim shrines before the 1940s, before the issue got hot. Likely, not many.

If the Jews' right to Jerusalem is disputed, what right do Palestinians have to it? They built nothing meaningful there. They were not the majority of the population there, nor had they been in the past two centuries. Why, of all Arabs, should the Palestinians control the Islamic shrines? Why preserve a modern Islamic temple and not restore the Jewish one, whose ruins are still on the same site? The Dome of the Rock was built

---

[159] William Penn insisted that, although the king of England gave him all of Pennsylvania, nonetheless the land had to be bought from the Indians at a fair price.

on the site of Mohammed's ascension into Heaven to celebrate the supposed triumph of Islam over Judaism.

The demand of sharing control over Jerusalem is hypocritical. The Palestinians do not let Israelis visit the Jewish holy places in their hands. But Arabs behave that way. The Saudis refuse to share control of Mecca and Medina with other Muslims.[160]

Said rejects the idea of putting the Muslim sacred places in Jerusalem under joint Islamic jurisdiction. Why? What special relation do the Palestinians have with them? Why should places holy to all Muslims belong to the one Arab nation all the rest despise? Said does not care about Muslim control of the shrines; he is fanning Palestinian nationalism. He thinks control will improve the Palestinians' status among Arabs. His meat is political gain, not principles. Israel prefers international control to Palestinian control for good reasons. It is one thing to deal with a representative body of Arabs at large and another to deal with minor enemy.

Said admits that though the Palestinians were allocated as many as *thirty thousand* housing units in East Jerusalem, they built nothing. They are not interested in Jerusalem.

Two of Said's propositions are incompatible: that the Jews' historical right to the land is a nuisance and that Palestinians have a right to the Muslim holy places. Yet Jewish archeological remains are both more extensive and older than the Islamic ones. Jerusalem is also more central to Judaism than to Islam, where she comes after Mecca and Medina. Arabs kept Jews from visiting their holy places until the Israelis reconquered the city in 1967, but Palestinians did not flock to Jerusalem *en masse* to visit Muslim sites.

The passion for the Dome of the Rock suggests that Palestinians are staunch Muslims, yet they are notoriously irreligious among Arabs.

Socialist values

Some passages in Said's book suggest that his nationalist rhetoric is about class struggle in the developing Palestinian society. He thinks Palestinian businessmen are speculators who collaborate with Israel. He admits that most Palestinians, certainly middle-class professionals, accept the present situation, and therefore only the lower classes hate Israel and espouse radical notions—and they enjoy the support of leftist radicals elsewhere.

Said blames the United States and Israel for liberalizing the Palestinian economy. In his view, producing goods for export is evil. He asserts that deregulation distorts the economy, while exactly the opposite is

---

[160] Indian Muslims first asked that from the Saudis seventy-five years ago, to no avail.

true. He prefers trade unions, government paternalism, and a heavily regulated, closed economy.

The size of the thirty- to fifty-thousand man Palestinian police force, the largest sector of the economy, shocks Said and indicates something wrong with Palestinian society.

Said says that on at least one occasion and presumably on others, anti-Israeli riots were really anti-Arafat demonstrations. The common radicalism of youth protesting the older generation's conservative values poses as the anti-occupation struggle. The real problem, however, is not Israeli rule but the clash of generations. Various organizations, including the U.N., fan that non-specific radicalism. Said gleefully reports that a senior U.N. diplomat in Palestine urged him to incite the young to anti-Israel acts.

In general, the war for liberation is a vent for social pressures. A Palestinian intellectual Said interviewed says nationalism is a disguise for social transformation. Israel may have to force democratic changes in Palestine.

Said is clear who his opponents are. He expressly calls the Adam Smith Institute his enemy, presumably on the ground of its liberal orientation. The list of foes includes the British Foreign Office and the former Arthur E. Andersen accounting and consulting firm. He abominates anything related to the free market and non-partisan politics.

Support for Arafat

Said says that life in Palestine got worse after the Oslo accords and attributes that to Israel's collaboration with Arafat. Yet with whom else was Israel to negotiate, if negotiate she must? Free Palestinians of New York perhaps? Instead of posing that question, Said says Israel somehow perpetuated Arafat's rule. Though it makes sense for Israel to stop subsidizing Palestine to force it to select reasonable leaders, the matter is an internal Palestinian question.

Said ignores the real reason Palestinian life worsened: the Palestinians got what they wanted, a measure of independence. That meant losing Israeli social and medical services, living with border restrictions that control labor migration, losing various kinds of direct funding and economic assistance. But the Palestinians want it both ways: political independence with economic integration with Israel. A good wish, but no right to it.

Colonialism

Said decries the damage colonial powers, including Israel, do their foreign subjects. He forgets the Arabs were colonists—and slavers to boot. Civilized colonialism has done more good than harm to indigenous people. Most of the territories that became European colonies were rife with tribal warfare, and the peace the colonial powers imposed saved many lives, though others were lost in police actions. Colonialism let savages leapfrog from the Bronze Age to modernity. Further, civilized rule was profitable for the colonies, as it spared military expenses, maintenance of a royal court, and various forms of corruption; and payment (which Said calls "colonial extortion") was usually taken in products of little or no value to the locals. As far as Israel is concerned, Palestinians today live far better than their ancestors did fifty years ago, better than other Arabs in countries without oil.

Said often argues both sides of an argument. On one hand, he favors Palestinian nationalism, but on the other he criticizes the colonial partitioning of the Middle East, which destroyed Arab unity. The Palestinian nation, however, resulted from that dissection, and Jews have argued in vain that there is no such thing as a Palestinian nation, that Palestinians are equally at home fifty miles away in Jordan. Beside, the mythical Arab unity, whose loss Said laments, never existed, since the region has almost always been split among different states and cultural influences: Egyptian, Assyrian, Greek, Roman, Persian, and Turkish, to name a few.

Palestinian society has never existed. The concept of a Palestinian nation first appeared in the 1960s. Earlier references are to Arabs living in Palestine. What kind of society was there in an always-occupied country? History records no Palestinian home rule of their own, nor did they develop any of the institutions of modern society. Similarly, Said's claims that the creation of Israel destroyed the Palestinian economy contradict his claim that the subsequent Arab technological and scientific development— presumably, based on decent economy—suffered because of the political climate Israel created. There is little evidence of Arab science and technology, none in modern times anyway—which Said admits when he says Arab civilization reached its apex in Andalusia,[161] specifically because it involved other nations.

The Palestinians are content with Israeli rule

Said repeatedly mentions the benefits Israel bestows on the Palestinians, such as when the Israeli trade union Histadrut turned the pension funds of Palestinians who worked in Israel over to Arafat—which Said opposed, implying that the Israeli institution is more reliable than the P.A. Palestinians would prefer having their money saved by a hostile government to having it stolen by their own. The Palestinian population increased six-fold in fifty years of Israeli oppression; seemingly, they are well-off.

Said notes that Israeli Palestinians refuse to discuss moving to a separate Palestinian state which he interprets as attachment to the land,

---

[161] A flourishing multicultural state under Muslim control in the south of Spain for some centuries. Its loss reverberates with Islamists today.

though they are clearly so much better off in Israel that they do not want to live in Palestine. Realizing that, Said harps on examples of discrimination against Palestinians in Israel. He reports that the Israeli army took a hundred acres of land from an Arab village in Israel and calls that racism. But how much land has Israel taken away from Jews for military purposes? Much, much more. In all probability, the Arabs were compensated for land urgently needed for defense. No Arab government would hesitate a second to expropriate its citizens' land for military needs.

Irresponsibility

Professor Said repeatedly disregards his fellow Arabs' irresponsible behavior while lamenting the natural consequences of their actions. The Arabs started the 1947 war, so they suffered. Said frets over the harsh refugee camp life of a family with *eight* children. Many Westerners would say that life can be hard with half that many. The Palestinian population explosion exemplifies Arab irresponsibility, which often requires special measures and preferential treatment to correct.

Said tells the story of a refugee family in the Shatila camp, "without hope and money" but with a week-old baby needing medical treatment. Did the child's parents not expect medical expenses when they bore the child? Condoms are cheaper than the socialist free health service Said advocates. And why is the child's family without work and money? Can neither adult find any job whatsoever? Arab women, of course do not usually work outside the home, but the Western world relaxed that cultural restraint dozens of years ago when men could no longer provide all their families needed. If Arab women prefer to sit at home, that is their right— but they choose poverty willingly. The main reason Palestinians are jobless is their dependence on welfare programs. While what they get may seem minuscule to Western journalists, it is far more than they earned from agriculture and comparable to the earnings of the rural population of Arab countries which do not have oil.

Of the family that needed medical treatment Said reports that a charity hospital refused to help because the child was Palestinian. Abominable as that is, it shows the hostility Palestinians arouse everywhere they live. Said also quotes a Lebanese official saying about Palestinians, "We cannot integrate them into society."

Another example of Palestinian unwillingness to take responsibility for actions is Said's blaming Israel for supporting Arafat. Israel fought Arafat when the Palestinians still supported him; Israel kept him under house arrest and was looking to exile him. Often Israeli politicians refused to talk to Arafat. Yet Said thinks Israel should have replaced Arafat or stopped supporting him. That would mean Israel should stop subsidizing Palestine with funds Arafat and his clique appropriated and spent on themselves. Never mind the resulting outcry against economic suffocation of their motherland.

Said rejects Israel's right to exist

Professor Said says the Arabs oppose Israel's presence but not her existence. Perhaps he proposes that Israel be relocated in Uganda, as some suggested a century or so ago.

He says the anniversary of the Balfour Declaration should be a day of mourning for Palestinians. When he criticizes Weizmann's remark that Jews had no need to ask Arab permission to establish the state, he admits that no permission would have been granted. That is more or less the position of most Palestinians. Why, then, should Jews sympathize with them?

If not for Balfour, there would have been no Palestinian state, because Jordan would have swallowed it. Yet Said does not want Palestinians re-settled there. Indeed, the Palestinians have not tried to seize a chunk of Jordan for themselves, nor would Jordan offer it; they found Israel a weaker negotiating partner than Jordan. The Palestinians support the partition resolution when it suits them and decry it when it suits the Jews.

Said argues against the U.N. partition resolution on the grounds that Jews bought less than 7% of the land at that time—though the Palestinians did not buy more, since most of the land was fallow. If the size of the purchase is relevant, then Jews today have indisputable right to the territories, where they bought vast tracts. Arabs say, however, that buying the land did not give Jews the right of statehood.

Conclusion

Said's book advances radical slogans. Never does he suggest anything practical for the Palestinians, nor did he fight Israel or demonstrate. From New York City, he encouraged the Palestinians to stick to their unrealistic demands instead of getting on with their lives under tolerant Israeli administration. He retained his American citizenship while supporting people who rejoiced at 9/11 and other attacks against America.

Said lacks realism because he does not understand history. National borders change constantly. Nations come and go or are dismantled. The balance of power is amoral, and power belongs to those who are willing to pursue their principles ruthlessly, especially when those principles involve no murder or looting but only a desire to reestablish the biblical entity. The Palestinians do not stand a chance. They have no distinctive culture, no attachment to the land, no national or religious identity. They are dispersed, disliked by Jews as sworn enemies and by other Arabs as rascals, brigands, and terrorists. Even if a Palestinian state is created, its Arab neighbors will swallow it up.

6887612R0

Made in the USA
Lexington, KY
29 September 2010